Architecture of Regionalism in the Age of Globalization

D1709769

The definitive introductory book on the theory and history of regionalist architecture in the context of globalization, this text addresses issues of identity, community, geopolitics, and sustainability along with a selection of the most outstanding examples of design from all over the world.

Through time, globalization and regionalism have been antagonistic. Globalization has tended to 'flatten' obstacles to the interaction between places, transforming a world of barriers and insular regions into a 'flat world' enabling creativity and bringing about unprecedented wealth but also producing inequality, wastefulness and ecological destruction. Regionalism by contrast has supported the singularity, autonomy and distinct identity of regions, enhancing differences between them, nurturing diversity, and contributing to a world of 'peaks and valleys', but it has also tended to confine, tearing apart societies and promoting destructive consumerist tourism.

Lefaivre and Tzonis retrace the multiple twists of the evolving conflict between globalization and regionalism within a vast critical historical perspective in relation to the design of the human-made environment. Engaging, vivid, and scholarly, the book demystifies this opposition and points to *critical* regionalism as a potential means of bringing together the two tendencies within a new framework of ecological complementarity.

Liane Lefaivre is the Chair of Architectural History and Theory at the University of Applied Arts in Vienna and a research associate at the Technical University of Delft.

Alexander Tzonis is Professor at Tsinghua University and Professor Emeritus at the Technical University of Delft.

Lefaivre and Tzonis have co-authored several books, including *The Emergence of Modern Architecture: A Documentary History, from 1000 to 1800*.

Architecture of Regionalism in the Age of Globalization

Peaks and Valleys in the Flat World

Liane Lefaivre and Alexander Tzonis

Routledge
Taylor & Francis Group

LONDON AND NEW YORK

First published 2012
by Routledge
2 Park Square, Milton Park, Abingdon, Oxon OX14 4RN

Simultaneously published in the USA and Canada
by Routledge
711 Third Avenue, New York, NY 10017

Routledge is an imprint of the Taylor & Francis Group, an informa business

British Library Cataloguing in Publication Data
A catalogue record for this book is available from the British Library

Library of Congress Cataloging in Publication Data
Lefaivre, Liane.
Architecture of regionalism in the age of globalization: peaks and valleys in the flat world/Liane Lefaivre and Alexander Tzonis.
    p. cm.
    Includes bibliographical references and index.
    1. Regionalism in architecture. 2. Architecture and globalization. I. Tzonis, Alexander. II. Title. III. Title: Peaks and valleys in the flat world.
    NA682.R44L438 2012
    724'.7–dc22
    2011016294

ISBN: 978-0-415-57578-2 (hbk)
ISBN: 978-0-415-57579-9 (pbk)

Typeset in Univers
by Wearset Ltd, Boldon, Tyne and Wear

Printed and bound in Great Britain by
TJ International Ltd, Padstow, Cornwall

Contents

Illustration credits

The authors and the publishers would like to thank the following individuals and institutions for giving permission to reproduce material in this book. We have made every effort to contact copyright holders, but if any errors have been made we would be happy to correct them at a later printing.

Chapter 4
From W. Halfpenny, *Rural Architecture in the Gothic Taste*, 1752: 4.02

Chapter 7
Jean Pers et Jean Ferlié, *Maisons pour Tous*, Variante septemtrionale et méridionale, Librairie Hachette, Septembre 1926: 7.05
P. Fauré, del. Digeon *Habitations modernes*, 1877, t. 1, pl. 161. From Jean-Claude Vigato, *L' Architecture Regionaliste. France 1890-1950*, Paris, 1994, pp. 160-161: 7.08

Chapter 8
Architektur Sammlung, TU Munchen: 8.01
Paul Schultze-Naumburg, *Kunst und Rasse*, Munich, J.F. Lehmanns Verlag, 1927: 8.02
Le Corbusier, Oeuvre complète, vol. 4, 1938-46. Wili Boesiger ed., 1946: 8.03
Photo Alexander Tzonis: 8.05
Anonymous photograph, 1895. From Margaret Richardson, *Architects of the Arts and Crafts Movement*, London, 1983, p. 54: 8.06

Chapter 9
Lewis Mumford Papers, with permission of the Annenberg Rare Book & Manuscript Library, University of Pennsylvania: 9.01
Photo Alexander Tzonis: 9.02

Chapter 10
Forum, June, 1955, p. 115: 10.06
Conrad N. Hilton College Archives and Library, University of Houston: 10.07
Walter Gropius Archive, Busch Reisinger Museum, Harvard University, University of Bagdad: 10.08, 10.09

Chapter 11
Alvar Aalto Museum, Jyväskylä. Photographer E. Mäkinen: 11.01
Hugo Segawa: 11.02, 11.03, 11.04

Marcel Gautherot: 11.05
Photo by Michel Moch: 11.06
El Eco Experimental Museum, Matias Goeritz, 1953. *Architectural Record*, August 1956: 11.08
James Stirling, House at Wolton, Study Sketch. From *Architect's Yearbook*, no. 8, 1957: 11.09
North elevation, Ashok Dilwali: 11.11
Architecture d'Aujourd'hui, Decembre, 1949: 11.12
from Minette de Silva, *Minnette de Silva*, Kandy, 1998: 11.13 and 11.14
Compliments of Charles Correa: 11.15
Photo Paolo Gasparini, Caracas: 11.18
By permission Tay Keng Soon: 11.22
Photo Alexander Tzonis: 11.23

Chapter 12
With permission from Ken Yeang: 12.09
Photo Alexander Tzonis: 12.10
With permission Moshe Safdie and associates: 12.11
Photo 2003 Hester + Hardaway, Texas: 12.12
With permission Wu Liangyong: 12.14
With permission Wang Lu: 12.15
With permission Wang Shu: 12.16
With permission Li Xiaodong: 12.17
With permission Zhang Ke: 12.18
With permission Yu Kongjian: 12.19

Preface

The Never-Ending Challenge of Regionalism

It has been more than a quarter of a century since *critical regionalism* was first introduced as a term – at the end of the 1970s – to draw attention to the work of a number of young architects in Europe who challenged post-modernism, the fashionable tendency of the period, proposing an alternative approach to design.[1]

As the name suggests, postmodernism claimed to replace modern-ism as the leading movement of architecture at that time, after modernism's countless failures since the end of World War II, a period during which it pro-duced large numbers of dysfunctional buildings and unsightly urban projects. At first, postmodernism enjoyed a meteoric rise in popularity; however, it did not take long for the public to realize that the 'postmodernist' projects were failing in the same way as the 'modernist' ones had done – because, like their 'modernist' predecessors, postmodernists continued to impose dogmatic, universal, global models disregarding the environmental particularity, the social individuality, and the cultural uniqueness of the places in which they were constructing their buildings.

By contrast, the younger architects whom we have referred to as regionalists have given priority to the identity – the ecological, social, and cul-tural features – of the specific site and region to which their projects belong.

In trying to present the special spirit of these architects, we recruited the term *regionalism*. 'Regionalism' was not the term used by these architects, nor was it a new concept. We chose it to express the fact that this new movement resembled in many respects the efforts of a long succession of architects who opposed an authoritarian, standard, and 'universal' approach to design and who tried an alternative way of making buildings, landscapes, and cities that treasured the particularity of a region, its unique environment and materials, the special character of its culture, and the way of life of its people.

On the other hand, we also wanted to demonstrate that regional-ism in our time has its own problems and priorities that make it different from the regionalism of previous periods in history. While consistently pursuing decentralization, autonomy, and particularity, regionalism was no longer focused on issues of 'ethnic emancipation' and 'nationalism', on 'chauvinism', 'separatism', and 'commercialism'.

Regionalism always opposes centralization and universalization, and instead supports decentralization and autonomy. But it has been aligned with different movements in history that have enhanced existing community ties, enabling the construction of new liberated communities and sustaining local resources and local cultures. At other times, it has also confined groups into gated belief systems, making them imagine that they were part of 'ghost communities'; 'retribalized' people, tearing apart existing communities. Then, at yet other times, it has been used as a prop to promote a kind of tourism bent on destroying the finite physical and cultural resources of regions.

Similarly, the idea of 'region' itself has gone through several shifts, although not as radical as those of regionalism. While for ancient geographers it meant an 'objective', 'natural' division of the earth's surface, an area defined by boundaries, landforms, paths, zones of vegetation, and climate, with administrative borders placed on top, by the end of the eighteenth century it had become associated with human rather than natural attributes, such as continuities and discontinuities of language, religion, ethnicity, and economy, or mental aspects significant for local people, aspects defining place, belonging, community.

To help grasp the apparently protean character of regionalism, similar to the elusive one of nationalism,[2] and distinguish the priorities of regionalism today from those embraced in the past, we felt it necessary to combine the notion of 'regionalism' with the philosophical, Kantian concept of a *critical* approach, stressing the need for reflection on the beliefs and assumptions of regionalist ideas before they were put into design practice. The historical investigation undertaken in this book is part of this *critical* approach.

The critical historical inquiry helps us understand the evolution of regionalism in the context of its changing cultural, social, and political uses. Through this study, regionalism emerges neither as a passing trend nor as a repetition of past campaigns, but as a continuous process creating new differentiated, diversified regions in dynamic confrontation with another major dynamic movement, equally protean through history: globalization.

At the moment, global or multinational corporations, global networks and alliances, as well as global institutions, dominate the making of buildings, cities, and landscapes. They promote universal, centralized design models, manifesting their creative but also destructive force on the environment, on cultural heritage, and on human community.

We believe that regionalism, critically understood, presents a vital complementary alternative for the world to come.

The story of the writing of this book is relatively brief compared to that of our three-decade-long engagement with researching and writing about regionalism. As regards this publication, we would like to thank colleagues and friends who have helped with this book as well as those who have inspired and supported us in our long-term project. For support in the very early critical stages we would like to thank Lucius and Annemarie Burckhardt, Charles Correa, Albie Sachs, Vanessa September, Ed Barnes, Luis Fernández Galiano, Juan-Antonio Fernandez-Alba, Michael Levin, Marvin Malecha, Spyro Amourgis, Toshio Nakamura, Lucien Hervé, André Schimmerling, Gerhard Fehl, Richard Pommer, and the Prince Claus Fund of the Netherlands. Later, for advice, stimulating discussions, and useful exchanges, special thanks are due to Wu Liangyong, and to Stan Anderson, Toshio Nakamura, Jeffrey Kwek, Roberto Segre, Bruno Stagno, Rick Diamond, Jean-François Drevon, Karla Britton,

Preface

Alberto Villar Movellan, Stella Papanicolau, Peter Rich, Ian Low, Hoang-El Jeng, Heng Chyekiang, Lu Yong Yi, Angeli Sachs, Philip Bay, Maggie Toy, Doug Kelbaugh, Gwendolyn Wright, John Loomis, Christopher Benninger, Ramprasad Nadu, Durganand Balsavar, Anne Whiston Spirn, Nezar AlSayyad, Michelangelo Sabatino, Isan Bilgin, Kongjian Yu, Zhang Ke, Wang Lu, Wang Shu, Li Xiaodong, Yu Li, Zheng Shiling, Tian Sun, Li Kaisheng, Enric Miralles, Santiago Calatrava, and Joeri Van Ommeren. Thanks for friendship and help to Fritz Schröder. Without Georgina Johnson's unflagging support, the publication would not have materialized.

Introduction

The End of Geography?

What will be the shape of the world to come? Some claim it is getting increasingly 'flat'. They don't mean flat in the sense the Flat Earth Society means it, that the earth is shaped like a plate; rather, they believe that the world is an ideal environment where obstacles to interaction such as distance, and peaks and valleys within and between regions, have been eliminated.[1]

To understand how regions are organized, Johann Heinrich von Thünen, a German landowner and writer, and one of the great pioneers of modern regional science and planning, wrote a seminal text, *The Isolated State* (1826). In it, he imagined an ideal 'isolated state' in the midst of an area with no peaks and valleys to obstruct the circulation of the inhabitants, and no roads to make their movement easier. It was a highly abstract and reductive view of the world: the middle of the state was occupied by a center that contained a market, and the surrounding land was divided into concentric zones at increasing distance from the center. The first yielded fruits, vegetables, and dairy products; the second, materials for fuel and construction; the third, field crops; and the last, animals for slaughter. Peasants traveled on foot, carrying goods and animals. His abstract description was a good representation of most of the German-speaking world at that time and it was able to help the landlords of the day better organize their estates. It was reductive but it introduced key planning categories such as 'center', 'location', and 'zones of land' differentiated by use, rent, and yield. More importantly, it related distance between places to cost and benefit. It is a solid point of departure for economists and planners in our own time, according to Paul Krugman. If you substitute commuters for farmers, he argues, the model helps us to understand better the spatial structure of cities and territories and the implications of centralization or decentralization of regions for land values and for the quality of life.

Of course, the model was too simple and too limited to be able grasp the entirety of people's lives and the complexity of contemporary buildings, cities, and regions as they work and evolve in space and time. Many researchers tried to go beyond its limitations, which reflected those of a closed agricultural economy. One of them was the geographer Walter Christaller. He developed an ingenious model consisting of a hierarchy of nested hexagonal patterns reflecting the multiplicity of scale of modern human settlements. Like Von Thünen's, Christaller's model assumed a physically flat land, which, rare as it may be, fitted very well the naturally flat regions of Poland and Ukraine. The Nazi army colonized both areas in the early 1940s with the help of Christaller's ideas in their globalization plans during World War II.[2]

Yet, like Von Thünen's, Christaller's model served as a major inspiration for a new generation of regional scientists, planners, and urbanists who became involved in the study of regions through a preoccupation with modern problems of urbanization, growth, and sprawl.[3] The new generation of researchers tried to build less reductive and more realistic models that could represent 'non-flat' regional landscapes, highly differentiated by intangible political, legal, and cultural 'frictions' to interaction, 'resistances' to the flattening of the world and to what was increasingly called 'globalization'.[4]

'Global', like 'flat', does not refer to a geometric shape. It does not refer to a sphere. Like 'flat', it helps us to visualize this future ideal universe where interaction between regions is maximized while resistance is minimized, where through transportation and electronic communication – including the internet and the web – there is no distinction between center and periphery, which has caused so much misery in the world,[5] where national borders, state regulations, and bureaucratic controls no longer enslave people, where every region is effortlessly, instantly, and equally accessible from any other region. 'Global', in the words of the chief economist of the American Express Bank, means 'the end of geography' (*New York Times*, March 28, 1992).

A flat, global world, it has been argued, leads to a better life, a life free from the cost and pain of having to surmount hurdles and distances to be in contact with other regions. But is the global world really like that?

There is an equally strong claim to the contrary, that the new technological and institutional developments that overcome resistances to interaction have not really brought about a truly flat *ecumene* when it comes to the distribution of affluence and to environmental or social quality, that there are in fact peaks in economic prosperity and environmental opulence that just keep rising, and valleys in poverty and environmental destruction that do nothing but deepen.

In addition, the claim goes that with global 'flattening', the only things that got leveled were the unique peaks and valleys of ecological diversity, ways of life, and cultural treasures, along with nature, ideas, and identities. The adversaries of the idea of 'the end of geography' claim that globalization brought about impoverishment, anxiety, and anger rather than happiness. They ask why *regionalism* – keeping the earth populated by diverse regions – is not a better alternative and the degree to which architecture could enable this alternative. And this is the quandary we would like to explore here.

Chapter 1

The Regional and the Classical Imperial

The question of 'regional' architecture – its environmental aspects and its political implications, hot topics today in the context of triumphant globalization – appears, probably for the first time in history, in a Roman text, *De Re Architectura*, written in the time of Augustus (63 BCE – 14 CE), the first Roman emperor. The text identifies 'regional' buildings and juxtaposes them with those of Greece and Rome which we call today 'classical', a word not used by Vitruvius.

Vitruvius dedicated his book to the *imperator*, Supreme Ruler, Caesar, named Augustus because he 'gained the empire of the world', praising Augustus because 'Rome gloried in [his] triumph and victory', but also because of his support for the construction of public buildings in Rome. In the words of the Roman historian Suetonius, Augustus 'found Rome a city of brick and left it a city of marble'.

De Re Architectura is the best written source we have on the architecture of antiquity. From what we know and from the tone of his book, Vitruvius aspired to be among the leading Roman intellectuals of his time busy constructing a political theory and a Roman identity as global imperial ruler. It is clear, therefore, that Vitruvius's goal in writing his book was practical and pressing: the new empire needed a universal toolbox of design and construction rules capable of serving a huge-scale construction program alongside the universal economic, legal, and cultural ones, establishing a centralized global order that was taking the first major step toward making the world flat.

The book tried to cover almost all aspects of design, from buildings and cities to machines and fortifications, with references to philosophy, natural science, astronomy, 'physiology', acoustics, and medicine. Vitruvius was an engineer, architect, and writer, who was trying to cover all these topics in the framework of the philosophy of Lucretius. Accordingly, he believed that architectural form is determined by natural causes. What cannot happen in nature, he wrote, cannot be forced in an artifact. In the fourth book of his text, he declared his intention to reduce architectural knowledge to 'a perfect order' (*perfectam ordinationem*), a universal rule system within which nothing was permitted to be 'inchoate' and everything was to follow rationally (*habet rationem*). In this spirit, he presented Greco-Roman architecture and its 'kinds' (he called them *genera*, in the Aristotelian sense of natural kinds) – Doric,

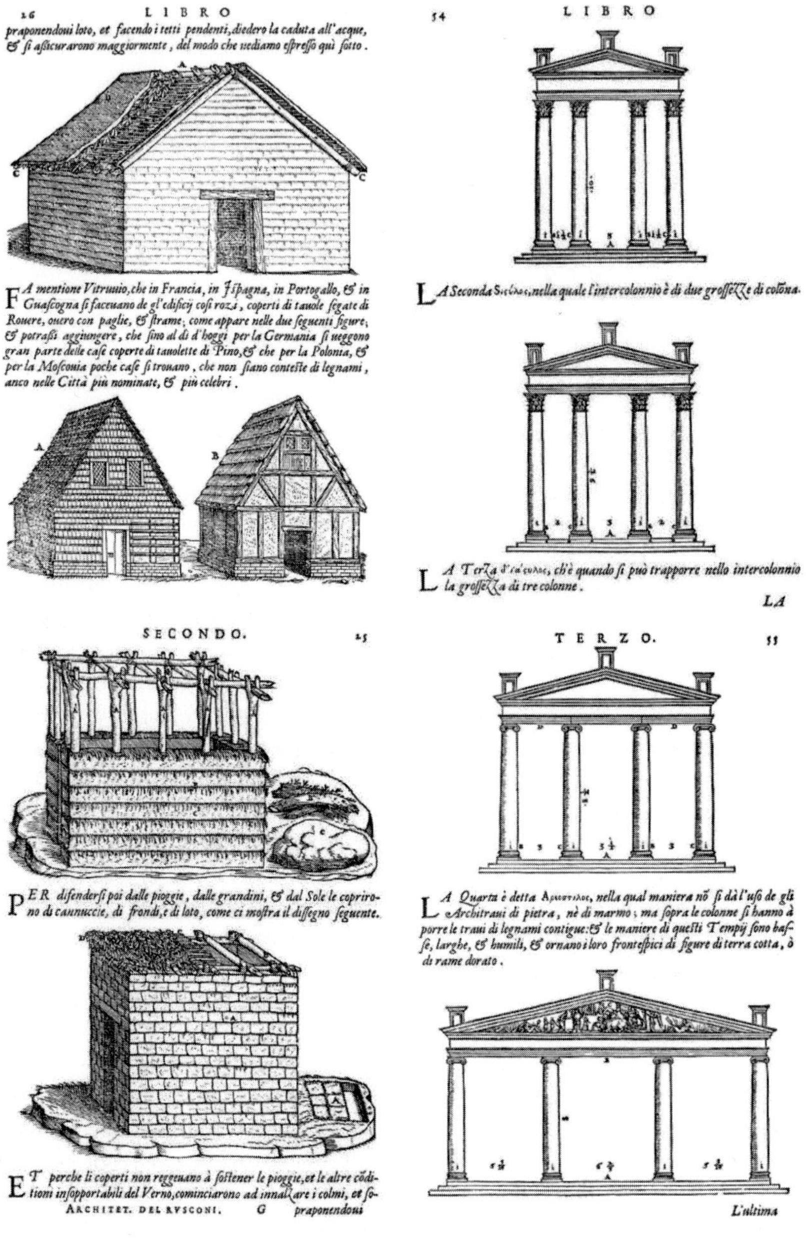

Figure 1.01 Four regional houses and four classical temples. Illustration for Vitruvius's text in Giovan Antonio Rusconi's *Dell'architettura* (1590).

Ionic, and Corinthian – their 'parts', their 'members', and their organization in terms proportion and symmetry. Then he turned to another 'kind' of building, not subject to the same rules, *regional* architecture.

As a rationalist, after classifying the kinds and describing their differences, Vitruvius tried to explain what made them different. He contrasted the 'regional' 'kinds' of buildings (*genera aedificiorum*), the ones that belong to a region (*regionum*), with the Greek and Roman ones, their diversity caused by their different characteristics 'ordained by Nature' ('proprietates locorum ab natura rerum … constituere aedificiorum qualitates'). In other words, the physical environment of the regions the buildings belong to accounts for their variety. The theory is not original. It goes at least as far back as a treatise by Hippocrates (460 BCE – 370 BCE), *On Airs, Waters, and Places*, a text that deals with the relation between humankind and the environment.

It is of particular interest that, in addition to architectural issues, Vitruvius also discusses the political implications of a world divided into regions of unequal quality. Thus, just as climate and physical conditions influence buildings, so do they shape human beings. Consequently, he claimed, just as the extreme physical conditions (*natura rerum*) of the North dictate buildings with strongly sloping roofs, among other features, and at the opposite extreme the physical conditions of the South lead to buildings with almost flat roofs, so these extreme environmental conditions create extremely different kinds of people, different in physical constitution and in behavior.

On the other hand, Vitruvius argued, there is a 'temperate' environment that produces temperate architecture and temperate people. This is the environment Romans inhabit and the architecture they build. The temperate environment is superior to the extreme ones, and so it is with the temperate buildings and people. The temperate architecture and people are more balanced, reflecting the balanced environmental characteristics of the region they inhabit. Again, elements of this theory are to be found in *The Histories* of Herodotus, where he argues that the climate of Greece is 'ideal', being temperate, in contrast to the very cold climate of Scythia and the very hot one of Egypt. Similarly, the Hippocratic treatise claimed that Europeans are more industrious than Asians, owing to the temperate climate of their region.

From these observations, Vitruvius draws a political conclusion arguing that because of their temperate region (*temperatamque regionem*), the Romans have special courage and strength and for this reason they can overcome the deficiencies of the people of the northern or southern regions, presumably Germans and Africans. Romans are allocated this 'excellent and temperate region in order to rule the world' (*terrarium imperii*). Interestingly, the Hippocratic treatise argued in addition that because of their environment and climate, Europeans do not depend on any despotic authority, whereas Asians are governed by despots (chaps. 14–22).

The architectural implications of this environmental-political theory were that, by Nature, Roman ('classical') architecture must be applied globally. It is obvious that Vitruvius's reasoning was inconsistent. On the one hand, from nature (*naturae deducta*) and on the basis of rationality (*disciplinae rationes*), it asserted that buildings, like people, are adapted to the environment of their regions, resulting in regional variety and diversity; on the other, it supported the political, 'imperial', universal normative doctrine that Roman ('classical') buildings, like the ruling Romans, ought to be imposed in a region without being adapted to its regional conditions, thereby creating a standard, classical, global world. History might have helped Vitruvius to understand that even classical Greco-Roman architecture was not universal and that its buildings were the result of regional adaptations. History occupies a small place in the *De Re Architectura* and it is frequently impressionistic even by the standards of its time.

In the years to come, Vitruvius's materialist theory of regional architecture would survive, associated with the role of architecture in shaping ethnic identity, and it would also live on incarnated in racist and chauvinistic theories in nineteenth-century or early-twentieth-century architecture. But it will also serve as a point of departure in the study of the relation between particular environmental climatic factors and the regional diversity of human habitat and the regionalist movements toward its achievement.

In contrast to Vitruvius's book, Plutarch's *On Music*, written soon after *De Re Architectura*, gives a detailed historical account of *armoniai*, 'modes', tonal scales, the 'kinds' of music used in antiquity, and the role of imports, originally Asian, Thracian, and Egyptian, that led to the Greek inventions. Vitruvius's discussion about the origin of the Doric, Ionic, and Corinthian kinds of architecture was brief, anecdotic, or fairy-tale-like. However, there is evidence from the great Greek historian Herodotus, who credited non-Greeks with the origin of most Greek achievements, that many key aspects of Greek architecture in fact came from other regions. Paradoxically, Herodotus was attacked by Plutarch, who called him 'friend of the barbarians',[1] even though Plutarch himself, as mentioned, was equally forthright in attributing to non-Greeks the origins of Greek music.

The Alleged Purity of the Classical

The question of whether Greco-Roman architecture was original, pure, and spontaneous as opposed to created through 'borrowings' became very important, as we will see later, in the context of nineteenth- and twentieth-century debates about whether the pure ethnic ancestry of some regionalist groups gave them the nationalist right to become legitimate states and the imperialist right to conquer territories and take control of other groups.[2]

In these debates, it was repeatedly claimed that Greek architecture and the classical tradition were the original and pure expression of a special kind of people, the Aryans, who had their origins in a special region of the North. The contemporary implications of this story were that Greek architecture and culture, on which Western architecture and culture were founded, were pure and unadulterated. We find this view, for example, expressed as late as 1940 by the prominent Talbot Hamlin[3] in describing the creation of classical architecture as resulting from the coming together of a people 'speaking a language which belongs to the Aryan linguistic group, that ... were blond ... Ionians and ... Dorians' and that they 'created the Ionic and Doric orders'. The notion of Aryan purity is combined with Aryan superiority in January 1943, when a German Nazi philosopher, Martin Heidegger, anxious about 'the planet in flames' as a result of the world war, compares the noble mission of Germany with that of ancient Greece, both being races 'of poets and thinkers' dedicated to 'saving the West'.[4]

The Impure Regional Roots of Greek Classical Architecture

In fact, Greek classical architecture is anything but pure. It is an amalgam of different regional architectures, as we will see in the rest of this chapter.

There is a mass of evidence that Greek architecture, like most expressions of Greek culture, was not the product of the genius of a single people working in isolation. The Greeks and before them the Minoans were part of the early Mediterranean world. They settled next to the sea and established long-range sea routes interlinking diverse coastal regions, distributed over regions in the 'water-washed islands' or on the coasts of the wine-dark sea (*oinopi ponto*), crossing it in 'deep blue-bow', 'black hollow ships', enabling widely spread communities to stay closely interlinked, weaving almost global networks that enabled the exchange of food, materials, artifacts, people, techniques, information.

Homer, one of the great architects of the Greek identity, in *The Odyssey* [XVII380] refers to carpenters and builders as men with a craft from several regions traveling 'all over the boundless earth' rather than sitting in one place. Aristotle also considered it normal that craftsmen were mobile, thus most of the time immigrants and not citizens. As their names reveal, the great potters and vase painters of Athens were foreign. Rather than worrying about purity and authenticity, the ancient Greeks consistently welcomed regional materials, appropriating them and recombining them into universal systems. Even their *dodecatheon*, the family of deities of Greek polytheism, had its origins in regions outside Greece, the Greeks importing the deities and fitting them into a system, a constructed conceptual framework through which they conceived and construed their physical, cultural, and social world.[5]

As we shall see, Greeks settled close to the sea and set up 'global' (for their time) communication networks, interconnecting diverse

Figure 1.02 Protected bays in the Mediterranean: 'Archipelago' by Jacobus Robyn (Amsterdam, 1694).

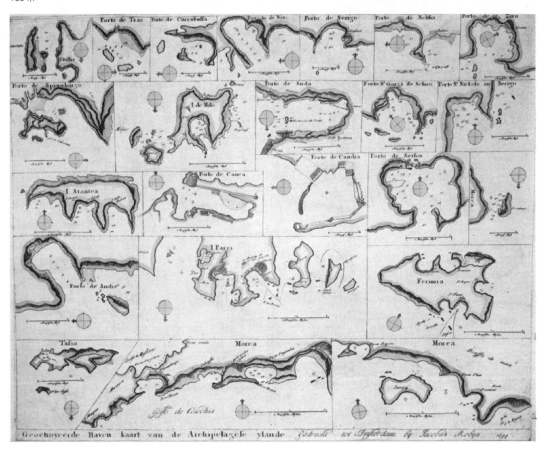

coastal regions of the Mediterranean, interacting with them, conquering them, and trading with them and, as a result, flattening the world. The unique characteristics of the 'Greek miracle' were exploration, discovery, recruitment, systematization, transformation, invention, through redesign and synthesis.

Between roughly 2000 and 1100 BCE, the area of what today is southern Greece possessed important settlements, densely built centers, inhabited by the so-called Minoans and Mycenaeans. Long-range sea routes linked their settlements, supplying food of higher nutritional value, superior construction materials and technology, artifacts, people, and information. In particular, the elements of novel knowledge imported from abroad recombined through 'fission and fusion' led to inventions that enabled a rise in the quality of the inhabited environment, constructing a built tissue with larger and more regularly configured spaces, and impressive domed burial structures. Painting was advanced, writing had become established, and the Mediterranean world was becoming increasingly flat.

Then, at around 1100, most of that social and cultural development vanished and was replaced by what has been called a Dark Age. For unknown reasons (although one of the contributing factors was the arrival of a new

Figure 1.03 Acropolis of Pylos, *c.*1300.

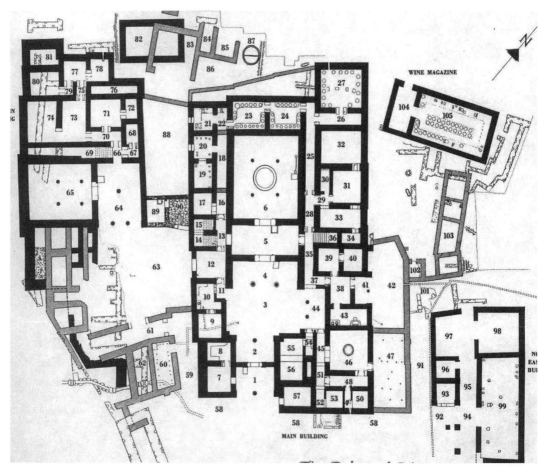

group, the Dorians), the densely populated 'urban', built centers were deurbanized, being replaced by distributed 'tribal' hamlets revealing a less structured, loosely coordinated society, and a lower level of division of labor. Writing was forgotten and significant knowledge, including sophisticated knowledge of design and construction techniques that we found practiced by Minoans and Mycenaeans, their maritime networks linking them with other Mediterranean regions, faded away.

The new Dark Age perhaps was not as dark as was once believed, but its settlements consisted mainly of communities turned inward on themselves, and the world of southern Greece entered a new phase of regional 'de-globalization'.[6]

Nevertheless, despite these prevailing conditions, after a period of about three centuries, for obscure reasons again (some experts suggest improvements in agricultural technology that were able to generate a surplus, enabling a revival of navigation, as a factor), the inhabitants of these distributed settlements consisting of old and new settlers appeared to become more organized collective entities, growing in size and wealth without signs of losing their autonomy. The era of the *polis* began. Not to be confused with the contemporary 'city', 'town', or 'city-state' – a type of settlement associated with dense, urban living – the *polis* could be a number of interlinked hamlets or villages spread out over a territory. Its identity was that of a relatively autonomous institution whose members participated in a relatively collective government. As such, the *polis* helped to bring together and anchor tribes that had previously been more decentralized and of a mobile nature.[7]

While these economic, legal, and political changes were occurring, during the eighth and seventh centuries, the inhabitants of several of these *poleis* became seafaring people. They turned to the Mediterranean, reestablishing commercial and cultural routes, founding colonies and once more transporting goods, people, and ways of thinking, designing, and constructing, and as a result raising their standards of construction and living.

The pattern of dispersed communities that made up the human geography of Greece after the time of the collapse of the Minoan and Mycenaean empires, the arrival of the new settlers, and the establishment of *polis* states was maintained during the archaic period.[8] The first communities located sanctuaries to define their claims over the land. The newcomers reused them to confirm the ethnic identity of their new communities as well as to establish borders.[9]

The function of sanctuaries as regional spatial-political markers was enhanced by rituals, processions, and periodic gatherings associated with the divinity of the sanctuary, displaying territorial control and spelling out stories confirming the legitimacy of this occupation, or even spelling out more nuanced relations of cooperation, conflict, or neutrality between a *polis* and its neighbors, as de Polignac suggests.

Very often, extra-urban sanctuaries and the ritual activities associated with them helped gather, reconstruct, or maintain the ethnic identity of a scattered community.

It is during these seminal years that the various dispersed micro-regional settlements in mainland Greece and their colonies, coexisting in a framework of cooperation, competition, but also conflict, developed various distinct styles of what was called later 'regional' architecture such as 'Doric' and 'Ionic', in turn the outcome of the 'fission and fusion' of imported architectures already developed in Mediterranean regions other than Greece.

From a Greece of Regions to a Panhellenic System

It was not until the various regions we have been looking at so far were brought together by the Athenians into one Panhellenic system that classical architecture begins to be conceived of as one system.

In a world of autonomous *poleis* related to each other in a framework of cooperation, competition, but also conflict, these freshly conceived design elements began to function as 'labels', identifying and representing their region of origin. Thus, the Greeks from Miletos in Antolia (Asia Minor) who founded Naucratis, the first Greek trading colony in Egypt, around 566 BC built their temple dedicated to the colonizing god Apollo using capital motifs, a girdle of hanging leaves and lotus flowers and buds around his neck, whose origin was their regional mother-city. As opposed to the colonies in southern Italy, which utilized a Doric style, a similar motif of palm-like hanging leaves was used by the Greeks originating from Anatolia who established the colony now known as Marseille, in order to represent the identity of their Anatolian regional origins. Centuries later, when in the second century King Attalos II from Pergamon donated the famous *stoa* (covered walkway) to the *polis* of Athens, he used the same capital – left unused for 350 years – to indicate the Anatolian identity of the donor and his region.

The representation of regional identity was important also in Panhellenic sanctuaries, institutions founded with the intention of bringing together the Greek tribes. The most important sanctuaries of this type were the site of the Panhellenic Olympic Games in Olympia and that of the Pythian Games.[10] The latter, established in 586 in Delphi, a place defined by the Greeks, modestly, as the 'navel' of the world, the seat of a 'global' institution claimed to have been founded by the god Apollo himself that invited 'people from all over the world' to have their questions about the future answered. Delphi, like Olympia, became a center initially for a periodic singing competition, which later turned into an athletic contest. The importance and popularity of Delphi is probably related to the first wave of colonization of the eighth century: the sanctuary specialized in giving advice about the foundation of colonies and the choice of their location, in this way forging a link between new communities and their parent communities.[11]

The Greek *poleis* were eager to participate during the festivals but also to be present in a more permanent way, erecting buildings, each *polis* competing with the rest in the quality of the design of their structure, its materials and execution. Interestingly, while the overall architectural idiom of these structures was universal – 'classical' – their details carried signs manifesting in these collective institutions their particular regional identity.

The choice of the location of Olympia and Delphi was very important. They had to be equally accessible from all the dispersed Greek communities and the same time outside the territorial orbit of individual ones. They had to serve all but favor none. Both the Olympic and the Delphic festivals were held in August or early September; their territory was regarded as inviolate, and the gathering of competing Greeks was accompanied with the observance of a sacred truce. Yet despite all these considerations, their capacity to centralize and unify the regional Greek tribes was limited.

Since the archaic period, there had been many attempts to form alliances. The Amphictyonic League, around the seventh century, was an early one that did not lead to a more permanent result. In 477 BCE, after the Persian defeat at the Battle of Plataea, the Athenians took the initiative in forming a league, bringing together more than 159 independent states with a center and treasury located on the island of Delos. On the other hand, it became increasingly clear that the alliance, initially founded as a defense organization against the Persians, was increasingly acquiring the characteristics of an empire under the Athenians, who controlled and taxed its members – a modern, as opposed to an Asiatic, empire, centralized but having no despot, and promoting democratic regimes for all its subservient member states.

Ictinus: out of the Regional, the Universal System

In 454, the Athenians took the initiative in moving the treasury of the Delian League to Athens. It was a few years before the construction of the Parthenon and the other buildings on the Acropolis, and it was rumored that they were built using the league's gold. An interesting fact is that while these political steps toward the integration of the Greek regions into a broad alliance were taking place, Ictinus designed the Parthenon, carrying out a very significant innovation the first step toward the integration of diverse regional architectural types, the Ionic and the Doric, into the same building, and thereby taking the first step toward the development of a universal architectural system.

Figure 1.04 Temple of Apollo, Bassae.

At about the same time, or perhaps earlier, he also designed the temple of Apollo at Bassae, carrying out the same experiment in integration by inserting in addition to the Doric and Ionic a new kind, the Corinthian. In 434, Mnesicles repeated the experiment in the Propylea, on the Acropolis of Athens. What was significant in these experiments was that they systematized the way a building was partitioned into parts or zones, associating each of the parts with each of the kinds of architecture: the Doric on the outside of the temple, the Ionic in the inside, and the Corinthian in the middle of the Ionic. This framework meant that the regional types were shedding their identity, becoming components of a universal system, the classical canon applicable to any building for all regions of the world.[12]

It is difficult to make out what the Athenians, and later the Greeks and the Romans, had in mind in synthesizing multiple regional kinds of Mediterranean design into the universal system, creating classical architecture. There is an intellectual explanation for this: just as in other domains of knowledge, philosophy, geometry, physics, and poetics, there is a quest for a coherent and total way for construing and constructing the world, so in building there is a search through history to find a universal system of architecture. In fact, the Greeks carried out a similar operation with the regional gods, creating, as was mentioned earlier, the *dodecatheon* system.

But there is also a strong political argument for the development of classical architecture. The Greeks, and in particular the Athenians, were driven by a desire to unify and dominate the Greek world. From this point of view, the drive for coherence that classical architecture stood for represented an ecumenical political order eliminating regional accidental anomalies, autonomies, and particularities.

In the end, the Delian League became a destabilizing factor in the family of Greek regional states, bringing about the Peloponnesian War. In 404, the league was dissolved. The Greeks maintained an identity juxtaposed to that of invading 'Asia', or 'the barbarian'. Other military coalitions tried to make a global union out of the autonomous regions and *poleis* of the Greeks. Yet for the Greeks, the loyalties to *polis* and to family remained stronger that those to a more global entity.[13]

The Greek states were finally brought together by force soon after their defeat by the army of Philip II in the Battle of Chaeronia (338 BCE). And around the time Vitruvius was writing *De Re Architectura* and about 'regional' architecture, the Greek city-states became regions of the Roman Empire. But even Rome and classical architecture did not escape the fate of being regional, as we shall see in the next chapter.

Chapter 2

The First Regionalist Building-Manifesto

One thousand two hundred years after Vitruvius wrote his book on architecture, we are back in Rome. But this Rome is no longer the seat of an empire. Officially, the capital of the empire, a Christian empire now, has been moved by the emperor Constantine to Constantinople, the New Rome, in 330 CE. What remains of Rome and its fourteen regions arranged by Augustus in 7 BCE is nothing but ruined structures and open fields.

The Roman Empire and the city of Rome had been declining for at least three hundred years. Left in the city were rudimentary pieces of imperial administration and the Christian bishop who claimed to be the successor to Saint Peter, the 'first bishop', and for this reason legal owner of the Lateran property of the city ceded to him by Emperor Constantine. The population of Rome at its lowest point had shrunk to a mere 30,000. Most people lived in the ancient ruins or in tenements between the ruins, some having lost the memory of who they were, some claiming that they descended from the ancient inhabitants of the city, but no longer one of what Oswald Spengler called the 'ruling races' (Herrenvölker).

It was in this Rome, in an ironic and tragic twist of history, that the first politically conscious regionalist building was erected using regional elements to defend the rights of the inhabitants of what was left of Rome to be independent from an encroaching new global empire in the making, the pope's new empire. The building, known today as the Casa dei Crescenzi, was a relatively small and strange-looking fortified mansion of weird configuration and, at first sight, bizarre decorations and arcane inscriptions covering its facades. The architectural historian W. S. Heckscher tried to decipher its meaning, reconstruct its story, and explain its inscriptions.

The Casa dei Crescenzi stands near the circular Temple of Hercules Victor and the Temple of Portunus, sometimes erroneously called the Temple of Fortuna Virilis, a masterpiece of Roman architecture. It was erected between 1040 and 1065, or perhaps as late as 1100.

In contrast to the classical order of these temples, the Casa dei Crescenzi is a chaotic collage of fragments cannibalized from antique Roman buildings, mixed with imitations of antique sculpture, antique friezes, arcane ornaments, volutes, foliage, and cryptic inscriptions, difficult to appreciate or understand today.

Figure 2.01 Casa dei Crescenzi, Rome.

One of these inscriptions on the facade of the building that can still be read states clearly in Leonine hexameters that the building was erected by Nicolaus, son of Crescens and Theodora, a member of the Crescenzi family. But who was this Nicolaus Crescenzi and why this Roman-looking architectural collage?

Heckscher claimed that, despite its chaotic appearance, the Casa dei Crescenzi was built with a clear intention: to support the idea of *renovatio* of ancient Rome, the Rome that produced the Casa de Crescenzi's two neighboring highly ordered temples.[1]

Crescenzi's idea of making a structure using ancient Roman fragments does not seem to be very original. Since 800, there had been an increasing number of buildings that, like the Casa dei Crescenzi, reused building fragments taken from ancient Roman buildings; the practice of cannibalization of antique structures had been permitted in Rome since 459, some of these scraps finding their way to Northern Europe.

Did this practice of *renovatio* in the North have the same meaning as in the Crescenzi mansion?

Reglobalization of the Classical

For Charlemagne, a ruler of the North who was crowned emperor of the Romans in Rome on Christmas Day 800 by Pope Leo III, *renovatio* meant reviving the Roman Empire under his aegis and thereby claiming the leadership for constructing a new global world in analogy to the global Roman Empire. His palace at Aachen, which began around the time of his coronation, ignored regional precedents and drew from the universal prototypes of the Roman Empire, including the basilica (*aula palatine*) at Trier, a palace built around 310 by Emperor Constantine, the emperor who brought together the old institution of the empire with the new institution of the Christian Church. While Charlemagne was building his palace, believing and having others believe that he was the new Constantine, Pope Leo III launched his own *renovatio* construction program in Rome, claiming for himself the leadership of the global empire under restoration. Like Charlemagne, he used for his Lateran palace an imperial precedent – more specifically, taking elements from the Imperial Palace of Constantinople.[2]

Charlemagne was not the first to take steps to forge this alliance with the pope. Before him, his father, Pepin the Short, the first king of the Franks (752–768) of the Carolingian dynasty, who was in theory elected to but in reality usurped the throne in 752, asked the pope to legalize his imperial status. Accordingly, Pope Stephen II, who anointed him at the Basilica of St.-Denis in Paris in 754, offered him the title *patricius Romanorum* (patrician of the Romans), a title associated with ancient Rome, in return for military protection. Consequently, Pepin descended on Italy to defend the pope against the Lombards and captured land that he 'donated' to the pope, consolidating the Papal (or Church) States in 751. Following the same cultural policy, Charlemagne solidified and expanded the popes' property, strengthening the alliance between king and pope, bringing the idea of a new global power, under the pretext of the *renovatio* of the Roman Empire, closer to reality. His coronation, which the pope inaugurated, set the foundations of the new *Holy* Roman global Empire as a bipolar condominium of emperor and pope. Functioning through separate courts and independent structures of administration, an arrangement quite different from the unipolar structure of the global Roman Empire, the condominium undertook the task of recentralization, reunification, and flattening of the fragmented regions of the ancient empire, the ruined city of Rome being one of these regions.

The project of reglobalizing the world under one central authority at the end of the first millennium was just as difficult as that of constructing the empire at the beginning of the millennium. While around the time of Vitruvius the military resistance of the archaic German tribes that presumably inhabited the regional huts referred to by Vitruvius was bloody (the Roman defeat at the Battle of the Teutoburg Forest and the revenge massacres that followed, littering the wild European landscape with corpses, was one of the most traumatic events in the history of humanity), the opposition to globalization by the more sophisticated militant German tribes of the time of Charlemagne was more complex and required hard diplomatic efforts as well as brute force. Their post-Roman Empire world, like the world that replaced the collapsed Minoan and Mycenaean Empires, consisted of self-sustained *castra* and *villae*, and a vast landscape of fragmented, depopulated, deurbanized regions occupied by illiterate tribes with local legal customs using no currency. Knowledge of how to make complex artifacts, and the classical cultural architectural canon of the Roman Empire, had been left to decline since the fifth century. The French art historian Focillon, in his masterpiece *The Year One Thousand* (1969), comments that around the year 1000, 'only formless and inept things' were produced and only buildings with 'rude' interiors and devoid of any order were erected. Many of the ancestors of the members of these tribes had welcomed the collapse of the Roman global 'order' and found no reason to collaborate in its resurrection and be flattened once more under a universal order, even if that meant the return of Pax Romana, the rediscovery of literacy, art, and law, and the reintroduction of currency. Neither a pope nor an emperor could overcome the resistance of their regions on his own.

The emperor could assemble an army but he needed the pope to provide an indisputably universal, 'holy' system of knowledge, law, and order. In 1155, when Frederick I, 'Barbarossa', became emperor, the empire began to be called 'holy', sealing the alliance between emperor and pope. Frederick I worked hard to establish common legal and administrative structures that could enable the centralization and globalization of areas inhabited by stubborn regional tribes but also Rome as a city.

Regionalism as Republicanism

It was about this time that the Casa dei Crescenzi was erected, using elements of Roman architecture in the design as an expression of the *renovatio*. However, for Crescenzi, *renovatio* stood for the opposite of the globalization program of the emperors and the pope.

Heckscher informs us that Crescenzi was a mid-twelfth-century citizen of Rome, leader of the 'regionalist' popular republican party revolting against Pope Innocent II in 1143 and struggling for the emancipation of Roman citizens from the 'imperial' and papal domination. In order to manifest his patriotic political regionalist movement, Nicolaus decided to employ architecture to express publicly his independent political views. He erected a new structure in which fragments of Roman ruins were reassembled into a new, proud composition. To make certain his objectives were understood, Nicolaus inserted in the facade an inscription in Leonine hexameters, 'Romae veterems *renovare* decorem'.

It is very important to add that for Crescenzi and his regionalist party, *renovatio* meant also 'renovation of the Senate'; that is, the creation of a republican regionalist government for a sovereign Rome. In its republican aspirations, Rome was part of a broader regionalist republican movement spreading among other towns in northern Italy at that time, which had already taken steps to establish municipal governing consuls to resist being flattened by the encroaching Holy Roman Empire. Around 1164, the Lombard League was formed to safeguard their autonomy. It included most important regional communes of the north, such as Milan, Bologna, Verona, and Venice. Just as the Holy Empire found legitimacy in the idea of *renovatio* of the original Roman Empire, so the communes of the league were inspired by republican Rome, which was ruled by a Senate.

In addition to the private initiative of Crescenzi, there were other architectural efforts in support of a regionalist Roman Republic such as those of the Orsini and the Catanei family. The most ambitious was by the Colonnas, the fiercest champions of republicanism in the face of what they saw as the foreign domination of a 'barbarian' imperial papacy.[3]

Krautheimer mentions the placing of a repaired obelisk 'from Roman times' on the Capitol Hill that 'may well have stood as a symbol of the *commune* and the Senate, the Roman Republic revived', and the Palazzo del Senatore itself, an arcaded imposing assembly hall for the commune.[4] The radicalism of the short-lived Commune of Rome went beyond regionalism and republicanism. One of the leaders of the movement, Arnold of Brescia (*c.*1090–1155), a student of Abelard, preached apostolic poverty and renounced ownership.[5]

However, the Senate and the dream of a regionalist republic did not last long. In 1155, with the help of Barbarossa, Pope Adrian IV (1154–1159) regained full control of Rome. Arnold of Brescia was tried by the Roman Curia as a rebel, hanged, and his corpse burned. The Commune was abolished. Rome, 'Mother of the Empire', the restored universal empire, was secured from its regionalist internal enemy. The conditions were ripe to focus on its project of globalization.

Chapter 3

A Flat Archipelago of Garden-Villas

Barbarossa put an end to the internal menace to Rome caused by the region-alist republicans, adhering to Charlemagne's pledge to secure the Rome of the popes from any threat. By 1155, Rome began to feel secure enough to pursue its rebuilding and reclaim its place as the unique universal center of the world.

As we have mentioned already, Pope Leo III – one might say in 'friendly competition' with Charlemagne's building program but also with Constantinople's superior architectural and urban achievements – began a major construction campaign during his papacy. Now the time had arrived for adding new types of buildings appropriate for the Church's growing operations by offering functionality, comfort, and a commanding image to represent its global power. By the beginning of the thirteenth century, a new architecture had emerged which aimed at providing for these new needs while maintaining the idea of *renovatio* and universality, so essential for the legitimacy of the globalization campaign of the Church.

Soon after his appointment, in 1198, Pope Nicholas III started modifying the interior of a palace that had previously belonged to Pope Innocent III, extending it and adding to it outside spaces. The architecture employed by Nicholas – who was of Roman origin, born Giovanni Gaetano Orsini – was classical Roman; that is, it expressed the claims of the Church to universality as a global institution. However, the plan of the building, opening onto the landscape and integrating the interior with the outdoor space, was 'regional'. Its scheme drew from local precedents designed to facilitate the enjoyment of the Mediterranean climate of Rome.

The project included a small enclosed garden to function as a 'secret' outdoor counterpart of the rooms of the building (*giardino segreto*). Further open areas were provided: a larger protected garden that contained specially chosen trees and animals. Nicholas did not invent the idea of these small and large gardens. As David Coffin remarked,[1] there was already a local tradition of such 'outdoor rooms' in 'princely Palaces'. On the other hand, there was also a strong link between these modern Roman gardens and the ancient Roman classical tradition of the *villa urbana*. In contrast to the *villa rustica*, the rural villa, which was a farm-estate, a *villa urbana* combined the character of an urban structure with that of the country. During Roman times, when this new building complex fusing building and garden was invented, it was aimed at emperors, a powerful elite, and the very rich, and was intended to enable, in a location not far from the urban center and in close contact with nature, enjoyment combined with business and administrative functions.

At the time of Nicholas III, Romans knew about the villas of antiquity from texts, the most important being the letters by Pliny the Younger, lawyer, writer, villa lover. He owned only three, while his uncle Pliny the Elder owned seven. The letters contained detailed descriptions of his Villa Tusci in Tuscany and the Laurentium, on the coast near Rome. Among the many projects that drew from his texts was Villa Madama on Monte Mario, designed by Raphael.[2]

In addition, Romans at the time of Nicholas could derive a first-hand, very incomplete, but real impression of how a villa/garden complex of antiquity was laid out from the ruins of Emperor Hadrian's villa at Tivoli, which contained gardens, courts, and about thirty buildings devoted to entertainment, administration, and study. Interestingly, the complex, though set out according to the universal classical Greco-Roman canon, had structures which related to the architecture of regions outside Italy that Hadrian ruled.

In employing elements from ancient Roman precedents, these new villas of papal Rome were expressing the political idea of *renovatio*, constructing a link between the elite of the Church and the ancient Roman elite, and at the same time offering a regional *villeggiatura*, a hedonistic way of elite life having very little to do with the values of Christianity, but appropriate as a summer vacation facility fit for administrative work, contemplation, study, and social-diplomatic entertainment, functions easily extendable to most parts of the year.

Figure 3.01 Papal garden of the Quirinale; engraving by Giovanni Battista Falda.

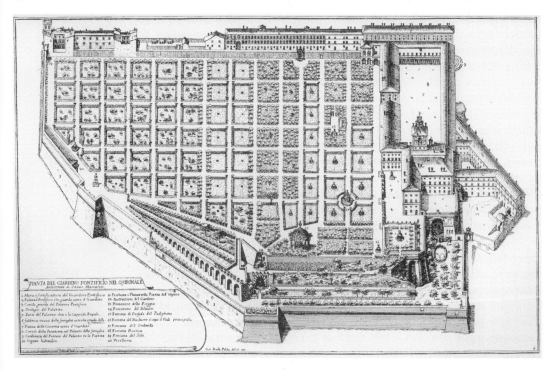

The newly invented outdoor spaces were particularly suitable for enhancing this amalgam of politics and pleasure embodied in newly designed ceremonies and feasts. The scenarios for these events, intended to be carried out mostly in garden settings, were reinforced by works of art, sculptures, wall paintings, and ornaments introduced into the surroundings. They were designed by contemporary artists according to specific iconographic political programs written by poets-historians-diplomats to give to the events a reconstructed, 'antiquated' character alluding to Roman or Greek mythology or history as universal models to justify the present and prescribe the future. In the 1570s, Pirro Ligorio in the Tivoli gardens drew parallels between Tivoli and Mt Parnassus; at around 1601, Giacomo della Porta introduced the Pillars of Hercules, a well-known classical symbol of global power, in the garden Villa Aldobrandini, and at around 1620, in the Villa Lante at Bagnaia, Bernini designed a sculptural group of Neptune and Triton drawing similar political parallels. The same effect was created without hiring contemporary artists by recruiting the real thing, inserting in the courts and gardens authentic ancient sculptures excavated from the ground of Rome, the most famous example being the early-sixteenth-century statue garden of the Vatican Palace of the Belvedere Court designed by Bramante around 1505. Even the trees placed in these outdoor spaces – laurel, olive, myrtle, bitter orange, and sycamore – were chosen on the basis of their presence in model classical texts.

On the other hand, there was also a deeper and a more abstract way of expressing, in the design of a garden-villa, the analogy between the new global empire being pursued by the Church and the earlier Roman Empire. This involved organizing the space of garden-villas according to the rules of the universal classical architectural canon. Better than in the existing gardens of Rome, which have been greatly modified over the years, one can see the application of the Vitruvian rules, but also of the Aristotelian classical poetics,[3] in the design of the garden/villa complexes in the books of the period that documented these projects through magnificent illustrations, especially the superb aerial views engraved by G. B. Falda.

One can also find the composition rules of thumb for arranging a garden corresponding to the design rules for laying out the parts of a building in treatises of the period. The most important text about architecture of the period, Alberti's *On Building* of 1452 (book IX, ch. IV), dedicated mostly to proportions in general, briefly discusses the design of gardens. Alberti recommends 'figures that are most commended in the Platforms of Houses, Circles, Semicircles, and the like' and 'trees [which] ought to be planted exactly even, and answering to one another'; that is, figures with bilateral symmetry. The basic message of the text is that the spatial organization of gardens should follow the same universal rules of regularity and order as buildings do.

Similarly, other texts of the period suggested not only simple geometric forms, such as perfect squares, circles and rectangles and evenly spaced divisions, but also more complex motifs such as quartered arrangements, foursquare compartments, and bipartite or tripartite divisions of the garden.

This led to a deep spatial unity between building and garden, as we saw in the garden-villa of Nicholas III, with the rooms and the outdoor spaces conceived of as complementary parts of a single composition. Numerable schemes were invented following the principle: in the ambitious composition of the Villa Medici garden, Bartolomeo Ammanati embedded the building within the tripartite and quadripartite landscape framework. More grandiose and complex was the composition of Belvedere Court. Here Bramante, intending to set up an analogy between Pope Julius and the Roman emperors, inserted in his composition architectural elements recruited from classical Rome: the Stadium of Domitian, the sanctuary of Palestrina, and the Palace of the Caesars on the Palatine Hill. Courts, terraces, supporting walls, and stairs were synthesized, producing an outdoor spatial effect far grander than any building could achieve at that time. Similar were the compositional achievements of the Farnese Gardens by Vignola around 1618, or the Villa Pamphili of 1645–1653, driven by the rules of classical composition with the goal of representing, no less, universal order abstractly.

However, in creating these amazing spatial compositions of abstract beauty and order, based on abstract norms, universal classical rules, and an internal logic from above, the architects of the period disregarded the identity and particularities of the existing grounds and the region. Such schemes required reshaping of the natural local landscape through massive excavations, leveling, and earth-moving – flattening the world in the most literal sense. The work elicited admiration, if not awe. An account of the Villa Albani in 1769 commented: '[H]ere everything is done against the nature of the site … originally everything was unequal and sloping, whereby it was necessary to take away earth from one part and carry it to another.'[4]

Within this inexorably ordered framework, the occasional 'disorder' was not only tolerated but actually welcomed, and even 'organized'. The most remarkable example involved placing symbolic objects according to an adventurous narrative scenario that was meant to entangle the viewer in the wilderness. This was the Sacro Bosco in Bomarzo, put together by Vicino Orsini. Orsini worked for about four decades until his death (in 1583) to achieve this complex project, and probably had as collaborator the architect, expert iconologist, and garden 'scenarist' Pirro Ligorio. But even here, the 'disorder' of the design was equally detached from the identity of the site.

The construction of ideal models on concrete sites entailed not only an act of violence against natural particularities, but also destruction of human-made regional structures, including old lanes and roads. Occasionally, this aggression elicited negative reactions from the local inhabitants, as in the case of Villa d'Este at Tivoli, where Cardinal Ippolito d'Este 'ruined the houses of the poor citizens against their wish', harassing them when 'they did not consent to his will'. In 1568, the cardinal was taken to court but the plaintiff was unsuccessful.[5] The regionalist party in Rome was long gone and there was no one to defend his property rights.

By the second part of the seventeenth century, the Roman villa/garden complexes were known, admired, and, as we shall see, imitated around Europe. However, the monopoly of Italian artists began to decline. For example, it was claimed that Villa Albani and its gardens were influenced by French designers and Villa Pamphili was attributed, wrongly, to the famous French garden architect André Le Nôtre. In reality, Le Nôtre did visit the garden in 1679, but that was all.

An important means of transmitting the classical architectural canon and establishing it as a global way of designing buildings and gardens outside of Italy was through books. Vitruvius became available in a French translation by the great French humanist Jean Martin in 1547. But more important was the exchange of people. Before Le Nôtre's visit, French architects and artists went to Rome to study. At the same time, Italian architects and artists went to France to work during the reigns of Charles VII and Louis XII. François I wanted to make certain that the most perfect works, designed according to the classical *renovatio*, were produced in France and, just as the pope and the Holy Roman Emperor had done earlier, he believed that architecture and art could legitimize and publicize his political program, his aspirations to construct a global empire.

Technically highly competent, architecture in France at that time continued to employ to a great extent regional, medieval, 'Gothic' methods, as one can see in the structure, many facade details, and the typical high roof of the château of Blois, François I's initial involvement with building, in 1515, and the Château de Chambord, which followed in 1519, designed probably by Domenico da Cortona, an Italian architect, who moved to France in 1495 with his teacher Giuliano da Sangallo. At the same time, both projects introduce functionally innovative elements, especially the Château de Chambord, but also import and establish the global classical canon.

Toward the same 'globalist' goal, in 1516 François I invited Leonardo da Vinci, by then an old man of mysterious reputation, and in 1540 and 1541 the Italian architect and author Sebastiano Serlio, after having read his books *I sette libri dell'architettura* (Seven books of architecture).

Philibert de L'Orme as Regionalist

French architects and artists also went to Rome to acquire first-hand knowledge of the 'new classical' design, among them Philibert de l'Orme. Son of a master mason, Philibert was born and educated in Lyon, a thriving economic center through which the achievements of the Italian Renaissance entered France. Philibert stayed in Italy between 1533 and 1536, and even worked there. Upon his return in France around 1541–1548, he worked at the Château de Fontainbleau. Given his growing reputation as a practitioner, but also as an intellectual with a deep knowledge of classical architecture and classical culture, Philibert was commissioned in 1547 by the mistress of Henry II, Diane de Poitiers, to design the Château d'Anet. The terrain, near Dreux, as in most cases in France, was more level than in most sites in and around Rome, a factor that made the universal classical doctrine easier to realize and the idea of global culture that it stood for easier to accept. The building and garden composition, as documented by an engraving by Jacques I Androuet du Cerceau, formed a rigorous classical synthesis. In this and in many of his projects, in the words of Anthony Blunt, '[Philibert] De L'Orme's design is classical but does not go back mimetically to any Roman model'.[6]

In fact, Philibert was very much preoccupied in developing an entirely new 'French order' which he applied in the chapel in the park of Villiers-Cotterêts, commissioned by Henry II about 1550. This was contrary to his first intentions when he returned from Italy, when, as he remarks in his *Instruction* (1559), he felt he had a mission 'to bring to France the art of good building' – that is, the universal canon of classical architecture – and 'remove the old barbarous ways' of the locals. In fact, when Henri II died, in 1559, and

Philibert, without a major client, turned to writing, he began investigating the problem of a 'French order'. In his treatise, the first by a Frenchman, he rejected the obedience to the established Italian universalist canon, inviting originality, innovation, and efficiency, and promoting a regionalist-nationalist point of view. He argued:

> In different nations and countries, architects felt free to invent new types of columns, as was the case with the Latins and Romans with the Tuscan and Composite columns; the Athenians the Athenian column. A long time before the Latins and the Romans, the Dorian architects invented the Doric column; the Ionian architects the Ionian columns; and the Corinthians the Corinthian. Who, then, would keep us, the French, from inventing some of our own and calling them French?

The basic point of departure, claimed Philibert, is difference and not universality. The new French columns must be carried out through 'the imitation ... of natural things that are God-given: trees, plants, birds, animals ... the way nature made them different from one another'. Further on, because France is lacking in the kind of marble that permitted Tuscans to erect monolithic columns, he suggested a structurally sound column made of superimposed modules made out of local French stone.[7]

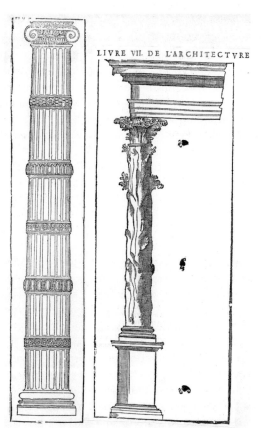

LIVRE VII. DE L'ARCHITECTVRE

Figure 3.02 Philibert de l'Orme: the 'French order' next to the natural order: *The First Volume of Architecture* (1567).

In a regionalist-nationalist spirit, Philibert went on to propose what a French column should look like. It has to 'be decorated and enriched with the things which are more inclined to Nature as she is to be found in the Kingdom of France'. For example, one can decorate bases, capitals, architraves, friezes, and cornices with elements that are 'particular to this Kingdom' such as 'fleurs de lys and other devices used by its Kings, Princes and Seigneurs'.[8]

Most French architects contemporary to Philibert were more focused on perfecting the classical canon or promoting it by producing books about it aimed at the French or a global audience rather than developing a regional architecture. Among the most important were the Mollets. Jacques Mollet, possibly a collaborator of Philibert, and his sons Claude and André designed, built, and wrote on classical gardens following universal norms.

Claude Mollet's book *Théâtre des plans et jardinages* (1652) was read in France but also beyond its borders. André Mollet's *Le Jardin de plaisir* was published in Sweden, where he was spreading the idea of the universal classical garden in Stockholm in 1651, working as a designer of gardens in Sweden for Queen Christina and in England for Charles I.

Probably the greatest promotion of the globalization of the universal classical canon was done by the superbly illustrated books of Jacques I Androuet du Cerceau, *Livre d'architecture* and *Les Plus Excellents Bastiments de France* (1576, 1579), which appeared in numerous editions in France and elsewhere.

Jacques I Androuet du Cerceau was also a prominent architect. Around 1558–1568, he designed Charleval for Charles IX. Our knowledge of the project is derived from his engravings, which show influences of Italian precedents, including Serlio's plan for the Louvre, but the compositional strictness and overall coherence of the work, its inventiveness in partitioning space, and its grandiose scale were uniquely French – regional but not necessarily regionalist (that is, consciously promoting regional values).

As with the architects and clients of the garden-villas of Rome, there was a major intellectual fascination among the French elite with the classical design canon as a great invention of a system of spatial order. However, as in Rome, together with this intellectual fascination there was also a political movement driven by the ideas of universality, centralization, and globalization under the aegis of François I.

Spatial Order and Absolutist Power

François I's globalization ambitions were twofold. They were international and they were simultaneously internal, related to the reorganization of the regions of the country. Indicative of his political visions and cultural universalism was the appointment in 1530 of Guillaume Postel, a scholar preoccupied with the development of a universal religion, expert in many languages and disciplines, as professor in his newly founded institution of public instruction and research, the Collège Royal de France, today the Collège de France. Postel's task was to teach mathematics and Hebrew.

In the founding of the Collège and the appointment of Postel, François strove to demonstrate that the universal center of knowledge and art was no longer Rome or Italy, but France. On the other hand, the practical value of the appointment was also revealed when François made moves in 1536 to set up a West–East global axis with Suleiman the Magnificent, Postel acting as a key adviser in the project.

At the same time, his plan to reorganize France focused on setting up the country in the manner of a sixteenth- and seventeenth-century classical château/garden complex, developing his scheme according to the internal logic of the universal classical canon, subjugating the uniqueness of the region and the individuality of the site within one scheme. This plan aimed at eliminating regional particularities and self-rule. Achieving such a harmonious state was a counterpart to his grand plan to create and lead an equally harmonious global empire. It involved putting under a central universal control mechanism over the highly particularized regions of the country, which up to that moment had been ruled by local nobility and whose inhabitants to a great extent did not even speak French. It also involved applying the same administrative measures to regional towns, which since the middle of the fifteenth century had been dominated by the wealthy bourgeois. Moreover, the king's plan was to contain the power of the local *parlements*, which defended regional economic interests, regional laws, regional styles of clothing, traditional local liberties, and rights that had been inherited from the time when regions were more autonomous and local governments had enjoyed greater freedom. Among other things, these seats of regional power also tended to back the pope's economic claims rather than the king's interests.

Designing absolutist universal laws, centralizing, and standardizing the French regions and towns also had an immediate pragmatic reason: creating an effective and efficient organization for the collection of taxes to finance increasingly costly military campaigns.

The regions resisted, and uprisings, whether urban or rural, were not uncommon. They were led by local nobility or by masses of peasants, the peasants being the group who suffered the most, being also victims of famines, epidemics, and the brutality of the state troops stationed temporarily in their region. A cluster of revolts occurred around 1636–1637 in the regions of Loire and Garonne, Angoulême, Burgundy, Périgord, and in the 1660s all over the regions of France: in 1662 in Boulonnais, in 1664 in Landes, Gascony, in 1665 in Lille and Soissons, in 1666 in Dunkirk, in 1669 in Amiens, in 1670 in Languedoc, in 1676 in Rennes, and a major rebellion in 1674–1675 in Bordeaux.

In the Holy Roman Empire, the situation was better. Regions and towns enjoyed more independence from the central imperial authority. There were numerous 'free', self-governing towns (Free Imperial Cities, *Freie Reichsstädte*), territorial towns (*Landstädte*), and autonomous communes governed by a council of elected citizens. However, the political regionalism that had operated since the middle of the fifteenth century became increasingly oligarchic-patrician and decreasingly independent toward the seventeenth century.

The New, Post-Westphalian World

In 1648, a most significant diplomatic event occurred that slowed down this tendency toward centralization and globalization, the Peace Treaties of Westphalia. Initially, the purpose of the congress that produced the treaties was to put an end to the bloody and senseless Thirty Years' War, which involved several European states, including France and the Holy Roman Empire, but also several Free Imperial Cities.

The implications of the Treaties of Westphalia were enormous. Most significantly of all, they initiated a new way of looking at a rigorous definition of sovereign state as an entity that has no authority superior to it. This meant abandoning prejudices inherited from the Middle Ages and the efforts to reconstruct the original Roman Empire. In addition, it established the idea that all sovereign states are equal from the legal point of view. This was intended to keep in check the forces of centralization and globalization by advancing the right to self-determination of regions and nations. On the other hand, the treaties referred to the sovereignty of a state and not the self-determination of a people or a nation, or how the sovereignty of a state emerges, issues that were to emerge a century and a half later.

As the Peace of Westphalia was being signed, major popular unrest and complex fighting between key members of the nobility shook Paris and France, with barricades appearing for the first time in Paris, under the name of the Fronde. It threatened to reverse all the progress made since François I toward the rationalization of the administration of France.

The hostilities were ignited by Cardinal Mazarin, the chief minister. He pursued the long-term policies of the Crown to centralize the administration and enrich the king's coffers. Reacting to demands concerning the lowering of taxes, the stopping of new bureaucratic appointments, and the strengthening of the power of the *parlement*, Mazarin arrested the leaders of the *parlement* of Paris and curtailed its operations in August 1648.

As we saw above, the *parlement* was a conservative institution supporting traditional regional sovereignty, and did not completely identify with the radical policies of the kings. As the pressure mounted, on January 6, 1649 Mazarin took a risk and, together with the ten-year-old king and his mother, fled Paris.

The panicky flight can be explained by the events that were taking place in England the same time. As was the case in France, regional uprisings were endemic. One of the issues contested was the policy of 'enclosures', which caused peasants to lose their traditional grazing rights over open common areas, turning those areas over to the landlords to increase their cultivable property and, as an overall result, increasing the efficiency of agriculture in the country. The 'Diggers' and 'Levellers' emerged at that time, radical groups who engaged in physically digging and leveling the boundaries of the enclosures. And while religious matters also played a major role in England, equally important was the confrontation between the encroaching centralist powers of the king, Charles I, and the regionalist opposition led by the Parliament. Like Mazarin, in 1629 Charles dissolved the Parliament, which to a great degree was responsible for the economy and taxation, and imprisoned some of its members. For the following eleven years, Charles I ruled as a 'personal ruler', or 'tyrant' as some called him.

Regionalist Revolts

The middle of the seventeenth century was a period of severe crises in Europe: from Andalucia to Sicily and Russia there were regional mobilizations, protests, and anti-feudal uprisings. In 1652, in Cordoba and Seville the local people set up a sort of commune government. In 1653, in Switzerland, a rebel army of 250,000 men, mostly peasants, was raised in few months.

The conditions in England were similar. The rural conflicts worsened rapidly around 1648 owing to poor weather, poor harvests, and high prices. Inside London, the radical Levellers collected 10,000 signatures within just a few days and on another occasion 100,000 signatures, vigorously promoting the rights of 'the free people of England'. Their *Standard* of April 20, 1649 contained a radical '*Declaration to the Powers of England*' but also '*to all the Powers of the World*':

> The Earth (which was made to be a Common Treasury of relief for all...) was hedged in to In-closures by the teachers and rulers, and the others were made Servants and Slaves: And that Earth that is within this Creation made a Common Store-house for all, is bought and sold, and kept in the hands of a few.

The 'Declaration' envisaged a global world where

> Enmity in all Lands will cease, for none shall dare to seek a Dominion over others, neither shall any dare to kill another, nor desire more of the Earth than another; for he that will rule over, imprison, oppress, and kill his fellow Creatures, under what pretence soever, is a destroyer of the Creation.

The same year, the song of the Diggers movement was a call for insurrection:

> You noble Diggers all, stand up now,...
> Your houses they pull down,...
> But the gentry must come down, and the poor shall wear the crown.
> With spades and hoes and plowes stand up now...
> ...we should now begin, our freedom for to win.
> ...stand up now.

But the song ends with a non-polemical invitation '[t]o conquer them by love'.

As the nervous Mazarin was moving the king out of Paris, the regime of Charles was ending and his trial under preparation. Charles argued along the lines of the French political philosopher Bodin, namely that as 'an absolute sovereign, [his] authority is ... not shared with any of [his] subjects'. In response, the court claimed that it was not the institution of the Crown that was being tried but the person Charles, two different things.

Charles was beheaded on January 30, 1649. The project of political centralization under the Crown was set aside and a new balance was created between the Crown, the Parliament, and the regions. But the question of centralization of rural property in the hands of relatively few landlords remained unanswered. The sense of discord, anger, horror and loss prevailing in England during this period was captured in a strange, ambiguous poem, 'Upon Appleton House', written in the year when Charles was executed and the

Levellers were defeated by Cromwell. It is dedicated to Lord Thomas Fairfax (1612–1671), a military man close to Cromwell but not always in agreement with him. The poet was Andrew Marvell (1621–1678), a tutor of Fairfax's daughter Mary.

The poem opens with a polemical statement criticizing the arrival of 'foreign' architects and models from Italy or France, applying a classical architecture of pomp and waste, something Fairfax avoided:

> Why should of all things Man unrul'd
> Such unproportion'd dwellings build?

Marvell juxtaposes to these absurd human structures a primitivist architecture that fits to the region and the environment, which is to say that it is functional and rigorous:

> The Beasts are by their Denns exprest:
> And Birds contrive an equal Nest;
> The low roof'd Tortoises do dwell
> In cases fit of Tortoise-shell:
> No Creature loves an empty space;
> Their Bodies measure out their Place.

In the Fairfax house, however,

> ...all things are composed...
> Like Nature, orderly and near:

without the absurd, superstitious Vitruvian classical rules that dominate the design of the Roman villas and the French châteaux/gardens we examined earlier.

> The *Circle* in the *Quadrature*!
> These *holy Mathematicks* can
> In ev'ry Figure equal Man.

as opposed to a settlement

> Where ev'ry Thing does answer Use?
> ...
> The House was built upon the Place
> Only as for a *Mark Of Grace*.

Design does not need rules to be produced; it emerges:

> ... Nature here hath been so free
> As if she said leave this to me.
> ...
> In fragrant Gardens, shady Woods,
> Deep Meadows, and transparent Floods.

The site and architecture Marvell praises is one where the traditional local community, social justice, and peace are restored and rule:

> For to this naked equal Flat,
> Which *Levellers* take Pattern at,
> The Villagers in common chase
> Their Cattle, which it closer raise.

Given this context, Mazarin was justified in removing the king from his capital. The same anger and chaos reigned in France as in England. However, at the same time the conditions were socially more stable and less anti-monarchical. The nobility was in-fighting. The bourgeois had placed their trust in an alliance with the king rather than with the confused factions of the nobility, from which they had nothing to gain, and for that reason were not willing to turn against the Crown. The peasants had great difficulty in findiing a reason to form a long-term association with any of the above. But the part of the Fronde that took place in Bordeaux, between 1648 and 1652, was one of the few regional movements where a broad alliance was formed that included the local *parlement*, *rentier* bourgeois, local commercial and artisan classes, as well as the lower classes, Catholics and Huguenots, declaring that it is 'equality that makes perfection' and identifying the 'wealth of the few' as the cause of trouble.

There have been many theories put forth about the causes and the nature of the Fronde. They range from a clear Marxist interpretation by Boris Porchnev,[9] who explained the event in the framework of class war, the bourgeois and proletariat fighting side by side against the government, to Roland Mousnier's opposite position interpreting the conflict as a more complex episode where parts of the nobility and a mixture of regionalist forces, but not class alliances, united against the rising control of France by the monarchy.[10] However, since each theory focused on a different set of data and one interpretation does not exclude the other, apart from ideological reasons, both theories can be accepted simultaneously. The unquestionable fact is that the growing tendency of the Crown to control the regions in an effort to extract larger amounts of taxes created a resentment that was shared by almost all classes and regional alliances, including regional nobility and peasants. The crisis exploded when the harsh economic demands of the Thirty Years War upon the population could no longer be borne.

Mazarin, with his schemes to centralize the government in order to perfect its tax collection mechanisms, was the main target of the revolt, and the population at large, the nobility, and crowds continued to be sympathetic to the king, although they favored the older conditions of regional autonomy. One of the reasons the French king was not in danger was that the groups that constituted what was referred as the Fronde frequently fought with each other without declaring real war, and never formed a front. The result was what Louis despised as 'chaos', a condition, to quote Hobbes about the dangers of anarchy, of 'every man against every man'. By October 1652, the king was back in Paris. It has been claimed that his aversion to 'chaos' and his determination to eradicate it influenced most of his political and cultural decisions.

Louis XIV Flattens the World

To erase the memory of the 'chaos' of the period of the Fronde, as Louis called it in his memoirs, in 1668 he went so far as to order the burning of all public documents related to the event, selectively 'recopying' only some of them. As head of state, he continued in the direction set out by François I, trying to bring order to the organization of the state and to centralize its regions, restrain the autonomy of their *parlements*, choose the mayors of the major cities himself, and squash any centrifugal forces. One of the earliest and most important cases in this campaign was the destruction of Nicolas Fouquet, his minister of finance and owner of the legendary garden-château of Vaux-le-Vicomte.

The project was one of many garden-châteaux that emerged after the end of the Italian wars during the second half of the sixteenth century and multiplied all over the landscape of France, forming by the seventeenth century, to borrow Erik Orsena's image, an 'archipelago' of proud, insular structures having very little to do with the region to which they belonged.[11] Some were the property of the king, manifesting his expanding universe. Some were seats of regional nobility, or even of bourgeoisie emulating the nobility. Through the perfect composition of these projects, France was showing off, claiming its central position in the world as Rome had done in an earlier era with the garden-villas. However, in the complex political-cultural landscape inside France, the projects were part of a competition – the king claiming his central position in relation to the nobility, the nobility seeking to signal their independence from the Crown while competing with their peers.

Vaux-le-Vicomte was constructed between 1658 and 1661 and designed by Le Nôtre together with the architect Louis Le Vau and the painter Charles Le Brun, three men who were close collaborators in bringing about the classical canon in France. As with several garden-châteaux, the grandiose classical scheme required the demolition of a large number of peasant houses, to be exact three whole villages. The result was the most spectacular and perfect project of its kind in France and Europe at that time. The designers paid the greatest attention to the smallest detail, each element being studied so that it would find its place in correspondence to the other elements and to the whole composition, a harmonious universe, a closed world within the world, as if the huge project were a Greek or Roman temple.

As soon as the project was ready, in August 1661, Fouquet decided to give a massive feast, which took place both inside the château and outdoors in the gardens. Apparently, he was foolish enough to provoke the envy, the fury, but also the suspicion of Louis by walking him through the buildings and gardens, displaying, together with the architecture, the best food, music, and entertainment available in France at that time. Louis, only 22 years old, had nothing to show that could be compared with Fouquet's property. Soon after, in September 1661, after careful personal preparation by Louis himself, Fouquet was arrested by the captain of the Musketeers, the famous d'Artagnan.

The fact is that Louis XIV, and his close adviser Jean-Baptiste Colbert, who had just been appointed a member of the king's council, found enormous financial irregularities in Fouquet's administration. More importantly, he found the post of 'superintendent' that Fouquet occupied to be ill-defined, dysfunctional, and contrary to the grand plan of a tighter, centralized organization running France, headed by the king. The administrative reasons that led to the arrest are apparent from a letter Louis wrote to his mother in September 1661, in which he clearly states that he would not have another 'superintendent' in the future and that he was planning to 'do his finances himself'.

The new administration, totally centered upon the king, relied on the assistantship of a number of highly qualified but 'vile' bourgeois of humble birth, as the members of the team appointed by Louis XIV were characterized by Saint-Simon. The high nobility were excluded from this group. One of the bourgeois upstarts was Colbert, who would go on to play a major role in the building program of the king in the future as Superintendent of Buildings, as well as Intendant of Finance in 1664.

To carry out the program of centralization and the 'flattening' of France, Colbert found necessary to develop a strong alliance between the king and the ingenious, energetic, and wealthy bourgeois population of Paris. He wanted the king to be a true resident of Paris in a new extension of the old palace of the Louvre. The initial choice for an architect of this project was Gianlorenzo Bernini, an Italian who was serving the pope and who was considered the best architect and artist of his time, and commonly thought to be divinely inspired.

However, Colbert was not impressed by these qualifications. He saw in the choice a continuation of the old dependence of France on Rome, the alleged guardian of the universal rules of art and architecture, and he wanted none of it. In the framework of the old long-term policy first conceived by François I, which placed France as the head of a global world, Colbert wanted the country to be the custodian and arbitrator of the universal rules of the arts and architecture. To this end, he persuaded the king to establish a number of academies: the Academy of Sciences (1666), the Academy of Music (1672), and the Academy of Architecture, which he founded himself in 1671. Through these academies, Colbert wanted to break not only the dependence of France on Rome as a center of knowledge but also the obligation to follow the dogmas and canons of Vitruvius. Thus, having set up the new royal institution, he instructed its members to redefine the universal rules of architecture, if they existed, on the basis of modern science. Allied with him in this project was Charles Perrault,[12] a medical doctor and member of the Academy of Science, who had an excellent knowledge of construction and was an expert on Vitruvius, whose book he retranslated from Latin. Perrault had just developed a new theory based on evidence, disproving the old theory of Vitruvius about the existence of universal norms in architecture. Opposing Vitruvius, he claimed that architectural rules were not constrained by the 'positive' laws of nature. They were like the rules of manners in the court: 'arbitrary' conventions instituted by the center of power, the royal authority. The implication of this modern theory was that the French were free from Rome and Vitruvius, free to develop, apply, and diffuse their norms of design. In this manner, Perrault liberated the king and his court from the classical Greco-Roman tradition and invited them to decide 'arbitrarily' on the rules that should order culture and society, everything that was not subject to nature. In a way, he was expressing the esoteric doctrine of Louis XIV, 'L'État c'est Moi' (I am the state), equating the state, a human artefact, with the manners of the court that Louis obsessively controlled and reinvented, with art. On the other hand, at the same time, implicitly, as a man of the proto-Enlightenment, with his stated belief in the 'arbitrary' rather than absolute foundation of power, he opened up the possibility for every individual and every region to declare their independence.

Claude Perrault failed to convince the members of the Academy that they should adopt his ideas. On the other hand, thanks to the support and machinations of Colbert, who succeeded in humiliating Bernini by withdrawing the commission for the Louvre and dispatching him back to Rome, Perrault was hired as the architect of the extension of the Louvre.

Colbert, however, failed to persuade Louis XIV to make the Louvre his base and home. Louis had another plan, which gradually became his major preoccupation: to build his own garden-château, the most perfect in the world, about 17 kilometers outside Paris at Versailles, where Louis's father had kept a hunting lodge. The choice of location, which was known for its good microclimate, indicated that the king was not abandoning Paris as a center of France but saw the world in a different framework from that of Colbert, a framework within which the bourgeoisie did not play such an important role. From this moment on, his plans diverged from those of Colbert.

Some said that Louis, still traumatized by the danger of another Fronde, wanted to stay away from Paris for his protection. He moved to Versailles as a result of his supposed continuing obsession with the 'chaos' of the Fronde. Louis was quite knowledgeable about military matters. He believed that in the event of a major insurrection, the Louvre could not provide serious security. He wanted construct a super-garden-château to co-opt, control, and coerce the centrifugal forces of the nobility by containing them physically. He turned his super-chateau into a kind of a super-prison for the nobility. From Colbert's point of view, the project was a mistaken move to the isolating 'suburbs', away from the teeming center of power.

Adamant and deeply envious of the high achievement of Vaux-le-Vicomte, Louis decided to recruit Le Nôtre for the Versailles project and give him all the means necessary to create the most beautiful capital, because he saw the Versailles château/garden complex not as a building and garden but as a new center of the world.

Le Nôtre worked to make Versailles, more than Vaux, a total environment. As in Vaux, so in Versailles. Gardens, buildings, and sculptures were positioned with supreme order. Trees, land formations, and water were cut, leveled, straightened, and gutted to conform to the preconceived formal stereotomy of the scheme. The more the composition was gaining in internal coherence, the more it was losing its contact with and relevance for the real world. By contrast, the real adjacent 'new town', which displaced the old village and was intended to accommodate services and houses for those who were attached to the palace, had all the open urban characteristics but it did not help to overcome the insulating effect of Versailles.

The court moved to Versailles in May 1682, and at first it functioned as planned. France constructed a capital that manifested in its form and the

Figure 3.03 The Marly-le-Roi garden and hermitage by Jules Hardoin-Mansard and Charles Le Brun, 1677 and 1684.

idea of a universal order and of a center from which the rest of the country's regions, and later the other states of the world, were to be controlled, harmonized and flattened.

However, as Colbert foresaw, even if in the short term Versailles succeeded in bringing about a new global world, in the long term it accelerated the decline of the regions and the decomposition of the country. What Colbert himself, who, with his commercial acuity and as the economic expert of the regime, failed in the end to comprehend was the real complexity of the French and international economy of his time. His mind was constrained by the economic models of the period, so-called mercantilism, according to which, for a country, money paid to import goods was like blood lost in bleeding. This is ultimately the reason he wanted, through his academies, to produce and control know-how regarding the design and manufacturing of artifacts, from clothes to architecture. Within this centripetal model, there was no room for the role of the regions except for that of bearers of a crushing tax burden.

Starving the Regions

Colbert did not realize that the economy was more complex. Someone who did was Charles Davenant (1656–1714). Investigating the facts about the English economy of the same time, he arrived at different, empirically based conclusions. In discussing the concept of 'balance of trade' in his 1696 *Essay on the East India Trade*, he argued against mercantilist protectionism and for what we might, anachronistically, call globalization (specifically, protecting English textiles against Indian imports), on the grounds that commerce was in the long run good for Britain's balance of trade. Davenant was also, unlike Colbert, against the policy of high taxation. He showed that in the long run it was ruining the regions, something that had started occurring in France at the time of Colbert.

Colbert's thinking about the regions of France was relatively simplistic. Like Louis XIV, he saw them as autarkic entities whose sole purpose was to feed the Crown. He did everything to enable this function administratively. Toward this end, Louis XIV had declared in his edicts that all landed estates had been granted to their tenants conditionally and that the state was the ultimate owner. As a result, when food shortages occurred, the logic of the structure of the regional organization of France did not permit direct linking between regions. This led to periodic catastrophic famines and chronic peasant revolts. It produced only a non-sustainable overall system that eventually would bring both the bourgeois of Paris and the so-called aristocrats of the *ancien régime*, not to mention the royal family itself, to their knees.

In England, seven years after the court of Louis XIV had moved to Versailles, the Bill of Rights 'Declaring the Rights and Liberties of the Subject' was passed by Parliament. It prohibited the king from 'assuming and exercising a power of dispensing with and suspending of laws and the execution of laws without consent of Parliament'. It also secured free 'election of members of Parliament' and 'the freedom of speech and debates or proceedings in Parliament'. In England, the power appeared to be moving in the opposite direction as compared with France, away from a centralized, flattening model and giving the power to a 'distributed', decentralized commercial and estate-owning class.

Chapter 4

'Consult the Genius of the Place in All'

At the dawn of the eighteenth century, there was no place more dissimilar to a classical garden-château in France than the Royal Exchange in London. At first glance, the two places are so dissimilar that it makes no sense to compare them or contrast them. One is a building type making up an entire archipelago in the French countryside, the other a unique place in London, the capital of England. Yet if we juxtapose them, we see on a more abstract level two distinct approaches to globalization and regionalism, two approaches to organizing the Western world at that time.

The garden-châteaux across the French territory, including Versailles, were designed top-down as versions of a universal model, as classical closed worlds within the world, suppressing regional particularities. The English Exchange, as described by Joseph Addison, a neophyte politician, playwright, and essayist,[1] was an emergent, free, open 'Assembly of Countrymen and Foreigners consulting together upon the private Business of Mankind', a 'Metropolis', and 'a kind of Emporium' for the 'whole Earth', a 'great Council' where 'all considerable Nations have their Representatives' and people 'divided from one another by Seas and Oceans, or live on the different Extremities of a Continent', keeping their particular regional identity, come together.

As opposed to the orderliness, the formal exclusiveness, and 'mathematical happiness' of the French landscape, to quote Orsenna once more, inside the Exchange one could 'see a Subject of the Great Mogul entering into a League with one of the Czar of Muscovy', 'distinguished by their different Walks and different Languages'. 'Sometimes', Addison continued, 'I am jostled among a Body of Armenians; sometimes I am lost in a Crowd of Jews; and sometimes make one in a Groupe of Dutchmen', to the degree that '[I think that] I am a Dane, Swede, or Frenchman at different times; or rather fancy my self like the old Philosopher, who upon being asked what Countryman he was, replied, That he was a Citizen of the World.' Welcoming global diversity, Addison adds:

> Nature seems to have taken a particular Care to disseminate her
> Blessings among the different Regions of the World, with an Eye
> to this mutual Intercourse and Traffick among Mankind, that the

>Natives of the several Parts of the Globe might have a kind of
>Dependence upon one another, and be united together by their
>common Interest.

Foreshadowing Adam Smith by sixty-five years, Addison added that even if
the 'Body of Men' were 'thriving in their own private Fortunes', at the same
time, without intending to do so, they were 'promoting the Publick Stock'.
'Trade, without enlarging the British Territories, has given us a kind of additional Empire' – ignoring the fact that at that moment the so-called War of the
Spanish Succession was going on, the English fighting against the French,
two years before Gibraltar was ceded to Britain.

Like Versailles, Addison's Royal Exchange comes forward as a
normative model for a world in flux, which 'multiplied the Number of the Rich,
made our Landed Estates infinitely more Valuable than they were formerly,
and added to them an Accession of other Estates as Valuable as the Lands
themselves'. In addition, in contrast to the imprisoning globalization of Versailles, Addison celebrated the new global environment of the Royal Exchange
as a vehicle of liberation, where the 'Vassals of some powerful Baron' in the
recent past are now 'negotiating like Princes for greater Sums of Money than
were formerly to be met with in the Royal Treasury!'

The Genius of the Place

Addison, not unlike Claude Perrault, rejected any kind of universal dogma
such as, for example, the classical one in architecture. But he also rejected
universal rules of design even if they were modern, as long as they were dictated from above. To him, this meant they were what Perrault had called 'artificial'. Instead, he wanted design inventions to emerge directly from the
forces of nature.

Perrault, an apolitical animal, found nothing wrong with following
artificial rules in the wake of the often fatal chaos of the Fronde. But Addison
– after the Parliamentary victory at Worcester on September 3, 1651, the
success of the Glorious Revolution of 1688, the English Bill of Rights, and the
more recent setting up of the Parliament of Great Britain on May 1, 1707, following the Act of Union between England and Scotland, to be housed in
Westminster in London, all events that contained the power of the monarchy,
enabled the forces of decentralization, and strengthened the power of a particularist Parliament – was overwhelmed with enthusiasm for the possibility
of a new way of life and a new kind of happiness to be found not in supersti-
tions and dogmas but in nature. His utopian optimism for a global world
grounded on Liberty had already been expressed, a year before (on April 20,
1710), in the *Tatler*, a periodical he had just founded with Richard Steele in
1709. The text narrates a dream about a free world he discovered flying above
the Alps, 'at the very Center of those broken Rocks and Precipices', and even
above them after he 'gained the Top ... another *Alps* of Snow' a 'Paradise ...
this happy Region ... inhabited by the Goddess of *Liberty* ... covered by profusion of flowers ... without being disposed into regular Borders and Par-
terres, grew promiscuously ... in their natural Luxuriancy and Disorder'.
However, the text comes to a critical conclusion that is turned not against the
French politics of centralization but against the English land policies of

'inclosure Acts' by means of local parliamentary decisions promoting centralization of local properties and exclusion of peasants from them. His flight affirms coming across a new happiness, 'wonderfully pleased ... in ranging through this delightful Place ... because it was not encumbered with Fences and Enclosures'.

Two years after the publication of Addison's 'dream' in the *Tatler*, Anthony, Earl of Shaftesbury (1671–1713), a Whig politician, philosopher, and writer, published a manifesto, *Characteristics of Men, Manners, Opinions, Times* (1711), that explicitly linked the new political ideas with the architectural ones. The *Characteristics* stressed that the universalist, classical, 'Vitruvian' doctrines practiced in France, as well as those imported and spread in England, were authoritarian and oppressive, in contrast to the liberating approaches based on nature and the identity of the particular place. The text, which has many similarities with the one by Addison quoted above, is even more panegyrical in support of the new political and design ideas:

> I sing of Nature's order in created beings, and celebrate the beauties which resolve in thee, the source and principle of all beauty and perfection ... Thy being is boundless, unsearchable, impenetrable. In thy immensity all thought is lost, fancy gives over its flight, and wearied imagination spends itself in vain, finding no coast nor limit of this ocean, nor, in the widest tract through which it soars, one point yet nearer the circumference than the first centre whence it parted.

While praising unruly Nature ('The wildness pleases.... We contemplate [Nature] with more delight in these original wilds'), he attacked 'the artificial labyrinths and feigned wildernesses of the palace', and in an optimistic turn announces that a new world that respects the particular, the natural, and freedom has arrived:

> the genius of the place, and the Great Genius have at last prevailed. I shall no longer resist the passion growing in me for things of a natural kind, where neither art nor the conceit or caprice of man has spoiled their genuine Order, by breaking in upon that primitive State. Even rude Rocks, the mossy caverns, the irregular unwrought Grotto's, and broken Falls of Waters, with all the horrid Graces of the Wilderness itself, as representing NATURE more, will be the more engaging and appear with a Magnificence beyond the formal Mockery of Princely Gardens.

The same year (1711), Alexander Pope, a classicist as a poet, published his anti-classical, pro-regionalist poem 'Essay on Criticism'.[2] Written in 1709, when Pope was twenty-one years old, the poem confirms that the creator must 'First follow Nature ... Unerring Nature': 'Rules of old, discover'd, not devised', which are 'Nature still, but Nature Methodized'. At the same time, Pope included many ideas that belonged to the heritage of the 'ancients' and a mini-history of the classical tradition, with the admittance that 'Critic Learning flourish'd most in France'; 'But we, brave Britons', as opposed to the servile French, 'foreign laws despis'd / And kept unconquer'd and unciviliz'd, / Fierce for the Liberties of Wit, and bold, / We still defy'd the Romans, as of old.' Pope's model circumscribed a region within which the norms of the universalist classical canon of composition were overtly and systematically reversed and negated.

In addition to his theoretical reflections, Pope also tried to design a garden. This is not strange, since a large number of the experiments to create a new landscape in eighteenth-century England were carried out by the owners of estates rather than professional gardeners. His project was a retreat in Twickenham and was carried out from 1719 on with the assistance of John Searle, a gardener by profession. The plan was published in 1745 after Pope's death by Searle, and one can admire a daring juxtaposition of classical motifs with irregular forms. The project included a grotto that attracted the admiration of his contemporaries, and a stream that an anonymous contemporary letter calls a 'fortunate Accident to Mr Pope', which he exploited as well as other features of 'the Place'. His intentions are described in a 1731 poem dedicated to the Earl of Burlington (1694–1753), an architect with whom he shared the same ideas about nature and particularity of place and region.

> [*Epistles to Several Persons: Epistle IV, To Richard Boyle, Earl of Burlington*]
> To build, to plant, whatever you intend,
> ... let Nature never be forgot ...
> Consult the genius of the place in all;
>
> ...
>
> Spontaneous beauties all around advance,
> ... strike from chance.

Further down he added a nationalist warning that the English way of design from the ground up will win through: 'proud Versailles! thy glory falls'.

A year later, Addison, again in the *Spectator* (June 23, 1712), returned to the question of the foundations of the rules of design, bringing together the idea of nature, the particular, and the regional with that of political freedom: 'The Mind of Man naturally hates every thing that looks like a restraint upon it, and is apt to fancy it self under a sort of Confinement' and 'a spacious Horizon is an Image of Liberty', and, stressing the importance of diversity, 'the Pleasure still grows upon us, as it rises from more than a single Principle'.

The ideas are elaborated further in the next issue of the *Spectator*. Here, however, Addison for the first time brings in another argument against the universalist classical dogma, the architectural traditions of another part of the world, namely China. The argument echoes a 1692 text by William Temple (1628–1699), a liberal politician, diplomat, and essayist, where for the first time the Chinese way of designing gardens is contrasted to the Western one:

> Among us, the beauty of building and planting is placed chiefly in some certain proportions, symmetries, or uniformities; our walks

and our trees ranged so as to answer one another, and at exact distances. The Chinese scorn this way of planting and say a boy who can count to a Hundred may plant walks of trees in straight lines and over against one another.[3]

Again, the world of nature is favorably compared to court classical design: 'Works of Nature and Art, as they are qualified to entertain the Imagination, we shall find the last very defective, in comparison of the former'; and further down Addison writes:

> There is something more bold and masterly in the rough careless Strokes of Nature, than in the nice Touches and Embellishments of Art. The Beauties of the most stately Garden or Palace lie in a narrow Compass, the Imagination immediately runs them over, and requires something else to gratify her; but, in the wide Fields of Nature, the Sight wanders up and down without Confinement.

He calls the classical European landscapes shaped through universal geometrical formulas 'laid out by the Rule and Line ... trees in equal Rows and uniform Figures', 'Trees ... in Cones, Globes, and Pyramids', 'trimmed into a Mathematical Figure' laughable in their simplemindedness, according to the Chinese.

By 1715, the new design movement was sufficiently developed for Stephen Switzer, garden designer and writer, to publish *The Nobleman, Gentleman, and Gardener's Recreation* (1715), which included an early attempt to provide a rough historical sketch of gardening in England. An enlarged version in *Ichnographia* (1718) followed. In his subsequent *Ichnographia Rustica* (1741–1742), Switzer does not hesitate to express his common sense puzzlement: '[W]hy should we be at that great Expence of levelling of Hills, or filling up of Dales, when they are the Beauty of Nature?' Why one should disfigure what a region supplied to apply a biased formula instead of thinking of the 'Goodness of the Land' and the 'Situation of a Seat' as an opportunity?

Switzer was credited as the person who introduced the term 'ferme ornée' to describe the practice of 'mixing the useful and profitable parts of Gard'ning with the Pleasurable'. Interestingly, he provides as an example 'the practice of some of the best Genius's of France', a country which, as we have seen, dominated up to that time with conservative ideas, asserting that he 'was always the promoter of this Farm-like Way of Gardening, before it was used by anybody in any place in *Great Britain*'. Historically his claim might be inaccurate; on the other hand, its value is that it stated clearly the emerging conflict in garden design between an approach aspiring to 'luxury and glory', represented mostly in the classical château-gardens of France during this period and one that targeted maximum profit, with which the gentry of England would be increasingly identified. Supporting Switzer, Batty Langley, a gardener and very popular writer, would assert in his *New Principles of Gardening* (1728), a most influential book at that time, that '[t]he End and Design of a good Garden is to be both profitable and delightful'.

The most read history of this distinctly English way of designing landscapes appeared much later, in 1771, with the *Essay on Modern*

Gardening by Horace Walpole. Walpole was an author, historian, politician, and amateur designer with very original and influential ideas. In his book, he tried to trace the rise of the new English regionalist movement and the decline of the globalist claims of the classical design dogma imported from France; the moment people realized that its 'absurdity' 'could go no farther ... the tide turned'. Walpole identified Charles Bridgeman as the designer representing the transition but credits as the real innovator William Kent (1685–1748). According to him, Kent studied and worked in Italy (from 1709 to 1729), returning to England with a unique proficiency in the classical canon of architecture as well as in the recent developments in landscape painting of the time led by the French painter Claude Lorrain.

Walpole both admired and criticized Kent. He considered him a major 'reformer' who set free the garden from its 'prim regularity', the classical norms, 'that it might assort to the wilder country without'. But he was also afraid of his innovations, a new 'fashion': 'new fashions like new religions (which are new fashions) often lead men to the most opposite excesses'. He even questioned Kent's honesty in having planted dead trees 'to give a greater air of truth' in an uninteresting spot. In the end, he admits that Kent was a major innovator, for having 'nature taken into the plan', coining the memorable phrase '[Kent] 'leaped the fence and saw that *all nature was a garden*', which epitomizes the deeper aspirations of the English movement to redefine the relation between culture, artifice, and nature. Although hesitant about the radical implications of the ideas of the new approach to design in England, Walpole admitted that the new way of designing was also intimately linked with a new way of life: 'the method of living is totally changed, and yet the same superb palaces are still created, becoming a pompous solitude to the owner, and transient entertainment to a few travelers'. And turning nationalist, he appears proud of 'how rich, how gay' and, using the term by which the new English way of designing would be known, 'how picturesque the face of the country' has become, with the 'demolition of walls laying open each improvement, every journey is made through a succession of pictures'. On the other hand, the visual effect of the disappearance of 'walls' as property boundaries, to be replaced by the ha-ha (a design device that Walpole attributed to the creativity of Kent, though Kent in fact took it over from French moat design), reflected the idea that the reality of the economic policies of the enclosures should become invisible. However, by 1768 George Mason, in his very influential *Essay on Design in Gardening*, finds that the effect of these '*sunk fences*' intended to do away with 'reference to actual property' is in itself disagreeable and 'necessarily destroys harmony of the landscape'.

On the other hand, Walpole himself, while maintaining his Whig optimism when envisaging the future of England ('what landscapes will dignify' every region in 'our island' when all these developments 'have attained venerable maturity'), he takes also the stance of the independent historian warning about a possible 'relapse to barbarism, formality, and seclusion'.

By the time Walpole's book was published, there were a considerable number of projects conceived and constructed according to the new English way that could be visited and admired, such as the landscapes of Rousham and Stowe, Kent having played an important part in their design.

Figure 4.01 Plan of Stowe garden from Benton Seeley's *Guidebook* (1744).

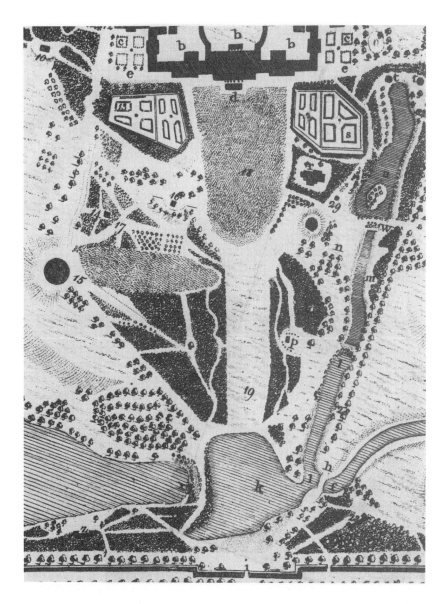

Touring the Regions

One of the visitors was William Gilpin, who wrote a descriptive guidebook to the project, with the title *A Dialogue upon the Gardens ... at Stow in Buckinghamshire*, published in 1748. Stowe became famous for its 'picturesque' qualities. However, as Gilpin, unlike the authors cited so far, was more attracted by the artifacts – a 'Palladian Bridge', an 'Obelisk rising', a 'Pyramid', 'the Temple of Friendship', the 'Temple of Liberty', an 'Imitation of the antient Taste of Architecture', 'a kind of Castle several Stories high' ('great Additions') – than by the natural landscape:

> There is something so vastly picturesque, and pleasing to the Imagination in such objects, that they are a great Addition to every

Landskip ... so great a Variety of beautiful Objects, and all so happily disposed, make a most delightful Picture.

Whereas the *Dialogue* focused more on structures and sculptures in Stowe, several years later, in 1782, Gilpin turned to nature and published *Observations on the River Wye and several parts of South Wales, etc. relative chiefly to Picturesque Beauty; made in the summer of the year 1770.* The aim of the book, accompanied with good illustrations by him, was to instruct people how to draw landscapes – in fact, it was to teach the English public a new 'mentality', how to look at nature as a picture, very much in the manner of Claude Lorrain's paintings.

The *Observations* contained very few lines about buildings, being devoted mostly to highly nominalistic descriptions of nature – 'forests, lakes, rocks, and mountains' – trying to capture the particular identity of the region in time, space, and atmosphere:

[S]ky, mountains, and vallies were all wrapt in one cloud of driving rain and obscurity. Our recompence consisted in following with our eye the rear of the storm; observing through its broken skirts a thousand beautiful effects and half-formed images, which were continually opening, lost, and varying, till the sun breaking out, the whole resplendent landscape appeared again with double radiance, under the leaden gloom of the retiring tempest.

Gilpin produced other books based on 'picturesque' tours, setting up a fashion for visiting the various regions of Britain and their unique landscapes. More books followed in the same vein by other authors. Even books satirizing the new fashion appeared, such as William Combe's *Tour of Dr Syntax in Search of the Picturesque* (1809).

Rarely can we find out with certainty how and why such fashions materialize. The easiest yet most doubtful way is to try to link such developments with material changes. Yet one is tempted to ask whether this fascination with the regions and their natural particularity had to do with the booming of the agricultural economy in the second part of the eighteenth century in Britain. Without doubt it was the result of the development of agricultural managerial techniques, together with the taking over of the estates by a new class, the so-called Whig gentry and nobility. In contrast to the aristocracy's 'obedience and the avoidance of change', dominant during the middle of the seventeenth century, their 'crushing burden of belief in the need for social stability', to quote Laurence Stone, that 'held all innovations and new ways suspicious' (ibid., quoting Sir Edward Coke),[4] the new class was active and realistic, and believed in the potential of any region for improvement and in any form of industry, including agriculture. The buoyancy of this new class was encouraged by the legislation of 'enclosures', the 1780 Enclosure Acts that made land cultivation highly profitable for the landlords, more profitable than at any time previously in Britain. On the other hand, this renaissance of the regions was not good for everyone. Enclosure, while increasing and unifying the cultivable property, was made possible only by peasants losing their traditional grazing rights.

After almost a century of such economic advances and improvements, the devastation of the natural landscape and the traditional communities brought about a wave of critical texts by leading writers in defense of the regions.

Already in 1728, Batty Langley, in his *New Principles*, in spite of the highly encyclopedic and didactic character of his book, did not hesitate to attack the self-congratulating fashionable improvers, 'those *wretched Creatures* (*regular Coxcombs*)' who have been destroying 'at a great Expense … in Leveling … the great beauties of Nature'.

As we saw earlier, the original creators of the idea of the new English landscape in the beginning of the eighteenth century had celebrated 'the genius of the place' and 'contemplate[d] nature with more delight in these original wilds' than in the 'artificial and feigned' artifices. About the middle of the century, the time William Gilpin wrote his book *A Dialogue upon the Gardens … at Stow …*, Studley Royal is praised in Philip Yorke's *Journal*, in 1744, for the fact that its temple of Venus, Hercules, its Gothic tower, its Chinese house and landscape have very little to do with 'nature', 'place', or region. The only authentic local object mentioned, the 'ruins of [an] Abbey', could not be purchased so that it could be included in the property, but if it had been included, the author reflected, it 'would indeed have been a noble addition'.

Figure 4.02 Gothic
entrance to a moat.

'Improvements' and Ruined Regions

Aiming to make the domains more productive or more according to the new aesthetic trend, the 'improvements' ignored the region and its people. In addition to moving ground and cutting trees, the improvements frequently involved demolition of local houses and removal of their inhabitants, who had been already deprived through 'enclosures' of land on which to live as independent peasants. The emerging poverty was not taken out of sight. It was made visible, so it would be easier to control. In 1697, a law required paupers, mainly originating from those enclosures and forced removals, to wear on their clothes a blue or red 'P'. As poverty rose during the second part of the eighteenth century, descriptions of deserted regions became more common. Gilpin's *Observations on the River Wye*, written in 1770, included next to the picturesque description of the Cistercian Tintern Abbey near Monmouth – an impressive ruin that would later be painted by Turner – 'among other things' a 'scene of desolation':

> The poverty and wretchedness of the inhabitants were remarkable. They occupy little huts, raised among the ruins of the monastery, and seem to have no employment but begging; as if the place once devoted to indolence could never again become the seat of industry.

Oliver Goldsmith's (1730–1774) poem 'The Deserted Village' (1770), written more than a century after Andrew Marvell's *Upon Appleton House*, about a village whose inhabitants were forced to move out, the land to be used for an improvement, is a lament and angry protest at the physically and socially destructive effects of the 'improvements' of the regions.

Goldsmith contrasted scenes of the happiness and prosperity of the locals of the village ('Sweet Auburn! Loveliest village of the plain, / where health and plenty cheer'd the labouring swain', 'where every sport could please', and 'where humble happiness endear'd each scene') before the 'improvements' with the current situation.

Like Proust, he evokes early sensual memories that he contrasts with the present; unlike Proust, he makes a critical political juxtaposition:

> Seats of my youth, ...
> How often have I loiter'd o'er thy green;
> ...
> How often have I paused on every charm,
> The shelter'd cot, the cultivated farm,
> The never-failing brook, the busy mill,
> The decent church that topp'd the neighbouring hill.

This was the world before the 'improvements', the old settlement a place for work and a place for play, where community brought together people of all ages:

> When toil, remitting, lent its turn to play,
> And all the village train, from labour free,
> Led up their sports beneath the spreading tree!
> While many a pastime circled in the shade,
> The young contending as the old survey'd.

But under the present conditions, 'all these charms are fled', and now 'Amidst thy bowers the tyrant's hand is seen, / And Desolation saddens all thy green: / One only master grasps the whole domain' – a 'tyrant', a description used until recently to refer only to absolutist despots.

This is no more the land of a united people. It is a land divided not by region but by economic status:

> Where wealth accumulates, and men decay.
> Princes and lords may flourish, or may fade;
> A breath can make them, as a breath has made;
> But a bold peasantry, their country's pride,
> When once destroy'd, can never be supplied.
> . . .
> But times are alter'd; Trade's unfeeling train
> Usurp the land and dispossess the swain;
> Along the lawn, where scatter'd hamlets rose,
> Unwieldy wealth and cumbrous pomp repose.

The human sensual-acoustic environment, the 'sweet sound' of the place, in the past, 'at evening's close', 'when oft up yonder hill the village murmur rose' is silenced; 'the sounds of population fail' and the community dialogue is suppressed.

> Low lies that house . . .
> Where village statesmen talk'd with looks profound,
> And news much older than their ale went round.
> . . .
> No more the farmer's news, the barber's tale,
> No more the woodman's ballad shall prevail'.

The close ties of the vanished local community are replaced by a new order of inequality where 'The rich man's joys increase, the poor's decay'.

> . . . The man of wealth and pride
> Takes up a space that many poor supplied;
> Space for his lake, his park's extended bounds;
> Space for his horses, equipage, and hounds;
> The robe that wraps his limbs in silken sloth
> Has robb'd the neighbouring fields of half their growth;
> His seat, where solitary sports are seen,
> Indignant spurns the cottage from the green;
> . . .
> Where, then, ah! where shall poverty reside?'

In reference to the enclosures, he added: '[E]ven the bare-worn common is denied', referring to the traditional open fields that supplied food for animals, access to which was now denied with the series of 'Inclosure Acts'.

Goldsmith's poem ends optimistically about the future world: 'that Trade's proud empire hastes to swift decay', while the oppressed, the 'self-dependent power can time defy'.

In other writings (William Cowper, 1731–1800, *The Task*, Book III: *The Garden*, 1785), the landscape designer Lancelot 'Capability' Brown (1716–1783), one of the most successful practitioners or 'improvers', is attacked as an 'omnipotent magician'. When he appears,

> Down falls the venerable pile, th'abode
> Of our forefathers, a grave whisker'd race,
> But tasteless. Springs a palace in its stead.

Cowper does not believe that the fashion of estate 'improvement', 'the idol of the age', is driven by the beauty of the regions and a genuine love of nature. Society is ruled by pecuniary interests and vanity. Contrary to claims about the attraction of the country landscapes making people want to own estates, estates are economic objects 'gazed upon awhile, / Then advertised, and auctioneer'd away'. There is no longer a peasant owner attached to the earth and to the region, only 'a transient guest, newly arrived, / And soon to be supplanted'. This is why in the end not the regions and nature, but cities, 'attract us'; 'nature pines' and is abandoned as 'unworthy of our love'. But Cowper asks the question, are not 'wholesome airs' and 'clear suns ... and groves'

> To be preferr'd to smoke, to the eclipse
> That metropolitan volcanoes make,
> Whose Stygian throats breathe darkness all day long;
> And to the stir of Commerce, driving slow,
> And thundering loud, with his ten thousand wheels?

Cowper included in the poem a kind of didactic story of an 'estate owner's progress' whose appetite for grander and frenetic, unstoppable additions of meaningless costly constructions ruin him. What follows is that finally, 'Drain'd to the last ... / He sighs, departs, and leaves the accomplish'd plan'. After unsuccessfully trying 'Ministerial grace', 'money from the public chest', and 'a usurious loan', he commits suicide.

As the eighteenth century came to an end, the political and cultural values that steered the English way of designing gardens, referred to increasingly as 'picturesque', began to fade away. The design of gardens became more standardized, following rules dictated from the top down, rather than from the ground up taking into account the idiosyncratic potentials of the site and the region.[5]

Authors reiterated with pride earlier anti-French arguments, more nationalist than regionalist, about the superiority of 'Old England's Genius' and the Englishness of the new English garden, more a formula than a new line of reasoning:

> Great Nature scorns controul: she will not bear
> One beauty foreign to the spot or soil.
> ...
> One native Glory, more than all sublime.[6]

Similarly, Sir Uvedale Price, in his widely read *Essays on the Picturesque, As Compared With The Sublime and The Beautiful* (1794) declared that 'there is no country... (if we except China) where the art of laying out grounds is so much cultivated as it now is in England', and that there is 'a decided superiority of British taste in Gardening', the country itself being 'a *School of Landscape*'.

However, there are moments when Price, one of the sharpest critics of form of the second part of the eighteenth century, becomes polemically critical of the state of the movement from the political, moral, and aesthetic points of view, not hesitating to point out the negative effects of the new kind of landscape practice. The picturesque, he argued, had abandoned its initial promise, now being driven by formalistic ideas and becoming just a fashion, assimilating all the bad qualities of the classical garden. 'Formerly, every thing was in squares and parallelograms; now every thing is in segments of circles, and ellipses: the formality still remains; the character of that formality alone is changed', the new fashion being 'deformity'.

> The intention of the new improvers was certainly meritorious; for they meant to banish formality, and to restore nature; but it must be remembered, that strongly marked, distinct, and regular curves, unbroken and undisguised, are hardly less unnatural or formal, though much less grand and simple, than strait lines; and that independently of monotony, the continual and indiscriminate use of such curves, has an appearance of affectation and of studied grace, which always creates disgust.

Price was critical even of the work of Kent from a conservative point of view. In his concluding chapter, he accused him of destroying rather than conserving a region, as was promised by the new movement. Kent, 'like other reformers', 'demolished without distinction'. There are echoes here of what was happening around 1794, when the Reign of Terror held sway in France, and in England at that time the Treason Trials were intended to destroy the reformers of English politics.

Yet Price was not just a simpleminded conservative. He was polemically against the local practice of 'improvement' in a passage that reads like a critique of any authoritarian planned globalization in the name of progress: 'There is, indeed, something despotic in the general system of improvement; all must be laid open; all that obstructs, levelled to the ground; houses, orchards, gardens, all swept away.' He is surprised that sometimes 'this method of levelling all distinctions, of making all places alike all equally tame and insipid' should not have been checked. Should not something have been done, given 'our repugnance to despotism'? His argument was quoted in post-World War II Britain when the central planning policies of the Labour government were criticized.

Price was wary of false patriotism in a time of war. He cautioned:

> It seems to me that there is something of patriotism in the praises which Mr. Walpole and Mr. Mason have bestowed on English gardening; and that zeal for the honour of their country, has made

them, in the general view of the subject, overlook defects, which they have themselves condemned... I feel anxious to free it from the disgrace of propagating a system, which, should it become universal, would disfigure the face of all Europe.

Walpole, by contrast, was content that it was England that 'has given the true model of gardening to the world' and more blasé about how 'other countries mimic and corrupt our taste; but let it reign here on its verdant throne'. Actually, in a snobbish way he believed that 'our style of garden' would not be adapted for 'general use in the continent. The expense is only suited to the opulence of a free country, where emulation reigns among independent particulars', with only one exception: the 'princes of Germany, who spare no profusion on their palaces and country houses, [are] most likely to be our imitators'. Indeed, with few exceptions that was the case.

Chapter 5

From the Decorated Farm to the Rise of Nationalist Regionalism

Many accounts by travelers returning from England to the Continent, and an increasing number of publications circulating in Europe during the first part of the eighteenth century, reported that something significant in landscape design was happening there: a new 'English way' in garden architecture that broke universal, classical dogmas and embraced natural regionalist values. The English welcomed the visitors who arrived to examine their 'English gardens' and, as Horace Walpole wrote to George Selwyn, they found this *anglomanie* flattering and amusing.[1]

In more than a passing fancy, and contrary to what Walpole expected, many people in Europe started considering the 'English way' as an intriguing alternative to design landscapes, and one that relieved them from the burden and demands of the classical canon.

Part of the French elite society in search of new sources of 'amusement', 'gaiety', and 'happiness', welcomed 'English regionalism' as a response to their search for a new genre to escape 'boredom'.[2] What they found appealing in it was the anti-classical spirit, the breaking of the rules. They had already experienced similar experiments in another recent import, this time from Italy: the 'decorative' *genre pittoresque*, applied mostly to the interior of buildings and to furniture design. By the mid-eighteenth century, the *pittoresque* had become an established trend, much to the dismay of the academician of architecture Gabriel-Germain Boffrand, who took no pleasure in this 'confused mixture of curved and straight lines' (1752–1757), finding it 'oppressive, frivolous, and flimsy' (1771), which, as another important architect and theoretician, J.-F. Blondel, in his *Book on Architecture* (1745), bitterly acknowledged, had become more important than 'classical correctness', a 'fashion'.[3]

Although also anti-classical, the 'English way' of landscape design, or the *picturesque*, as the new genre was referred to more frequently, in England and on the Continent, was different from what the French initially meant by *pittoresque*. The *pittoresque*, as one can see in the famous book of designs published by Juste-Aurèle Meissonnier, *Dessinateur de la chambre et du cabinet du roi*, was abstract, formalist, generating distortions of classical shapes in a rigorous way, employing newly developed techniques of projective geometry.[4]

The Regions of the *Philosophes*

On the other hand, the new, English way of designing landscapes, despite the criticisms it received in England itself for turning into a formalist fashion during the second part of the eighteenth century, stood, at least during its early phase, for a set of new ideals: freedom, nature, and region. This was what a group of French intellectuals, who did not see it as a frivolous passing fashion, found fascinating. For the *Philosophes*, an emergent group of 'public intellectuals' who expressed their critical ideas in writings, but also for a group of reformist bureaucrats and aristocrats, the Englishness of the English land-scape had a meaning beyond formalist and hedonism. They saw in it a fresh way of thinking that was not only aesthetic but also political: both an opposi-tion to despotic dogmas and centralization and globalization, and a support for *laissez-faire, laissez-passer* economic policies, for regionalist management of the country, and for law founded on nature.

One of these intellectuals was Charles-Louis de Secondat, baron de La Brède et de Montesquieu, a most influential political philosopher whose ideas influenced the American Constitution and who is still quoted in major debates by the European Union about the future of its regions. In his most influential book, *The Spirit of the Laws* (*De l'esprit des lois*, 1748), Mon-tesquieu tried to explain why there are such deep differences between people and nations around the earth. Excluding race and heredity as having an influ-ence on human constitution or behavior, he presented a theory that human diversity was a product of the environment. The idea, as we have already seen, was not original, its roots going back to antiquity and to the French poli-tical philosopher Jean Bodin.[5]

At around 1731, after returning from an eighteen-month visit to England – where he became familiar with the people, the institutions, the intellectual movements, and the landscape architecture – Montesquieu con-structed one of the earliest gardens in France created according to the English way of landscaping in La Brède. While the garden was under construction, Montesquieu was preparing *The Spirit of the Laws*. In the book, he criticized the idea of universality of laws to govern a country. The point had already been suggested in his earlier book, written before his trip to England, the *Lettres persanes* (1721), an amusing but also tragic epistolary novel confront-ing a Western and a non-Western point of view in politics and in ways of living. At moments, the novel implied that cultures can be incommensurable, and as a result the idea of understanding between different peoples is mean-ingless. However, his conclusions were not the inevitability of conflict but tol-erance and the need to explore the other.

Furthermore, Montesquieu stressed the importance of the climate of a region in shaping a people's character and determining the appropriate-ness of a kind of government for them. He argued that climate of the differ-ent regions influences the fibers of the human body, which in turn leads to differences in character, in feelings, and in the way people act, some becom-ing fearful, some amorous, some susceptible to temptations of pleasure. 'You must whip a Muscovite ... to make him feel,' he remarked. After attending the same opera in England and in Italy, the same parts played by the same actors, he was surprised to note the contrasting effect on the two publics' experiences. One was calmed down and the other agitated (XIV, ii). Finally, on the basis of his environmentalist-regionalist theory, he claimed that '[m]onarchy ... is more common in fertile countries', while republican government is for countries with barren soil, 'as in ancient Athens', as if political freedom was a compensation for the pain of cultivating the land.

Finally, as in the *Lettres persanes*, Montesquieu preached pluralism, tolerance, and respect for the particularity of the region, as well as skepticism about the *uniformity* of laws (XXIX, xviii), disapproving even of the universal application of weights and measures in trade and the imposition of the same religion 'without exception'. However, being open to all kinds of ideas and systems, he accepted that in 'China [where] people value tranquility [most]', it makes 'no difference' to them if their whole country is governed by 'laws that are universal'. However, his personal preference was for freedom, regionalist diversity, and anti-universalism ideas linked with the 'English way' he chose for designing his estate in La Brède.

The new political and economic views are even more explicit in the design in the 'English way' of Moulin Joly at Colombes in Hauts-de-Seine (1754–1772). The owner and designer was Claude-Henri Watelet (1718–1786), a rich collector of duties for the king, and a writer, painter, and expert on gardens. Watelet's estate was conceived as a 'decorated' farm (*ferme ornée*), which, as we have seen, is a term referred to by Switzer, which meant it was designed for leisure but also included productive facilities such as regionalist structures, a rustic house, a mill, stables, an apiary, and a dairy. Moulin Joly was a public success. It was visited by important contemporary artists, such as Hubert Robert and François Boucher (who admired the project and probably influenced its design), as well as the nobility, including Marie Antoinette.

The Regions and the Physiocrats

Watelet is known today more for his influential book *Essai sur les jardins* (1774) than for his garden. Many of the ideas in the book originated from English authors, especially Thomas Whateley's *Observations on Modern Gardening* (London, 1770), which he translated into French. Following the English authors, Watelet declared that the disorder of nature pleases more than 'regularity'. But the book is more than a formalist manifesto. It contains practical detailed instructions on how to construct such a new kind of garden, along with philosophical and political ideas about the revitalization of the French countryside. Watelet's book claimed that there was strong desire among contemporary urban dwellers 'to return to nature' and demonstrated how a farm out in the regions could, 'if one employs the art of management', be a useful and beautiful settlement combining 'economy' with 'sensuality', a challenge to the design of Versailles. Watelet's ideas were drawn not only from English authors but also from the Physiocrats, also known as *les économistes*, who were particularly interested in agricultural reform and the revitalization of the French regions. They were an informal reformist group that emerged around 1760 in response to the crisis of the French countryside – economic, political, and social. Although the problems were very practical, they were among the first to develop theoretical models for solving them. Pierre-Samuel du Pont encapsulated their ideas in his book *Physiocratie* (Governance of nature) (1768), from which they drew their name.

Preoccupied with the same problem but more pragmatically focused on practical scientific methods of farming were the *Agronomes*. Yet in their approach they were also concerned with the happiness and dignity of the worker-peasant, whose prosperity, as Béardé de l'Abbaye argued in 1762, they saw as the best measure of the economic well-being of a country.

One of the first Physiocrats was Charles-Irénée Castel de Saint-Pierre (1658–1743), who introduced the concept of 'utility' to describe how the feudal system, the existing system for structuring French regions, had no future. Even more significant was the contribution of François Quesnay, a pioneer of modern economics, who studied the flow of money inside France and identified the 'sterile classes' outside this flow. He was against serfdom, which he claimed 'extinguishes all competition and activity' in a state, in addition to being a 'detestable crime'.

Like the rest of the Physiocrats, Quesnay was also highly critical of the agrarian policies of the French government, which neglected the regions for the sake of the capital. He admired the political philosophy of Confucius and looked to China as an alternative model for organizing a state. The Physiocrats wanted a strong and effective administration around the king to be the prime motor of change. However, at the same time they were enthusiastic supporters of the *laissez-faire, laissez-passer* system and against government intervention in the economy.

They came close to establishing such a system when, in 1754, Louis XV, advised by Quesnay, curtailed tolls and regulations on the price of cereals, and in 1764 the export of grains was left to the control of the mechanism of supply and demand. However, exogenous forces such as bad harvests revealed the limited applicability of the system, and by 1770 the free trade edicts had been revoked.

As well as Watelet's Moulin Joly, there were other experimental projects in France during this period, inspired by the Physiocratic ideas of 'rethinking the regions'. One of the most important was Ermenonville Park (1763–1776), designed by René Louis de Girardin, marquis de Vauvray (1735–1808). While sympathetic to the ideas of the Physiocrats, Girardin was also known for his admiration of the notorious Jean-Jacques Rousseau (1712–1778), one of the *Philosophes* and very often critical of the Physiocrats.

Like Montesquieu and Watelet, Girardin visited England and its new gardens, including Stow, and in 1763 he decided to settle at Ermenonville, a village not far from Paris, and design a garden according to the English way. With the help of the painter Hubert Robert, a Scottish gardener, and the contribution of 100 workers brought from England, Girardin, following the English approach, tried to interpret and integrate the new garden within the existing natural landscape. However, like Watelet he also looked at the critical political, social, and philosophical meaning embodied in the project, drawn from the radical ideas contained in the writings of Rousseau. And also like Watelet, a year after the project was completed (1776) Girardin published a book, *De la composition des paysages* (1777), about the new kind of garden design and invited Rousseau to visit his work.

Rousseau arrived on May 28, 1778 with his companion Thérèse Levasseur, bringing with him his manuscripts, among them *Les Rêveries du promeneur solitaire*, his last text, which he had been working on since 1776.

Thrilled by what he saw in Ermenonville, he declared he would have liked to stay there for ever. A little more than a month after his arrival, Rousseau died, leaving behind the manuscripts of his works, including the *Rêveries*, which was to be published after his death.

Rousseau's Regionalist Manifesto

In relation to his previous works, which shocked, inspired, and agitated young Europeans, Rousseau's *Rêveries* appears apolitical, melancholic, and introspective, almost autobiographical, reflecting on his experiences of exile, loss of community, and the 'therapeutic' return to nature. Especially in his Fifth and Seventh 'Promenade',[6] written after his stay on a small island on the lake of Bienne following his expulsion from Geneva, Rousseau narrates how the wound of social isolation was gradually healed by his coming into contact with nature – not with the universal idea of nature but with particular, concrete, sensual experiences of the place and the region as he walked around without an aim or as he let his boat take him away, drifting without a plan or destination, 'doing nothing', deliberately idling.

Rousseau, like the Physiocrats, favored a return to a world of creative, autarkic regions, but the means of achieving it that he suggested were radically different from theirs. The Physiocrats sought efficient agricultural production and a regionalist reform through the application of modern knowledge and technology, but they did not want to change the foundations of the system of landownership or touch the institution of the Crown. Rousseau believed that France and the world needed to change their way of living, and believed in the distribution of power across a territory, reversing the present tendency for centralization of the state in favor of sovereign regional communities.

A quarter of a century earlier, he had shocked Europe through the publication of his *Discours sur l'origine et les fondements de l'inégalité parmi les hommes* in 1755, which looked head-on at the yawning gap between the wealthy and the poor. The idea had come to him a few years before, in 1737, while walking down the streets in Montpellier and deeply pained by the succession of superb mansions next to 'miserable humble cottages' built with 'manure and mud'. He felt they were 'wretched', 'the most squalid and filthiest [way of living] one can imagine'. He argued for the elimination of all inequalities and of the privileges of any central place such as Paris. Also, he advocated a sweeping redefinition of the institutions of property and the state as inherited through history and a return to natural conditions.

He repeated the same ideas in an amplified way a few years later in his most significant political text, a true manifesto: *Du contract social* (1762). In it, he points to Corsica as an island inhabited by brave people, defenders of their freedom, claiming that one day the little island would render Europe speechless. Two years later, in 1765, he was busy writing the *Projet de constitution pour la Corse*, applying in a concrete case his ideas about the liquidation of the state and the comeback of the regions.

He was asked to contribute his ideas following the Corsican insurrections of 1729 and 1755, and the proclamation of Corsica as a sovereign nation by its own people. His text is a mixture of political ideas, anthropological speculations, and concrete pragmatic suggestions for Corsica. As in his previous writings, in *The Corsican Constitution* Rousseau saw regionalism not just as an alternative to centralization and globalization but as a superior way to organize human settlements anywhere in the world. Breaking the tradition of political texts of his time that identified fame and glory as the highest values of the nation, Rousseau declared that Corsica 'will not be famous but it will be happy', the 'happiest people in the world [consisting of] bands of peasants regulating the affairs of state under an oak tree' (Bk. iv).

Although, in comparison to contemporary writers on politics, he made few references to history, Rousseau drew extensively on the case of Switzerland as a basic precedent, especially its ancient highly autonomous self-sufficient communities, when he wrote his constitution. Stressing their successful autarky as regions, he described the country's hard winter, lasting six long months, during which people worked hard to create for themselves all the crafts and tools needed for their household, in this way becoming 'independent'.

Switzerland, like Corsica, is small, rural, without aristocracy and without a despotic centre. Small regions with good governance, fragmentation of settlements, and decentralization of power are good things, better than 'the richness of large states', he asserted, because they are not obliged to produce 'laws that fit many regions' with different customs and climate or to produce large number of different laws to fit all these regions individually, causing misunderstandings and confusion, or leaving it to the state 'clerks' to impose laws at the expense of the weak and the poor.

Discussing the problem of measuring richness and poverty, Rousseau claimed, as many modern economists believe today, that they were not objective states. They are perceived according to points of view inherited through history. Consequently, they should not be used as indicators to measure progress. People *sensed* 'poverty in Switzerland at a certain point in its history only when money begun circulating', dividing people unequally, a condition that led them to 'desert the country', neglect the land, becoming 'useless consumers producing nothing', causing the decline of the population of the countryside, the swelling of the cities, the need for foreign imports, and finally the replacement of 'the love for the country … by the love for money'.

For Rousseau, the worst evil the Corsicans suffered under the Genovese occupation was that they were obliged to import useless machines and objects of 'fantasy and luxury', a 'tyrannical invasion' that did not improve their quality of life. 'Commerce brings wealth, agriculture freedom.' One can reverse this state of mind through a 'system' that alters people's perception of 'pleasures, desires, tastes', and provides 'a national character'.

Rousseau's constitution was never applied in Corsica, and Corsica's dream of independence was brief. In 1769, it was annexed by France without a plebiscite, as was done later for other regions that France incorporated, such as Avignon and Comtat in 1791.

Yet the '*regionalist*' approach in most of these projects did not take into account the particular attributes of the given 'region', its distinctive needs and constraints, and its unique identity. To return to the critique of the picturesque 'improvement' by Price that we quoted in the previous chapter, the designers were 'levelling all distinctions … making all places alike' in a similar way to that of their classical predecessors – hence the great number of 'English' landscapes on the Continent that had a modern English look but were not modern in their thinking.

Parc Monceau, created by the French painter, architect, and writer Louis Carrogis Carmontelle for the Duc de Chartres in 1773, employed 'regionalist' elements that, as Carmontelle showed in his book *Jardin de Monceau* (Paris, 1779), were intended to constitute an 'encyclopedia of botany', a learning garden resembling, in the words of Jurgis Baltrusaitis, a 'Kunst- und Wunderkammer' or 'cabinet of curiosities' (Carmontelle, *Jardins en France, 1760–1820*, Hotel de Sully, 1977). To support the idea, Carmontelle transported from several regions around the world antiquity-like, Chinese-like, Turkish-like structures which he mixed with rustic artifacts and plants from all over the world: berries from Buenos Aires, fig trees from North Africa, sycamores from China. The idea of the project was to 'unite' all the varieties that Nature supplies in 'all places and all times' in one place, a 'land of illusion', as if 'one was at the opera', where, as Carmontelle wrote, 'everything becomes a fête'.

The regional spectacle character is also dominant in the design of the estate of the Château de Chantilly belonging to the prince de Condé, who in 1774 commissioned the architect Jean-François Leroy to design and build a place where the prince intended to entertain French and foreign dignitaries. Accordingly, the project imported a regionalist Normandy village-farm with thatched roof buildings, a *trompe-l'œil* made out of regional objects removed from their region. In effect, what was regional about them was that they were from identifiable 'regions' of the world: Normandy, Bretagne, China, and Siberia.

Figure 5.01 Peasant hamlet designed for the retreat of Marie Antoinette in the gardens of Versailles designed by Richard Mique (*c.*1774).

Regionalist Fantasies: Regions without a Region

Even more extreme was the case of the retreat commissioned by Marie Antoinette in 1774 – about the same time that Girardin and the prince de Condé started constructing their gardens – on a site given to her by her husband, Louis XVI, not far from the graceful, classical Petit Trianon, designed by Ange-Jacques Gabriel for Madame de Pompadour. But instead of a classical retreat, like Madame de Pompadour's, Marie Antoinette followed the new regionalist fashion and asked her architect, Richard Mique, to design a peasant hamlet in the manner of the agricultural settlements of the Normandy region and to accompany it with an English garden. The project included a mill, a farmhouse, and a dairy, all adhering to a regionalist style, but instead of accommodating peasants, it enabled Marie Antoinette and the ladies of her entourage, dressed in regionalist peasant clothes, to act out bucolic roles such as milking cows using utensils specially ordered from the royal porcelain manufactory at the Manufacture Royal at Sèvres. In fact, in spite of her effort to stay away from the spirit of the court at Versailles, Marie Antoinette was repeating the tradition of court spectacles involving acting, music, and dancing organized by Louis XIV, in which courtiers exchanged roles between spectators and actors, Louis XIV himself assuming a leading role, very often impersonating King Alexander of ancient Greece. However, instead of classical drama, Marie Antoinette offered 'regional' peasant folk 'gaiety'. A number of important painters of the period such as Hubert Robert (designer of the Temple of Philosophy and Rousseau's tomb in the estate of Girardin), Fragonard, Greuze, and Boucher, commemorated such princely *trompe-l'œil* regional fantasy events as much as helping to stage them.

Similar 'English way' gardens, 'converting every natural spot into a beautiful portrait of nature', as a contemporary author, Johann Jacob Volkmann,[7]

Figure 5.02 Château du Raincy, Paris, *Maisons Russes*, imitations of Russian *isbas* (log houses), together with the English garden, designed by the Scottish gardener Thomas Blaikie (*c*.1770).

remarked, spread in various regions of the German-speaking world. Thus, the second half of the eighteenth century confirmed Alexander Pope's prophecy: '[P]roud Versailles! thy glory falls'.[8]

The German Version of Being English Regionalist

As in France, some of these parks in the German-speaking regions had a serious intention: to manifest, symbolically, new political and cultural ideas. Prince Leopold Friedrich Franz von Anhalt was one of the first German nobles or princes to become fascinated with English gardens. Like Girardin before him, von Anhalt traveled to England in the early 1770s, and, returning to his home in Wörlitz, near Dessau, he decided to design a park following the 'English way'. Before that, Leopold had joined the Prussian army, but after witnessing the barbarity of the Battle of Kolin (fought on June 18, 1757), he resigned from the army, declaring the neutrality of his quasi-independent region. He became involved with the education of the people inhabiting his state and initiated a small number of important political reforms. Like Ermenonville, Wörlitz included a 'Rousseau island', demonstrating Leopold's political views. But he also took in a synagogue designed and built by Friedrich Wilhelm von Erdmannsdorff in 1790, the only synagogue in the area serving the Jewish community. The scheme was inspired by the Temple of Vesta in Tivoli. The garden also contained a strange, eclectic building that fused rococo with Gothic. Because of the novelty of the design, it soon became a point of attraction for travelers, among them the young Johann Wolfgang von Goethe, who in 1778 responded very positively to the innovations of Wörlitz.

But these were exceptions. Most of the 'English' regionalist parks in Germany at that time had no other goal but pleasure, by generating a certain mood, mostly melancholic, a sense of loss of a bygone era, a feeling enabled by inserting Gothic-like ruins, as in the Neuer Garten in Potsdam, designed by Carl Gotthard Langhans for Frederick William II around 1775, or as in the park at Wilhelmshöhe, built by William IX of Hesse.[9]

The trend was assisted by two publications. The first was *Gothic Architecture Improved by Rules and Proportions ... Geometrically Explained* (1742), by Batty and Thomas Langley, which included many examples of Gothic ruins. The second was an equally influential book by Horace Walpole, *A Description of the Villa of Mr Horace Walpole ... at Strawberry Hill* (1784), which described 'Strawberry Hill', a strange 'Gothic' villa, or 'little Gothic castle', as Walpole referred to it, that the author had designed almost by himself. In 1747, the structure began growing out of an existing building that Walpole was leasing; he purchased it in 1748. He continued to add to and rebuild it in stages according to his own Gothic-like specifications. The alterations were completed to the designs of a professional architect, James Essex, in 1776.

The product was a curious assemblage of irregularly Gothic-like structures that served mainly to house Walpole's vast collection of historical objects, related mostly to Walpole's family or to the history of England, exhaustively cataloged and described in the book. Walpole chose to use the Gothic style in his design because he thought it appropriate to the character of the site and the Gothic's capability to evoke narratives; he wrote a romantic novel, *The Castle of Otranto* (1765), while building his house/museum. There is little evidence that his Gothic preference had to do with patriotism, although he once referred to the Gothic as 'our architecture'. At Stowe, also, there is a Gothic Temple of Liberty designed by James Gibbs, a Catholic architect, that was adored by Walpole and is supposed to be a reference to Lord Cobham's ancestors.

Walpole incorporated many exterior details from cathedrals into the interior of the house. In the scheme of the exterior, he mixed two kinds of elements: one based on castles, with turrets and battlements, the other based on Gothic cathedrals, with arched windows and stained glass. The building evolved over time like a medieval cathedral, there being no fixed a priori plan. Walpole added new features to it over a period of thirty years.[10]

Because of the reputation of its owner and the strangeness and novelty of its design, it was known and discussed all over Europe and is considered to be the starting point of the Gothic Revival mania.

The appearance of Gothic structures in German aristocratic gardens in the second part of the eighteenth century seemed purposeless. In addition to creating an association with England, they seemed to be intended to induce a mood in the landscape. And in most cases, they had very little to do with the site or the region. In fact, initially, Germans reacted negatively to the trend. The German writer and popular professor Johann Georg Jacobi ridiculed the meaningless idea of collecting pavilions from all over the word, including Gothic structures, within the same landscape.[11]

Against Enchanted Islands

Even more critical was Justus Möser from Osnabrück, a small, industrious state surrounded by Prussia. Möser was a lawyer, bureaucrat, brilliant author, and one of the earliest theoreticians of modern regionalism. Möser called these gardens 'enchanted islands' where one could find 'nothing that one searched for' and 'everything one did not search for'. For example, next to 'the Grandma's laundry' stood a 'charming little Gothic Dom'.[12]

Möser's passage ridiculing the English garden fashion was included in his major work, *Patriotische Phantasien* (1774–1778), written about the time Rousseau was writing his last text, *Les Rêveries du promeneur solitaire*. Möser introduced the concept of *Heimat*, the regional homeland, which was to play a most important role in the political and cultural development of regionalism in the German-speaking territories and in German regionalist architecture at a time when German nationalist politics was pursuing the goal of a modern super-regional German state.

Like Rousseau, Möser was concerned about the growing trends toward centralization and globalization, and their impact on community. But unlike Rousseau, he defined community in a conservative way, defending the traditional way of life and the 'virtue' of his homeland, Osnabrück, during a golden age of almost self-sustained economy. He cared very little about human rights, equality, and the 'way of living ... courage, and ... freedom' of primitive tribes that Rousseau admired so much.

Möser's 'patriotism' and his defense of regional autonomy referred to the *Heimat*, the traditional semi-closed community originally created by free settlers, who cultivated the land independently, decided voluntarily to use the forest collectively, and finally formed a community of guilds and peasants based on honor, which was now threatened by the merchants (*Krämer*), the peddlers, the Jews, and their imported commodities, which were ruining morals and promoting 'fashion, the great pillager of provincial towns'. Möser did not hesitate to reveal his nostalgia for the old times when 'our ancestors banned Jews from the diocese'. Yet Möser was a regionalist rather than a nationalist. His closed world was regional, and, with few exceptions where he accepted migrant labor, it was made out of a single center supporting rural/ service concentric rings, resembling Von Thünen's idealized 'isolated state' of 1826, referred to on p. 13.

The 'enchanted' garden islands imported from England upset him because, as they were applied in Germany, they represented idleness and fri- volity, undermining the traditional German work ethic. But he was equally hostile to the freewheeling commercial and industrial centers that were on the rise, advancing toward capitalism, such as Frankfurt, and to the politically centralizing tendencies of 'monarchist' Berlin.

A year after Möser wrote his caustic comments about the useless 'Gothic Dom' in the garden, a short text of his about Osnabrück appeared in an anthology of texts edited by Johann Gottfried von Herder (1744–1803), *Von deutscher Art und Kunst*, in 1773, next to a text about the Gothic Dom (Cathe- dral) of Strasbourg under the title *Von deutscher Baukunst*, written by a German author only nineteen years old, Johann Wolfgang von Goethe, the future great poet. The text, a manifesto more than an essay, a slow starter at first, had a tremendous impact in the years to come, influencing not only how people viewed 'Gothic' architecture but also how they looked at buildings in general, introducing a new approach to architecture founded on regionalism and the idea of the nation. Shockingly, Goethe, rather than calling Strasbourg Cathedral Gothic, as was the convention up to that time, called it German. So why did Goethe claim this new identity for an old building?

The Construction of the New Gothic

In his autobiography, Goethe says that he was born in Frankfurt, one of those Free Imperial Cities mentioned earlier, subject to the Holy Roman Emperor and not to a regional ruler, a 'city of three religions' known for its international commerce which, as we saw above, disturbed Möser so much. Goethe's family was cosmopolitan; its members spoke many languages, and his father's library contained Latin, Italian, English, and French books. But Goethe also recounts how he was brought up in an atmosphere of 'telling and retell- ing' stories about Charlemagne, the 'German Empire', the magnificent impe- rial elections and coronations, and his visiting with his father the old 'Roman' town, the imperial election hall, and the cathedral, by then being turned into 'a warehouse' for storing beams, poles, and scaffolding.

In 1756, at the age of seven, he experienced the Seven Years War (Prussia and England fighting against an alliance that included a coalition of small German states joined with Austria, Saxony, Russia, and France), the occupation of the city by the French, and the requisitioning of his family house by the French king's lieutenant, giving the young Goethe the opportunity to become more familiar with the French language and French culture, especially theater, but also to experience the humiliation and oppression of the occupa- tion by a foreign – French – power.

By 1763, the war was over, and Goethe's appetite for becoming acquainted with foreign cultures grew to include the English language and English literature as well as Yiddish and Hebrew. The period of these explorations in Frankfurt ended in 1765 when Goethe was sent to Leipzig to study law. According to *Poetry and Truth*, Goethe there entered a phase of identity crisis – a personal crisis, but also a crisis of his generation, a post-war generation struggling to develop something new 'by opposition to the preceding epoch'. For over two centuries, wrote Goethe, many German-speaking states had been overrun by foreigners. Their inhabitants were obliged by other nations to use foreign languages and foreign expressions for diplomacy, science, and business, a 'ridiculous' condition and a cause of 'misery and confusion'. However, noted Goethe, the situation was changing. A new generation 'were beginning to assert themselves', demonstrating 'the German independence of mind' and drive for 'enjoyment of life'. For Goethe, that was the outcome of the Thirty Years War and the inspiring personality of Frederick the Great, despite the fact that Frederick had not hidden the fact that he despised 'everything German'. Goethe joined the activities of this new generation in Leipzig, devoting most of his energies to them, which did not much help his legal studies. Consequently, in 1768 he was asked by his father to return to Frankfurt, and after spending two years there, during which time Goethe suffered a breakdown, he was sent to Strasbourg to finish his studies in the local university.

It was there that Goethe became involved with Strasbourg Cathedral,[13] first using it as a therapeutic object to overcome his fear of heights (he climbed 'the highest pinnacle of the cathedral spire' and remained there for a quarter of an hour), then by using the cathedral as a therapeutic object of another kind, enabling him to overcome the deep trauma of national humiliation, and his personal identity crisis related to his age. The same therapeutic role would be played by his essay when it was read by Germans of his generation and of the generations to come.

His first impression of the city's old medieval cathedral was one of anxiety, generated by what appeared to him 'huge', 'malformed', 'confused', 'unregulated', 'arbitrary', 'squashed with ornament', a 'curly-bristled ogre'. Yet he soon realized that his negative reaction was due to 'hearsay', a bias resulting from his education, in thrall to foreign classical models. Despite the frivolous fashion for using Gothic ruins and minor Gothic structures in 'English' gardens, and the writings by (mainly French) critics of architecture, such as Amédée-François Frézier, Michel de Frémin, Jean-Louis de Cordemoy, and Marc-Antoine Laugier, who praised Gothic structures from the point of view of technical ingenuity, the predominant point of view about Gothic architecture in Germany was that it was a 'barbaric mass', inferior to the classical French or Italian style.

Undaunted, Goethe was driven to return to the cathedral several times, during different hours of day or night, until the 'masses stood before [his] soul', gradually 'unfolding in enjoyment and understanding'. Everything became even more clear when, during a night of contemplation, he was visited, 'in faint divining', by 'the genius of the great master mason', the medieval architect Erwin von Steinbach. After this call, the cathedral no longer appeared to Goethe as a savage structure but rather as an artefact with unity

Figure 5.03 Strasbourg, with a view of the cathedral in the background (postcard *c.*1900).

(he uses the term *Gestalt* that he was later to make famous as an aesthetic and psychological category expressing the holistic nature of organisms and cognition).

One of the important points made here by Goethe is that in contrast to the universalist, rationalist, 'paternalist' ways through which classical buildings were designed, following a canon imposed from 'another region of the world', producing a 'uniformity' 'that presses upon the soul', the cathedral can be admired without any knowledge of rules, 'without the need for an interpreter'. Opening up a new approach to understanding a work, Goethe suggests that one needs only to 'feel one's way in', an idea that Herder would call *Einfühlung*.

Forming this emotional alliance with the building helps the spectator imagine being part of a forlorn region and an absent community, and as a result to rise above feelings of rejection, shame, impotence, and alienation imposed by foreign oppressors, developing a sense of pride, empowerment, and liberation. As the morning sun touched the cathedral's façade, Goethe stretched out his arms toward it, shouting: '[T]his is German architecture, this is ours.'

Thus, as opposed to classical buildings, which can be analyzed and judged explicitly and rationally, because they are grounded on a universal objective canon – the precondition being that the spectator has to have prior knowledge of this canon – someone looking at Strasbourg Cathedral is invited to be drawn into an intimate state of *familiarization*; Goethe called it 'faint divining', an emotional, subjective, inexplicable relationship with the building, establishing an affective affinity bond with it.

Pushing the subjectivist point further, Goethe suggested that there are no universal criteria by which to judge architecture but only particular, 'regional' ones corresponding to a people. The suggestion had implications beyond architecture, as a further pointer to the fact that cultural products are incommensurable with each other.

Goethe's text was first published anonymously in pamphlet form in 1772/1773.[14] Soon afterwards, as was mentioned earlier, it was included in *Von deutscher Art und Kunst* (1773) by Johann Gottfried Herder. Why did Herder include it in this book? What were his ideas about the Gothic and the Germans, the regional and the classical?

Chapter 6

From Regions to Nation

Johann Gottfried Herder was five years older than Goethe. He was a student of Kant and a follower of Johann Georg Hamann, a radical writer who coined the term 'metacritique', and a member of the *Sturm und Drang* ('Storm and Stress') movement that valued subjectivity and emotion above rationality. Between 1769 and 1770, he traveled to France – where he became acquainted with the pre-revolutionary climate, remaining attached to the French revolutionary ideas until his death – and then to Strasbourg, where he met Goethe.

The Genius of the People

He came to value Gothic architecture as a collective creation by 'the people' rather than the invention of a single individual. For him, 'Gothic architecture' – which he did not particularly like aesthetically – 'would never have attained its flourishing state' without the republics and the wealthy commercial cities, the free cities of the Middle Ages 'that built town halls and cathedrals'. Herder even claimed that 'the better Gothic architecture is most easily explicable from the constitution that governed these cities'. For people build and inhabit in the same way that they live and think. For him, the remarkable Gothic architecture 'would never have originated in convents or in castles of knights'. Next to the political dimension of the Gothic architecture, Herder praised it also as a product free from the yoke of foreign models, its creation embedded in the local context and needs, 'the same way every bird constructs her nest to accommodate her figure and her way of life'.

Herder circulated these ideas in his book *On the Changes of Taste*, published in 1766, prior to the 1773 publication of his essays that included a reprint of Goethe's essay. He believed that 'a poet is the creator of the nation around him ... he gives [the people] a world to see and has their souls in his hand to lead them to that world'. Probably that was the reason for including the Goethe essay, which, although it paid homage to the creator architect Erwin von Steinbach, reserved the deepest praise for the 'German soul' collectively, the German *people*, the *Volk*, the ultimate creator of the cathedral.

At this moment in history, while Goethe was interested in the German people, Herder was more interested in the *people*. A year after *Von deutscher Art und Kunst*, Herder published *Volkslieder* (1774), a collection of translations of popular songs in which he celebrated the creative contribution of 'people', unique and particular, in regions around the world, and in which he believed he was demonstrating their genius.

For Herder, 'the people' was not an amorphous crowd but a well-defined group, a classless body distinguished by a collective spirit (*Volksgeist*) and language. For a people, Herder declared, language, 'the speech of their fathers', is the dearest thing. Anticipating contemporary philosophers and sociologists, Herder saw residing in a language 'a whole world of thinking', tradition, history, religion, and the foundations of life. To deprive a people of its speech, he warned, is to deprive it of its 'single eternal good'. No greater injury can be inflicted on the people of a nation than to rob that nation of its language. Similarly, people have their own way of settling, and if removed from it they feel miserable. The Bedouin 'shudders at the thought of inhabiting a town', and the Abiponian (a member of a particular South American tribe) hates 'the idea of being interred in a church'.

However, just as a people are attached to their language, they are also 'attached to their soil'. 'Deprive them their country, and you deprive them of everything.'[1] He sites the traveler Cranz, who described in the most moving manner how six Greenlanders brought over to Denmark sought in vain to return, first mentally, then by trying to run away, to their country; 'their eyes often turned towards the north', and they eventually died of grief despite the friendliness of the Danes and the good food they were given. The same happened with 'Negro slaves'. The 'painful recollection and the irreparable loss of their country and their freedom' prompted them to murder, he believed. Whatever the efforts of the Europeans to compensate them by 'adopting them as children' and 'impressing upon them their seal', they were still bent on becoming 'robbers and thieves'. They were unable to 'suppress the feeling' that white men harbored the thought that 'this land is ours; you have no business here'.

Echoing previous environmental determinists, Herder believed that the diversity of people, and the process through which a 'people' becomes a *nation* characterized by unique beliefs, concepts, and ways of viewing the world, is the result of being attached to a distinct piece of land, a region, characterized by a specific climate and geomorphology, and organized by particular education and tradition. He even suggested that research should be dedicated to the 'the physical-geographical history of the descent and diversification of our species'.[2]

This history would tell us how a group of people was associated with a region. 'Earth is a globe', not flat, and it is not smooth, being divided by the sea and mountains raised above the sea in different 'regions', different 'climatic communities' where 'most living beings act in the mode best adapted to them'.[3] 'Every nation bears in itself the standard of its perfection, totally independent ... of others.' But environmental constraints shape the way people think and act. 'The ideas of every indigenous nation are confined to its own region': the hunter 'takes lessons of architecture from the beaver of his lakes, others build their huts like nests on the ground'; 'the canoe takes its form from the fish'. 'The shepherd beholds nature with different eyes from the fisherman or hunter' ... 'the dweller of a tent considers the inhabitant of a hut as a shackled beast of burden.'[4]

Herder felt that a people are happy and creative when left to be united and to be attached to a region. When these conditions are not met, then they are miserable. Germans, even if they are fragmented and dispersed in many regions, are a single people, a group, because they share a language and a common history.

> The tribes of Germany have been degraded by mingling with others; they have sacrificed their natural disposition in protracted intellectual servitude; and since they have, in contrast to others, imitated a tyrannical prototype for a long time, they are, among all the nations of Europe, the least true to themselves.[5]

'No two leaves of any one tree in nature are to be found perfectly alike and still less ... two human faces'; however, 'the human intellect seeks unity in every kind of variety ... the mind ... has stamped the most innumerable multiplicity upon earth with unity ... *all mankind are only one and the same species*'. '[E]very nation is one people, having its own national form, as well as its language', which has to be acknowledged and respected, yet, as opposed to the divisions between species in nature, the diversity of people does not imply inequality. Herder rejected the term 'race' as 'referring to something that does not exist' and 'all mankind are only one and the same species' ... 'therefore thou shouldst not oppress, or murder, or steal'.[6]

Preempting the possibility that national liberation is turned into aggression against other people, he stressed that the recognition of a people's uniqueness and value does not imply the subjugation, humiliation, and lessening of the other.

Herder supported the idea of particularity of human communities and even the desirability of allowing these communities to stay independent, occupying a singular region which, like each person and each group, has its own particularity. If that happened, he argued, the earth would become one garden where each 'national' plant could bloom 'in its proper form', and each 'national animal' could pursue its course 'according to its instincts and character', leading to a universe of diversity.

He abhorred the efforts by the pope to centralize and globalize the world, and destroy the 'rights of nations' and the traditional 'German principles' of liberty and security. For the same reason, he detested the Crusades, 'a mere phantom of the brain' lasting a period of two centuries of plundering and including massacres of thousands of Jews 'on the banks of the Rhine' – and 'what are its consequences?' Answering this question, Herder suggested that 'it was an unfortunate experiment ... that created a precedent for similar wars in Europe' – that is, wars in support of globalization – 'which have since extended to other quarters of the globe'.

However, by bringing diverse people together, having them 'emerge from the narrow circle which climate and education have drawn around the mind', Herder argued that 'the mind ... expands' and 'learns from other nations'. Thus it is that in history, 'the Negro, the Greek, the troglodyte, and the Chinese' have formed their own 'society' and, driven by 'experience, equity and reason', they 'will be led ... further'.

> Let it not be imagined that human art can with despotic power convert at once a region into another Europe by cutting down forests and cultivating its soil. As attested by American Swedes, the speedy destruction of the woods, and the cultivation of the land not only lessened the number of edible birds ... and of fishes [but also] diminished the lakes, streams, rivulets ... the grass of the woods ... and seemed to affect the health and longevity of the inhabitants and influence the seasons.[7]

Two years before Rousseau visited Ermenonville, his last destination, in 1776, Herder moved to Weimar, a small duchy of Saxe-Weimar, to take up the post of general superintendent of the Lutheran clergy, at the recommendation of Goethe, who had been invited there the previous year to serve at the liberal court of Carl August. He held the post until the end of his life, 1803. Before he died, he endorsed the French Revolution.

The Political Enjoyment of Folk Songs

Before moving to Weimar, in 1774, Herder published a book on folk songs, *Stimmen der Völker in ihren Liedern*, 1773, a project he worked on for several years following the period when he lived in Strasbourg. The authenticity of the material collected is dubious. It is known that he was not above editing it, and even rewriting it. However, the book succeeded in making the point that the folk poems by medieval German *Meistersingers*, as well as by folk poets from other countries such as England, Peru, and the Limousin or Provence in France, were 'masterworks'.

Although his publication was a landmark in the German language, the idea was not completely original. In France, Jean-Baptiste de La Curne de Sainte-Palaye (1697–1781), a French historian and philologist without the philosophical and cultural anxieties of Herder, in 1741 began studying previously unnoticed medieval manuscripts by Jean de Joinville. In 1751, before Herder visited France, he published *Le Goût dans les arts*, in which he argued for the aesthetic superiority of these works written in Provençal, a regional language.[8]

Before Sainte-Palaye's studies and publications, Camille Falconet, a member of the Académie des Inscriptions, was working on the history of the 'French nation', basing his study on documents of the period. In a paper of 1724, he proposed the systematic documentation of French regional laws, customs, traditions, and, interestingly, of French medieval buildings, as well as of the literature of the troubadours. Regional history, linked with 'medieval' studies, was already on the way.

These new studies on medieval regional popular literature emerged at a time when studies in France on classical Greek and Roman art, architecture, and literature, like those of Comte Anne-Claude-Philippe de Caylus or Julien-David Le Roy, were at their peak. Certainly a debate along the lines of the old *Anciens/Modernes* quarrel during the Louis XIV era did occur, neither side suffering from it.

The classical studies continued to be the backbone of the official French claim to global leadership; the regional popular ones had commercial success. Around the time Herder that published his folksongs, a large number of 'vieux romans' were printed in France and appealed to a wide audience, including Marie Antoinette.

But there were also other, more serious reasons for the rise of this interest in medieval history – as in the case of Herder, political ones. The historical documents published in the mid-eighteenth century revealed information that began to have an impact in the debates about the future of French institutions and the French way of life. In fact, the French understood the value of history in constructing a political argument and started very early to dig into past records to discover material that could be used in the struggle between the king, trying to create a global centralized state, and the regional nobility.

The documents presented competing views, with each side eager to unearth new material in support of their interests. In one of the first studies of this kind, *Franco-Gallia* (1573), François Hotman (1524–1590) brought to light documents that showed that the power of the French Crown was illegitimate because it had usurped it. Even less legitimate were its efforts to centralize the country and subjugate the regions. Hotman was a French lawyer and writer, a Protestant who moved to Geneva to become John Calvin's secretary. In another book, *Monarchomach*, Hotman supported a type of government whereby the people had the right of rebellion as well as of tyrannicide, the right to kill a prince who usurped the state by force.

Anne Gabriel Henri Bernard (1658–1722), a historian and scientist, presented a picture of decentralized, independent regions in early France, the Franks being originally free, their king just a civil magistrate chosen to resolve conflicts. Similarly, the picture of France that emerged out of the historical works of Henri de Boulainvillier, published in the first part of the eighteenth century, is one of a highly decentralized organization of regions, a unique 'masterpiece' of the human mind that Aristotle failed to conceive of which was destroyed by the kings who introduced monetary rewards for services deforming its order.

But there was also historical evidence in support of the Crown that demonstrated that nobility had no rights conerning the regional lands they claimed they owned. The material Sainte-Palaye brought out described an aristocracy dominated by amorality, violence, and brutality, but the same time it also offered an attractive picture of early chivalry at a moment of increasing antagonism between absolutist centralization and regionalist autonomy of the nobility.

It is no surprise that the Académie des Inscriptions, one of the centers of this perpetual industry bringing to light new documents, founded in 1663 by Louvois with only four members initially, by 1713 had forty.

In 1743, Abbé Dubos, a historian, diplomat, and pioneer writer on aesthetics, having carried out further research, argued that the origin of the nobility as a class was recent; they had seized their privileges at the expense of the king and the bourgeois class. He offered a picture of the regions of early France in a state not of independence but of 'feudal anarchy' and arbitrary excesses, the great vassals 'galloping through the countryside, pursuing and cutting to pieces unarmed travelers and peasants', which the kings tried to control through centralization of government. The king appears in this case as a civilizing, centralizing, and modernizing force operating in alliance with the regional bourgeois class.

Regions before the Revolution

The most interesting document describing the condition of the regions in France before the Revolution, which documented the effects of the royal policies, the condition of the peasants, and the preoccupations of the nobility, was written by an Englishman, Arthur Young (1741–1820). Young was an admirer of Rousseau and he included in the book wonderful vignettes of the countryside and the structures built by people without any formal education in architecture. This book, *Voyages en France pendant les années 1787, 1788, 1789* (1792) was intended to record the condition of agricultural development in the various regions of France. It was part of a larger empirical comparative study Young conceived and undertook on the state of farming techniques in Great Britain, Ireland, and France.

Young's involvement with agriculture began in 1767, when he assumed the management of a farm in Essex. He began to carry out experiments to find ways of improving the productivity of an estate. Three years later, there were not many practical results, but there was a book, *A Course of Experimental Agriculture*, which launched Young's a prolific career as a writer and researcher, a pioneer in the development of regional surveys.

Young's *Travels in France*, published in 1792, was based on his tours before, during, and immediately after the revolution. The book went beyond descriptions of technical aspects of agriculture, touching on management, economic, political, and social issues. But it also touched on issues related to the rights of the laboring classes, the desperate state of the poor, and the minorities. Young's mother was Jewish, and throughout his writings he became very interested in the position of the Irish, Catholics, and Jews in the agricultural society of his time.

His descriptions constitute a unique document on techniques of agricultural practices applied at that time, their role in the evolution of 'public prosperity', regional customs, prejudices, and everyday life. The book showed the unexploited potential of the French regions, the 'pitiable agricultural land' such as 'Loge and its houses of misery', the incompetence and apathy of the landowners, like the owner from the 'frozen, miserable province of Sologne' whom Young met at the 'feast in Versailles the other day', and the indifference of the state, which occasionally contributed to the downgrading of fertile lands to deserts. Young went beyond his prescribed cultivation comparisons to contrast the carefree and ignorant eighteenth-century regional aristocracy in Aix, Dijon, Montpellier, Poitier, Strasbourg, and Rennes, absorbed in dancing, eating, making love, and importing the English garden, with the serious and well-informed communities in Amsterdam, Rotterdam, and Utrecht, mixing Calvinists, Quakers, and Jews.

He juxtaposed the appalling conditions of the poor living in buildings without glass to cover their windows, next to the superb royal stud farm of Pompadour, a contrast he claimed to be unthinkable in England.

Having spent a night in Montauban, the place of 'total poverty', he reflected, ironically, what a 'terrible burden' this region, with its thousands of industrious people left in misery and laziness, must be on the 'conscience of the king and his ministers', blinded by the dogmas of 'despotism and bias, not worse than in the time of feudalism'.

Visiting Chambord and seeing the progress in agriculture made there, he questioned the utility of the French academies, the prominence of the orators-academicians, and their armchair official reports as opposed to experimentation and fieldwork.

The book is perhaps the best document about the conditions in regional France moments before the 'long-impending storm' of the revolution arrived. Young felt that the problems he had witnessed were deeper than could be fixed rapidly just by a revolution. Indeed, the revolution reestablished communes and citizens in their properties and gave them back rights of which they had been deprived by the 'feudal power'. The revolution also abolished tithes and feudal dues and tried to do away with regions, replacing them with the nation. Jacques Godechot wrote about the characteristic 1789 event whereby 1,200 National Guards, originating from three different regions, publicly cast aside their regional identities and declared themselves to be nothing but Frenchmen. The regions had become a nation.[9]

All these developments were well received. But many of these actions were too limited, arrived too late, and were not understood by the population of the regions at large, most of whose inhabitants, as Young attested, were illiterate. With Paris in a state of terror and chaos, a post-revolutionary, counter-revolutionary movement began to grow in the regions, turning against any universalistic efforts to rationalize and centralize the country, efforts that, as we have seen, had roots going back to long before before the revolution, championed by the Physiocrats and even by the monarchy.

In fact, the conservative, traditionalist, but also penetrating observer and analyst of politics Alexis de Tocqueville claimed that the reforms the French Revolution introduced, seemingly radical, were not original.[10] They 'made far fewer changes than is generally supposed', and did not improve life. 'The old regime provided the revolution with many of its methods ... all the Revolution added was ... savagery', introducing 'a central authority with powers wider, stricter, and more absolute than those which any French King had ever wielded', annihilating all individuality of the regions and 'imposing drab uniformity ... dingy monochrome'. France was already highly centralized in the eighteenth century, with the central government 'issuing permits or vetoes ... promises and subsidies' before the revolution. In fact, Tocqueville asserted that during the *ancien régime* there was 'far more freedom than there is today'.

Regionalism against the Revolution

Like the revolt of the Fronde, the new insurrections involved local aristocrats as well as peasants in fluid and complex alliances.[11]

Godechot argues that the regionalist reaction and resistance took place in regions that were geographically isolated and where the peasants were most obedient, tied to the 'seigneur-proprietor'. The peasants, especially in western France, could not identify with bourgeois values. They were scared by the hostility of the revolution to 'the religion of our fathers', its efforts to abolish religious practices and cult services. They mistrusted reforms, and they were traditionally opposed to any kind of centralization from the 'royal despotism' of Louis XIV to the most recent measures promoted by the revolution.

In 1793, a 'federalist' wave bringing together a loose coalition of conservative provincial aristocrats, local clergy, some freethinkers, and peasants spread in Toulouse, Jura, Haute-Garonne, Basses-Alps, Hautes-Alps, Normandy, Brittany, and the Vendée. After the fall of Robespierre, in 1795, churches were reopened, political prisoners were liberated, and royalist émigrés returned. What followed was a broader counter-Enlightenment, anti-universalist reaction, particularly popular in the regions as well as outside France, given the fact that Jacobinism had become an almost global movement, attracting supporters in the German-speaking world, in England, and Italy. A peasant war was unleashed in Belgium, Jacobins were arrested in Siena, and the town's Jewish population, becoming a particular target of the regionalist counter-revolution, was massacred. After 1799, Jews were deprived of their newly acquired civil and political rights, and Liberty Trees, planted all over the country by the revolutionaries, were chopped down. As Godechot remarks, 'troubadourism' – the medieval literature glorifying conservative chivalric anarchist regionalism – became fashionable, from Poland to Switzerland.

Abbé Henri-Baptiste Grégoire (1750–1831) identified the deep cause of the regionalist counter-revolution as being the absence of linguistic uniformity among the inhabitants of France. He undertook systematic research and presented the results to the National Convention in June 1794. In his twenty-eight-page report, he claimed that out of the eighty-three *départements* into which France was subdivided, only fifteen spoke French. What he called the 'national language' was ignored by at least 6 million inhabitants and spoken only by 3 million, in a country of 28 million. Grégoire did not believe in preserving regional or ethnic ways of life. He thought they were the cause of discord, treachery, and moral decadence, and argued for the universalization of the French language. The project was not easy to apply under the chaotic conditions that continued to prevail until the end of the eighteenth century. The counter-revolution was unable to bring back order in France, either in the capital or in the regions.

The 1799 *coup d'état* that Napoleon staged to install himself as first consul brought relative internal order, reunifying and recentralizing the country. However, it initiated a long series of external wars, occupations, and institutional changes that shook the whole of Europe for a decade and a half. Napoleon's aim was to bring back in a definitive way a modern version of the Roman Empire with its universal legal, political, and cultural system. His very first title echoed the title of the highest political officer of the Roman Republic, and his 'consecration' as an emperor was carried out by the pope, although the pope did not crown him.

Contracting a Nationalist Gothic

Bonaparte declared France an empire on 18 May 1804 and crowned himself emperor at Notre-Dame on 2 December. He entered Berlin on 27 October 1806. The same year, his army marched into Weimar. Goethe's house was invaded by French troops, who maltreated him. Two years later, Goethe had an amiable meeting with Napoleon. He received the Légion d'Honneur, which he continued wearing after Napoleon's demise, but, unlike Herder, he distanced himself from the violence of the politics of the revolution and of Napoleon.

Napoleon's campaign, destroying previous oppressive administrative structures and states, was initially successful and popular, especially among the young, sympathetic to the ideas of the French Revolution. However, by the beginning of the new century, numerous centers of local resistance appeared in most occupied countries, including Spain and Germany. The German wars of liberation took place in 1813 and 1814, mobilizing the young and intellectuals. During this struggle, Germans from the different regions and regional states began to work on a new political and cultural program, to construct a new united state. Indicative of the spirit of resistance and optimism was the response of the regionalist/nationalist painter Caspar David Friedrich (1774–1840). When, c.1807–9, Gotthilf Henrich von Schubert visited his studio and, upon seeing his painting *Eagle over the Fog*, inquired about its meaning, Friedrich replied: '[T]he German spirit will manage to work its way out of the storm and the clouds ... there are mountain peaks up here. Yet he will also represent the German nation during this period as an "uprooted oak".' Johann Gottlieb Fichte (1762–1814), a German writer, a champion of freedom and supporter of the French Revolution until the occupation of Germany by Napoleon, became what today we call a 'nationalist', dedicated to the idea of uniting the numerous German-speaking political units into a sovereign German nation.

In his *Addresses to the German Nation* (1806), delivered in French in occupied Berlin, echoing Herder's theory about language and group cohesion, Fichte argued that the underlying 'internal' bondage that unites people into 'an inseparable whole' is language. Clearly, the Germans living under different states and in different regions possessed this union. In contrast, the inhabitants of France at that time, although living within a single state, did not share a single language.

A common language, Fichte stressed, united the German nation, but it also, 'sharply enough, severed it from the other peoples in Middle Europe'. This is a point Herder did not stress. Also, in contrast to Herder, who was not looking to identify foreign enemies responsible for the problems of the Germans, Fichte accused the foreign countries 'whose calculations' and 'foreign cunning won an easy victory over German ingenuousness and lack of suspicion'. They 'broke up the tight German inner unity into separate and disconnected parts'. To overcome this damage, Fichte argued, Germany 'ought to make an alliance with itself'; 'we must become Germans' – 'the salvation of all is to be found ... solely in the unity of the Germans among themselves'.

To realize this unity, Fichte tried to construct a new collective memory for the Germans by reusing old historical material to be found in the text *Germania* by the Roman writer Tacitus, but also in bits of memory still remaining in the communal mind of the Germans, such as recall of the Battle of the Teutoburg Forest, mentioned on p. 15. The great twentieth-century political scientist Karl Deutsch once remarked that a nation is 'a group of people united by a mistaken view about the past and a hatred of their neighbor'. What Fichte was trying to do was to construct a new nation along those lines.[12]

Like Möser, Fichte opposed 'world trade' and what he called 'participation in the booty of other worlds ... drawing profit from the sweat and blood of a poor slave from across the sea'. Clearly, he was not interested in the rebirth of a new, German-driven global empire. He was even against the 'freedom of the seas ... so frequently preached in our times'. He found it 'foreign to the Germans', who do 'not need it ... given the abundant supplies of their land', which with their own intelligence and diligence could offer them everything they needed to live a life of a 'civilized man'. His view of a new German state based on a pan-German nation was of a mega-region made out of all German-speaking regions with 'internal autonomy and commercial independence'. He rejected 'manufacturing for the world market ... to suit the foreigner'. In other words, his vision was one of an 'isolated' von Thünen 'mega-state'.

Within the framework of this movement, pursuing the unification of the German-speaking states, the claim that Gothic architecture is German rather than 'Gothic', first put forward, as we have seen, by Goethe in 1773, was a very useful instrument with which to construct, or 'reconstruct', this unity, a strong patriotic icon capturing the imagined German community. Thus, Goethe's idea acquired a new urgency and political use. Similarly, the studies of Gothic architecture by Germans inspired by intellectual or aesthetic interests that came to prominence toward the end of the eighteenth century were, after the decline and fall of Napoleon early in the new century, increasingly driven by political motivations.

Thus, in one of the most interesting texts about the Cologne Dom, by Georg Adam Forster (1754–1794), a German explorer, ethnologist, naturalist, scholar, revolutionary, and briefly republican politician in the Mainz Republic, the first republican state in Germany, published in 1790, the Dom is presented as a most impressive, powerful structure without any references to a Germanic identity.[13] Similarly, Christian Ludwig Stieglitz, jurist, architect, and writer, writing on Gothic architecture in the 1790s before Napoleon's invasion of German territory, argued that the claim that Gothic originated in Germany is false, Germany being the last country to receive the Gothic, which, according to him, originated in Spain and subsequently arrived in France and England.[14] Stieglitz had a very broad outlook on architecture and believed that to understand in depth the Gothic style, it is necessary to study the social conditions of the Middle Ages. However, in a new text, *Von altdeutscher Baukunst* (1820), part of the strong stream of German patriotic writings, Stieglitz declared that the Gothic was an original product of Germany, of the particularity of the German mind, and of the Germans, the only people able to create it.

Friedrich Schlegel, a German writer and scholar in his *Poetisches Taschenbuch auf das Jahr 1806*, published later in Vienna in 1823, arrived at the same conclusions. His text was written after visiting, in 1804, Cologne and the Dom with the brothers Boisserée, who were busy studying German medieval art at the time. In it he argued that as 'every nation' and every region has its own 'specific and uniquely appropriate' architecture, so the German people have their own architecture, and, giving his argument a nationalist twist, he claimed that it was 'more perfect' than the 'Constantine-Byzantine' one, which was still under 'Hellenistic influence'.

Schlegel thus rejected the theory that the origins of the Gothic were Arabic. Instead, the roots of the Gothic, he claimed, are to be found in the German interpretation of Christian ideas, in a uniquely Germanic way that is more 'spiritual' than that of other nations. Like the early Goethe, Schlegel promoted the idea that feelings associated with the Cologne Dom were beyond words, 'indescribable and inexplicable', related to German moral-religious superiority. In later writings, he claimed that the Gothic buildings to be found in other European countries were conceived and constructed by German architects.

Attention was increasingly drawn to the Cologne Dom as the most significant building with a German identity, which was in a ruinous state at that time. Clearly, its geopolitical position in relation to the nationalist movement for German unification played an important role, making it to be preferred to the cathedrals of Strasbourg or Vienna. Cologne was liberated in 1814. The Napoleonic Wars were ended and a new German union, the German Confederation, was established in 1815. By 1814, a discussion had started about the need for a national monument, a kind of Valhalla, to commemorate the victory and the dead. The painter Friedrich wrote to the patriotic poet Ernst Moritz Arndt that 'as long as we remain the thralls of princes nothing great ... can come about. When people have no voice they are not permitted to feel or honor themselves'. The idea of the liberation monument was joined with the growing demand that the Cologne Dom had to be restored, with the suggestion that rather than designing a new structure, restoring the old cathedral was the best way to celebrate the German idea.

Cologne was believed to be the original place from where the ancient German tribes branched out to triumph over Europe and bring to it their spirituality, before declining and becoming scattered in regional fragments. The Dom, like the German state, the Reich, lay in fragments, an unfinished structure, waiting for its restoration, resembling the allegory of Germany as the cathedral emerging triumphal in a landscape of devastation painted by Friedrich.

The debate led King Frederick William III to commission Friedrich Schinkel – known for his design for the mausoleum of Queen Louisa of Prussia and for his beliefs in the spirituality of the Gothic and its German origins – in 1816 to examine the state of the cathedral and look into the possibility of its restoration.

A few years later, in 1823, Sulpiz Boisserée prepared the publication of the much-awaited *Ansichten*, a series of unique documents representing the Cologne Dom that communicated the high quality of the building to a wide public. Boisserée asked Goethe to write the introduction. In his autobiography *Dichtung und Wahrheit* (1811–1833), reflecting on his 1773 text, Goethe considered his renaming of Gothic architecture as German architecture, 'not a foreign ... but a native one' not to be compared with the Greek, one of the key contributions. Goethe agreed to write the introduction for Boisserée and in his text he returned to the question of 'German versus Gothic' architecture, asserting with equal force that the so-called Gothic was nothing but *alt deutsch*. The only change in his initial position was to adopt the idea of Herder that the cathedral was the product not of a single genius but of a collective effort.

Yet the project of restoration had to wait. Finally, in 1842, King Friedrick William commissioned the restoration of the building, and *der Dom von Köln* soon became a national cause for an imagined united German community. While the Strasbourg Minster sparked the search for a German regional nationalist architecture, the Cologne Dom brought it to a conclusion.

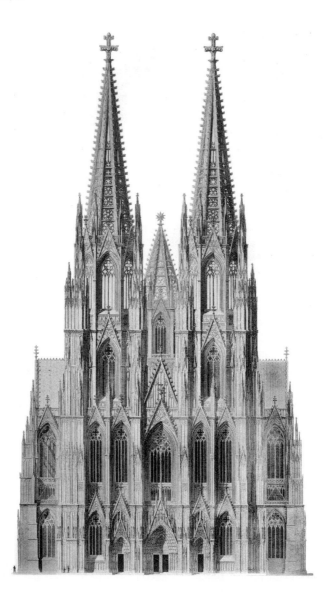

Figure 6.01 The Cologne Dom, from Sulpiz Boisserée, *Ansichten* (1823).

Sulpiz Boisserée was decorated both by King Frederick William and by the king of Bavaria, Ludwig, who aspired to be the cultural and political leader of the new German Reich. Its restoration and completion was the best representation of the German aspirations coming together in one complete whole. Joseph Görres asserted in *Der Dom von Köln* (1842) that the work was an 'all-German artifact' representing 'unity of purpose'. Unfortunately for the argument constructed by Görres and his contemporary nationalist writers, however, a year before the publication Görres's book, Frantz Mertens published his *Ueber den Dom zu Köln* (1841), in which he proved beyond any dispute that the Gothic had its origins in the French St-Denis Cathedral in Paris.[15]

One of the most enthusiastic supporters of the Cologne Dom project was the radical German poet Heinrich Heine. Writing about it as early as

1818, he considered it to be a genuine product of the German people. He even became a leading founding member of the Dombauverein, the society devoted to completing the cathedral. However, by 1828 he began to have his doubts. With the rapid growth of the nationalist movement and the advance of irrational chauvinist theories such as the one about the Gothic cathedrals being the exclusive invention of the uniquely endowed 'spiritual' Germans, he felt that the ideas of German rebirth, with the reconstruction of the Dom as its symbol, were being betrayed. Writing in 1832, he envisioned the cathedral's hollow space, despite its 'graceful' and 'transparent' workmanship, as an 'instrument of martyrdom', a 'symbol of ... intolerance and superstition', and in 1844 he compared it to a 'Bastille of the German spirit' within which the German reason was to be impaired.[16] It was a prophetic vision about the path the regionalist/nationalist cultural/architectural movement was to take in the German nation by the end of the nineteenth century.

Chapter 7

Gothic Communalism and Nationalist Regionalism

The 'English garden' movement, the first major architectural movement in Europe to challenge the doctrine of the universality of classical architecture and to support the particular, the natural, and the regional, was more than a century old when the Napoleonic Wars ended, in 1815.

As we have already seen, the movement, mostly under the name 'picturesque', spread around the world as a set of design rules, a style, with the original political regionalist intentions of the movement hardly being remembered. The new political reality that followed the Napoleonic Wars left behind eighteenth-century preoccupations for new targets, one of them the 'redrawing of the map' of Europe and the future of its regions.

This new list of problems made up the agenda of the Congress of European leaders that convened in Vienna on October 1, 1814, a year before Napoleon's final collapse. Among the participants were Britain, France, Prussia, Russia, and a number of smaller states including the Helvetic Republic, represented by a group consisting of one delegate from each canton of the republic. The reason the organizers, chaired by von Metternich, admitted the Swiss crowd was to demonstrate that the Congress respected the particularist reality of the European regions and that it was not bound to the old formulas.

During these meetings, the continental Europeans were confronting the decline and possible decomposition of the old empires, the emergence of new 'national'/regional identities, and the redefinition of the idea of state and sovereignty. The British appeared to be less attracted by these questions, being interested mainly in the issues of freedom of navigation and keeping the seas open, conditions advancing globalization.

Perhaps for this reason, the question of the 'Gothic', which played such an important role in the construction of the new German identity in the German-speaking territories during the second part of the eighteenth century, did not play such a vital political and cultural role in Britain. The Gothic ruins and Gothic structures used in English 'picturesque' gardens rarely carried an important regionalist/nationalist political message, as the English way of designing gardens had once done.

Most of the groups who praised and employed Gothic architecture, such as the undergraduate 'Ecclesiological Society', known also as the Cambridge Camden Society, founded in 1839, did so because they believed it stood for 'tradition and order' rather than patriotism or regionalism. Similarly, during the animated debate in the Royal Commission of 1835 about the future style of the British Parliament in the Palace of Westminster, the preference of the committee was for Gothic or Elizabethan, not classical, because Gothic style conformed with the neighboring buildings but also because they feared that a classical public building would be associated with French or American republicanism. In 1836, the commission was awarded to Sir Charles Barry, who predictably designed a Gothic building.

Similarly, Sir George Gilbert Scott (1811–1878), pursuing the job for the design of the new Foreign Office (1830–1842), proposed a Gothic project, a kind of architecture his client, the Liberal prime minister Lord Palmerston, did not approve of, afraid that the Gothic aroused High Tory associations, preferring a classical scheme. Without much difficulty, Scott made his project classical, believing that the Gothic and classical styles were like dresses, interchangeable.

Likewise, the criteria used by Charles Robert Cockerell (1788–1836) in copying the Parthenon for the most significant national structure, the National Monument at Calton Hill, Edinburgh (1826), to commemorate the fallen soldiers of the Napoleonic War, were not regionalist or nationalist. Cockerell, like Leo von Klenze, who designed another 'post-Napoleonic' monument at about the same time, the Walhalla temple overlooking the Danube, built to honor famous Germans such as Arminius, the victor of the Battle of the Teutoburg Forest, and Erwin von Steinbach, architect of Strasbourg Cathedral, believed that the classical model, notably the Parthenon in Athens, represented the highest point in a universal value system.

In designing the Palace of Westminster, Barry, who had extensive knowledge of Mediterranean and Middle Eastern architecture but was not an expert on the Gothic, employed as collaborator Augustus Welby Northmore Pugin (1812–1852), who was proficient in Gothic structures. However, for Pugin, Gothic was not just another style. It had a deeper meaning – religious, cultural, and moral.

The 'restoration of ancient art' (that is, Gothic), Pugin had declared in 1836, while working on Palace of Westminster, should not be considered 'a mere matter of taste ... it is most closely connected with the revival of faith itself'. Consistent with this belief, in 1835 Pugin converted to Catholicism, a minority church in England. To promote his ideas, he published a vitriolic illustrated cultural-political manifesto, *Contrasts, or, A Parallel between the Noble Edifices of the Fourteenth and Fifteenth Centuries, and Similar Buildings of the Present Day, Shewing the Present Decay of Taste* (1836), intended to be read not only by architects but by the wider public. Comparing, pair-wise, medieval building types and contemporary buildings of similar function, he tried to show the inferiority of contemporary mainstream architecture but also the greedy nature of British institutions. In contrast to the architecture of medieval times, Pugin claimed, contemporary architecture had ignored the fact that 'the great test of Architectural beauty is the fitness of the design to the purpose for which it is intended'. And praising regionalist diversity prerequisite to 'fitness', as opposed to universalist standardization – classical or even Gothic – he argued that 'different nations have given birth to so many various styles of Architecture, each suited to their climate, customs, and religion'.

By 1841, Pugin had another book ready, *The True Principles of Pointed or Christian Architecture*, in which he spelled out regionalist ideas, objecting to the transfer of Italian ways of design to England, calling them 'burlesque or false', ill adapted to the local climate, concluding with the question, 'what does an Italian house do in England? Is there any similarity between our climate and that of Italy?' And further down, he wondered what kind of 'ideas ever occur to those who design Italian gardens on the moorland of England'.

Pugin did not hesitate also to bring in a nationalist criterion: 'we are not Italians, we are Englishmen ... we should always cultivate this feeling ... we should never forget our land' – he himself being the son of a French draftsman. Worried about the effects of globalization, he stressed: 'England is rapidly losing its venerable garb; all places become alike ... national feelings and national architecture are at so low ebb, that it becomes an absolute duty in every Englishmen to attempt their revival.'

However, although Pugin appealed to the regionalist or nationalist feelings of the public, he was neither a nationalist nor a regionalist. His values were on a different level, as became clear in a later book, *An Apology for the Revival of Christian Architecture in England* (1843). Here he argued that the cause of the problem was the architects 'showing off' instead of 'carrying out what was required', and even more so the pecuniary attitude both of the architects and also of contemporary English society.

There was indeed a problem. While the memory of the Napoleonic adventure was fading away and while continental Europe remained busy with resolving its dynastic and regionalist conflicts, Britain, the real winner of the wars, pursued its pecuniary ideals, expanding and solidifying its lucrative colonial empire, while unemployment, famine, and destructive economic volatility were endemic in London and in the regions.

Pecuniary interests invited cheap foreign imports to compete with the products of the local regions. In 1815, the government introduced protectionist Corn Laws imposing tariffs, reversing its previous position. However, the protection the government offered was beneficial for the local landlords but did not improve the condition of the population at large. This created resentment in the regional population, which demanded fair representation in the decision making of the government. The protests led to the bloody 'Battle of Peterloo', the Peterloo Massacre in Manchester in which cavalry armed with sabres charged an unarmed crowd, shockingly just four years after the Battle of Waterloo.

Pugin's writings do not refer directly to these dramatic events, which remain implicit in the illustrations of the *Contrasts*, where Pugin did not hesitate to juxtapose the Panopticon scheme, the utilitarian Jeremy Bentham's notorious multifunctional combined workplace and prison, advertised by Bentham as a universal solution to the problem of the poor and the unemployed, with the social welfare institutions 'for the humble classes' provided by medieval communities, 'when England was merry England' and architecture was 'strong and hospitable'; the Gothic structures in the picture represented the values of a society and of a way of life rather than a style only.[1] It is no wonder that in 1846 the *Ecclesiologist*, believing in a dogmatic, mimetic use of the Gothic, ignoring its dynamic social history, criticized Pugin and warned its readers that Pugin's churches were 'conventional and modernized reflections' of Gothic structures and not the real Gothic, an abstract ideal.

Consistent with this was the Ecclesiological Society's reaction to the problem of building churches for the expanding global British Empire, ignoring regional needs and suggesting absurdly the selection of model Gothic church-types to be applied in Australia. Soon after, however, in 1845, the society had to listen to Benjamin Webb reading his 'Adaptation of Pointed Architecture to Tropical Climates', recognizing that there is a regional problem in architecture and that the idea of universal solutions had to be modified. In 1851, the Reverend William Scott discussed in the society regional subtropical architecture and, even more shockingly, argued for the need to learn from non-European inventions. However, the society remained oblivious to the disturbing economic, social, and political events reflected in Pugin's writings. By contrast, these were the issues that fired a younger generation of architects by the middle of the nineteenth century. For them, Pugin's message was most inspiring and relevant.

One of these younger people was John Ruskin. Unlike Pugin, Ruskin was not an architect. He was very active lecturer and a prolific critical writer. He conceived his first book and began writing it in 1837 when he was only eighteen years old. The subject was the regional cottages of Westmorland, which he contrasted with those of Italy. The idea grew to include cases from other parts of Europe, and the text was published a year later in the *Architectural Magazine* under the title 'Essays on the Poetry of Architecture,' by 'Kata Phusin', Ruskin's nom de plume, meaning 'according to nature' in ancient Greek.

The director of the magazine in which Ruskin's text was published was John Claudius Loudon (1783–1843), a successful professional gardener, designer, and writer, who had just published *The Encyclopedia of Cottage, Farm, Villa Architecture* (1834). In his introduction, the young Ruskin reacted to the encyclopedic character of Loudon's book without mentioning his name, declaring that the intention of his essay, about the 'Science of Architecture, followed out to its full extent', was to criticize contemporary architecture, 'so morally debased' and at such 'low ebb in England'. Describing the vacuousness of this architecture, he said:

> We have Corinthian columns placed beside pilasters of no order at all, surmounted by … pepper-boxes, Gothic in form and Grecian in detail, in a building nominally and peculiarly 'National'; we have Swiss cottages, falsely and calumniously so entitled, dropped in the brick-fields round the metropolis.

Censuring the passive attitude of the architectural profession in face of the demands of 'every citizen' to 'box himself up in as barbarous a tenement as suits his taste or inclination', he called the architect a 'vassal', identifying, like Pugin, the cause of this crisis, the 'economy … the order of the day'. Clearly, although on record as having criticized Pugin's design, probably because of

Pugin's fixation with the Catholic Church, and even claiming, falsely, that he had not read Pugin's writings, Ruskin shared Pugin's enthusiasm for the Gothic as well as his social and moral approach to architecture.

Moral Regionalism: Ruskin

Ruskin's text 'The Lowland Cottage: England and France' was intended to be an in-depth analysis of case projects within their context, to show through successful examples how building can be driven by regionalist ideals and not by the forces of the market: 'Perfectly ... singularly, the distinctive characters of these ... cottages agree with those of the countries in which they are built; and of the people for whose use they are constructed.'

The conclusion young Ruskin drew from these cases was not a design prototype but a general regionalist principle, a contradiction in terms:

> If our object ... is to embellish a scene, the character of which is peaceful and unpretending, we must not erect a building fit for the abode of wealth or pride, ... beautiful or imposing in itself, such an object immediately indicates the presence of a kind of existence unsuited to the scenery which it inhabits.

On the other hand, despite the fact that Ruskin was not a practicing architect, he was determined to influence architectural practice by making practitioners become aware of specific aspects of design that make a building fit into its site and region. Thus, in the next chapter he concentrated on 'the first remarkable point of the building ... the roof ... an excellent example of what should

Figure 7.01 Cottage types: James Malton, *An Essay on British Architecture* (1789).

always be kept in mind, that everything will be found beautiful, which climate or situation render useful'.

The third part of his book was entitled 'The Mountain Cottage: Switzerland'. This is one of the most moving texts Ruskin wrote, Switzerland being one of the regions that impressed him most. Although the chapter was written when he was no more than eighteen years old, the text has the nostalgic aura of an older man's recollections, to be found years later in his *Praeterita* around 1885:

> Well do I remember the thrilling and exquisite moment when first, first in my life (which had not been over long), I encountered, in a calm and shadowy dingle, darkened with the thick spreading of tall pines, and voiceful with the singing of a rock-encumbered stream, and passing up towards the flank of a smooth green mountain, whose swarded summit shone in the summer snow like an emerald set in silver; when, I say, I first encountered in this calm defile of the Jura, the unobtrusive, yet beautiful, front of the Swiss cottage ... the loveliest piece of architecture I had ever had the felicity of contemplating; yet it was nothing in itself, nothing but a few mossy fir trunks, loosely nailed together, with one or two gray stones on the roof: but its power was the power of association; its beauty, that of fitness and humility.

Figure 7.02 Alpine glacier: John Ruskin, *Modern Painters* (1843).

Figure 7.03 Alpine profiles: from John Ruskin, *Modern Painters* (1843).

Reflecting on the lesson to be drawn from the Swiss cottage, he asserts that it was its relationship to its environment and not the object itself that had impressed him so strongly. As a result, he recommended that it is not

> a thing to be imitated; it is always, when out of its own country, incongruous; it never harmonizes with anything around it, and can therefore be employed only in mimicry of what does not exist, not in improvement of what does.

After having gone through the cases, Ruskin's general conclusion was as follows:

> The inequalities of the ground, the character and color of those inequalities, the nature of the air, the exposure, and the consequent fall of the light, the quantity and form of near and distant foliage, all have their effect on the design, and should have their influence on the designer, inducing, as they do, a perfect change of

> circumstance in every locality.... only one general rule can be given ... the house must not be a noun substantive, it must not stand by itself, it must be part and parcel of a proportioned whole.

Ironically, in the years to come, as we will see later, the regionalist Swiss cottage became one of the most imitated buildings, transported over long distances away from its region, a 'regionalist' architecture without a region, or, in the words of Ruskin, 'a bit of Switzerland as a toy'.

Sixteen years after his publication on ordinary cottage architecture, Ruskin turned to the Gothic. 'The Nature of Gothic' is the title of the sixth chapter of the second volume of his *Stones of Venice* (1853). The book contains most penetrating aesthetic analyses of Gothic structures; however, like Pugin's, Ruskin's fascination with the Middle Ages was inextricably linked with his ultimate interest, the development of a critical assessment of the way people were obliged to live under the British Empire.

Like Pugin, Ruskin admired the 'Gothic spirit' because it was liberating and particularist. It did not obey any top-down universal system.

> It broke through that law wherever it found it in existence; it not only dared, but delighted in, the infringement of every servile principle; and invented a series of forms of which the merit was not merely that they were new, but that they were *capable of perpetual novelty.*

Yet the most important contribution of the text is that it looked at the Gothic not only in terms of the quality of its products but also in terms of the quality of the process of production. Ruskin challenged his readers to bring to mind their own private room 'they have been proud so often because the work of it was so good, and strong, and the ornaments so finished ... [the] accurate moldings, and perfect polishings, ... [the] unerring adjustments of the seasoned wood and tempered steel' and recall 'many a time' they have been 'exulted over them, and thought how great England was ... Alas!' In its perfections there are the 'signs of slavery in our England a thousand times bitterer and more degrading than that of the scourged African, or helot Greek'. The slavery Ruskin refers to is that of the 'operative' who produced them, who has been degraded 'into a machine ... which, more than any other evil of the times, is leading ... into ... incoherent, destructive struggling for a freedom' which is meaningless; 'the kind of labor to which they are condemned ... makes them less than men'. Attacking the fashionable ideas of the economists of his time about the benefits of division of labor, Ruskin identified as the cause of the wickedness 'the great civilized invention of the division of labor' which did not divide labor 'but men'. 'Our manufacturing cities ... manufacture everything there except men.'

By 1860, a growing number of young architects, although still admiring Gothic structures, felt that all types of 'revivalism' were exhausted. Even 'restoration' of Gothic buildings, the product of the 'uprising of ecclesiastical zeal' – not regionalist or nationalist – was seen mostly as 'destructive'. In the words of Ruskin, 'restoration' was 'a lie from beginning to end' driven by commercialism, resulting in polished 'forgeries'.[2] William Richard Lethaby

(1857–1931), architect, writer, and civil servant, accused Sir George Gilbert Scott of 'violence and stupidities ... [which were] done in the name of "restoration"', a practice consisting 'of producing professional office-made' drawings of 'any century which passed as the art itself'.

For Ruskin, what was of the essence was to enable buildings to preserve memory by preserving buildings. 'We may live without [architecture],' he wrote in *The Seven Lamps of Architecture*, 'worship without her, but we cannot remember without her.' This is because buildings, if they are old, with 'walls ... long ... washed by the passing waves of humanity', can 'admit ... a richness of record altogether unlimited'; they have that unique 'deep sense of voicefulness'. Ruskin's passage generalizes Goethe's thoughts about Strasbourg Cathedral and the competence of the building to embody memory and function as an agent for preserving the identity of a community and a region. However, in contrast to Goethe, who had in mind the reconstruction of a collective memory for the purpose of reuniting the population of the fragmented German-speaking regions into one mega-regional state, for Ruskin the idea of community was both fuzzier and more universal.

For Ruskin, 'scraping' historical buildings to 'restore' them destroyed their most valuable quality, the traces of touch by humans of the past. Thus, he helped the establishment of the 'Anti-Scrape Society', the Society for the Protection of Ancient Buildings, to save historical buildings from 'scraping', 'restoration', and commercialization. Key founders were the writer and designer William Morris (1834–1896) and the architect Philip Webb (1831–1815), whose politics were less theoretical and more concrete than those of Ruskin.

Environmental Regionalism: Viollet-le-Duc

More concrete – that is, leading to design products – was the contribution of the Lausanne-born architect Eugène Emmanuel Viollet-le-Duc (1814–1879), a contemporary of Ruskin, who has been several times compared with him.[3] Like Ruskin, Viollet-le-Duc has been often referred to as a supporter of the 'Gothic revival' movement, but, like Ruskin's, his approach to the Gothic was in fact deeper and more critical. Like Ruskin, Viollet-le-Duc was a prolific author and an adversary of classical dogma. His books were aimed at professionals and the wider public, advocating a critical, particularist, regionalist approach to design, ideas very close to Ruskin's.

Ruskin's appreciation of Viollet-le-Duc's knowledge and attitude to architecture was enormous. In a letter to Percy Morley Horder, who asked him to recommend a text about architecture, Ruskin wrote: '[T]here is only one book on architecture of any value ... Viollet-le-Duc's *Dictionary* ... my books are historical or sentimental ... you must learn from the things themselves.' Perhaps Ruskin's appreciation of Viollet-le-Duc resulted from having heard that Viollet-le-Duc had resigned from his prestigious post as professor of the École des Beaux-Arts a few days after he had been appointed in 1863, refusing to compromise with the institution's conservative program and objectives. (Similarly, Ruskin had refused the Royal Institute of British Architects' Gold Medal in 1874, declaring in a letter to Thomas Carlyle that he could not 'accept medals from people who let themselves out to build Gothic Advertisements for Railroads', and preferring to teach at the Working Men's

College.) Although founded in 1795 as a republican institution, taking the place of the Académie d'Architecture, which had been abolished as royalist by the revolution through a dramatic act on the part of Jacques-Louis David in 1793, the architecture section of the École des Beaux-Arts by the middle of the nineteenth century had become a center of conservatism.

Both traditionalists and radical Jacobins adopted the classical dogma and its application of abstract universal principles 'from above'. Both rejected particularist and regionalist values in design. A reaction occurred around the middle of the first half of the nineteenth century among the younger generation, especially leading students such as Henri Labrouste (1801–1875), away from Paris as Grand Prix de Rome-winning pensioners in the Villa Medici. But the impact inside the École was minimal, which remained sclerotic, authoritarian, and alienating toward young people.

Given this climate, Viollet-le-Duc refused to attend the École des Beaux-Arts and preferred to develop his ideas independently. He was attracted by Gothic architecture, as Ruskin was, not only for the formal excellence of its products but also for the process through which they were produced. He admired the guilds and the way they worked because, in contrast to classical architects, who controlled top-down the totality of the building, they gave the freedom to each technician to apply his creativity from the ground up, in the individual parts he was assigned to construct. There was no place at the École for such an approach.

Instead of enlisting in the École, Viollet-le-Duc participated in the 1830 July Revolution, building a barricade, which he later declared to be a most useful technical experience for the rest of his life. After this event, he continued his self-education by traveling inside France, in the Loire and Pyrenees regions, studying and documenting their medieval buildings, paying special attention to the particular details and their relation to their unique environment. Interestingly, soon after Viollet-le-Duc's resignation, two appointments followed: that of Julien Guadet, a student of Henri Labrouste, to teach theory and design, who promoted the importance of regional climatic conditions and regional materials in architecture; and that of Hippolyte Taine, a philosopher and writer, technically the direct successor to Viollet-le-Duc's post.

Taine taught aesthetics and theory, introducing some regionalist ideas from a conservative point of view. A protégé of de Tocqueville, he was opposed to the politics of centralization of the revolution and the Jacobins. He also opposed the French constitution of 1793 and supported the decentralization and autonomy of the regions of France, a view which, as we will see later, played an increasingly important role in the conservative politics and cultural politics of France.

Despite his radical youth, Viollet-le-Duc was respected, trusted, and supported by people of the establishment, among them Napoleon III and the great author, and inspector-general of historical monuments of France, Prosper Mérimée. This gave him the opportunity to pursue his pioneering investigations in the restoration of medieval buildings, to write, and to study nature. In 1868, he started investigating the morphology and structure of the Alps. He interrupted his work to participate in the defense of Paris against the Prussians, and came back to continue between 1871 and 1876. One of the themes of his studies was the process of the formation and erosion of mountains, a theme not alien to Ruskin. Like Ruskin, he tried to discover through this research the configuration of buildings as a result of environmental forces. Part of the research focused on Alpine architecture and its relation to the constraints of the site and of the region. He came to the conclusion that similar environments produce similar architectural results; thus, the chalets of the Swiss mountains were closely similar to those one sees on the slopes of the Himalayas. Toward the end of his life, in 1874–1876, he put his ideas about Alpine regional architecture into practice in the design of La Vedette, his residence in Lausanne, the profile of the building and its openings being shaped according to environmental and site-specific conditions, just as the massif of the Alps was shaped by the interplay between materials and environment.

Viollet-le-Duc's few buildings were widely imitated, but his major influence was through his numerous books: the *Histoire de l'habitation humaine depuis les temps préhistoriques jusqu'à nos jours* (1875), a voluminous history of the evolution of the human 'dwelling-place' – a much broader category than 'architecture' – from prehistory to the present. The same year, he published the definitive edition of the book that Ruskin admired, *Dictionnaire raisonné de l'architecture française du XIe au XVIe siècle* (an earlier version had appeared between 1854 and 1868), and between 1863 and 1872 he published *Entretiens*, discourses on architecture, a mixture of history, archaeology, and instructions for the design of buildings according to rational, evidence-based, regional principles. In the book, he asked architects to adapt their buildings to the hydrothermal conditions of a region, opening a new chapter in the definition of regionalism.

Figure 7.04 Alpine regional architecture: La Vedette, residence by Eugène Viollet-le-Duc (1874–1876).

The microclimatic control of buildings was already the subject of research and experimental design, being discussed among doctors, ship designers, and engineers during the second part of the eighteenth century.[4] Viollet-le-Duc did not deal with such specialized cases, being interested in bringing the new microclimatic knowledge to residential design and linking it to the general problem of architecture and regional adaptation. He asked architects to be creative and avoid importing schemes that belonged to other locations, a practice becoming fashionable 'in France, building cottages in Cannes and chalets in Paris', like the skeleton Potemkin villages that were built for the entertainment of Catherine the Great while she traveled through monotonous, unfriendly landscapes in Russia.

Without doubt, Viollet-le-Duc was an innovator and inspired innovative architects during the nineteenth and the early twentieth centuries; on the other hand, he warned that younger architects were obsessed with innovation without a cause, driven by reasons of 'false luxury and appearance', whereas they could easily follow the example of the builders in the Languedoc and Agenois, keeping regional traditions when there was no reason to change them, or, as 'the English did, being more practical than we, having conserved from their old private architecture what was still good'. At the same time, he warned that importing these English prototypes – or even the technicians who built them, a practice that had been started in France by people 'jealous of the *comfort* of the English houses' – does not work: 'This is not where we should search to find examples', he concluded.

Although he was an admirer of English architecture, there are passages in Viollet-le-Duc's *Entretiens* where regionalism turns into patriotism, when he was speaking about the importance of architecture for France. But there is also a long discussion about the rise and fall of races and nations and the perilous condition of France. Here Viollet-le-Duc is not original. He borrows his ideas from a contemporary book, *An Essay on the Inequality of the Human Races* (1853–1855), by a curious novelist and diplomat, Joseph Arthur Comte de Gobineau (1816–1882), notorious for developing the theory of the superior qualities of the Aryan master-race. Gobineau attributed much of the economic disorder in France to the mixing of races. The insertion of this theory into the *Entretiens* is peculiar because it does not serve in the development of any of the regionalist theories of Viollet-le-Duc.

Gobineau's book did not have any substantial influence on Viollet-le-Duc, but, as we shall see, it had an impact on other authors and politicians at the end of the nineteenth century, providing them with justification for the colonial campaigns to come. Its racism provided a therapeutic antidote to the after-effects of the 'Spring of Nations', 1848, the year of violent regionalist/nationalist uprisings and class-driven revolutions that shook Europe, with the exception of Britain, despite the social conflicts and the strong movement of dissent referred to earlier.

The Spring of Nations, 1848

The year 1848, the 'Spring of Nations' or 'Spring of Peoples', was a year of polycentric revolutions. In contrast to the vision of a universalist world revolution of the *Communist Manifesto* by Marx and Engels, published that year, the 1848 wave of uprisings did not originate in and was not directed from one place. The revolutions were initiated by urban poor and peasants, young radical students, regionalists, and nationalists. Some of these groups were violent and irrational, like those who a few years before, in 1817, had organized the 'Wartburg festival', which included the burning of books.

Four years later, Heine, a future radical, wrote in his 1821 play *Almansor*: 'where they burn books, they will ultimately burn people also'. Yet the 1848 revolutions were not a chaotic assemblage of ferocious explosions without coherence, like the mid-seventeenth-century peasant uprisings. There was a consistent pattern in a chain of eruptions driven by the desire to put an end to the 'world order' established by the 1814 Congress of Vienna and express the pain and frustrations of the regions.

The first uprising, a genuinely regionalist one, erupted in Sicily on January 12, 1848. Its aim was to topple Bourbon rule, and it succeeded in establishing a short-lived independent republic. The next uprising took place in Paris on February 12 of the same year. By then, France was a monarchy again. The revolution of 1848 toppled the monarchy, bringing to power the Second Republic, which did not last long but established 'the right to work' and National Workshops for the unemployed and homeless, and officially adopted the motto *Liberté, égalité, fraternité*. The next revolutionary event broke out in Vienna, on March 13. Although it resulted in the resignation of Metternich and his escape to London, it did not achieve long-lasting fundamental political changes in the Austrian Empire. The same month there was an uprising in Berlin, to be followed by one in Frankfurt and, in May, in Dresden. The young Richard Wagner was one of the leaders who commissioned the young architect Gottfried Semper to construct barricades, as Viollet-le-Duc had done in 1830 in Paris.

In Hungary, the 1848 revolution erupted on March 15 and soon led to a declaration of independence by the country. Before this declaration, Hungary, once part of the Holy Roman Empire, had since 1806 been a kingdom within the Austrian Empire. The 1848 revolution was preceded by the nationalist/regionalist revolution of 1843–1844 when the parliament of the Hungarian Kingdom – a non-democratic assembly of the nobility – adopted the regional Magyar as the official language, whereas previously its members had spoken the global language of the empire, Latin. However, since the parliament, like Hungary itself, was multi-ethnic, including Croats, Germans, Serbs, Slovaks, and Vlachs, not to mention of course the Jews and the Roma, the move to privilege one of the languages of the region caused conflicts between the ethnic groups, weakening any prospects of independence.

As with the unification movement of the German-speaking regions, the Hungarian nationalist movement had a strong impact on the development of regionalist architecture. Next to language, buildings, as we have seen, are excellent devices through which to construct a fictional collective identity and encourage regionalist separatism, setting up an identity apart from the long classical tradition, which had been prolonged by the Holy Roman Empire and then the Austrian Empire. One of the most important representatives of this development was Ödön Lechner.[5]

Born in Buda in 1845, Lechner studied in Berlin but worked in Paris between 1875 and 1878 before the eruption of the art nouveau movement. He returned to Hungary, where he established a successful practice, the facades of his buildings and their interiors being full of 'excessive decorative patterns' and curious colorful configurations. The use of these patterns caused many critics to classify his work as typical of the Vienna Secession movement. However, this characterization conceals the intentions of Lechner, his clients, and later followers who adopted his manners: to construct a regionalist Hungarian collective identity. Thus, far from being freewheeling imaginative patterns, these motifs were recruited from traditional regional folk art – Transylvanian, Magyar, Turkic, Syrian, and even Persian – in an effort to construct a dignified ancestry for the modern Hungarian imagined community. In 1893, Lechner tried to implement these rain bough, radiant 'magical' motifs through a brand-new experimental porcelain tiling technology using the eosin process. The most interesting examples of his work are the Thonet business house on Váci utca in Budapest (1889), the Postal Savings Bank (1901), and the Schmidl crypt at the Kozma Street Cemetery, which he designed together with Béla Lajta, another young Hungarian in search of an architecture of distinctive regional/national identity.

A number of regionalist architects younger than Lechner were even more insistent and imaginative in their research for regional/ethnic sources. István Medgyaszay, a student of Otto Wagner, traveled around the country studying ethnographic material. He extended his research to European museums, trying to find artifacts designed by the Hun people from whom the Hungarians were descended. Like Lechner, he applied this 'ancestral wisdom' using modern materials.

Given the new liberal policies of the empire, the Jewish community of Budapest commissioned the Viennese architect Ludwig Christian Friedrich (von) Förster (1797–1863), assisted by Theophil von Hansen, to build the Dohány Street Synagogue. Förster and Hansen, following the example of Friedrich von Gärtner, who in 1832 had designed the Münich synagogue using Moorish features, opted to draw from Byzantine-Moorish precedents, arriving at a highly polychromic building with onion domes, double towers, and arched gates, built between 1854 and 1859. Similarly, for the Rumbach Street Synagogue, Otto Wagner in 1872 used Muslim decorative motifs to approximate an 'oriental regional identity' for his Jewish clients.

Austria remained faithful to the classical tradition and relatively unmoved by this regionalist wave. Still, at least in name the center of an empire that had once aspired to becoming the single global power, it struggled to preserve what was left of its old dominion together with its unquestionably significant classical tradition.

In 1853, a Hungarian nationalist tried to assassinate Emperor Franz Joseph, and almost succeeded. The emperor was saved and a votive church was built as 'a monument to patriotism' and the devotion of the people to the emperor. Following an international competition, the commission was given in 1855 to the twenty-six-year-old architect Heinrich Freiherr von Ferstel, who submitted a Gothic scheme. Clearly, the choice indicated a 'return to the roots' of the empire. Toward the same goal, in 1859 the Austrian government invited Friedrich von Schmidt, who worked as a guild builder for the restoration of Cologne Cathedral, to work on the restoration of St Stephen's, Vienna's medieval cathedral. In 1872, Von Schmidt was asked to design the new town hall, which he did, applying the Gothic idiom. The choice of Gothic was not missed by Austrian reformers and radicals, who did not hesitate to criticize the scheme, which they saw as a regression to the old conservatism of the empire. Nevertheless, a few more 'Gothic' projects were added to the city without altering its fundamental classical character or arresting the arrival of a new experimental architecture.[6]

Regionalist Nationalism

After the 1848 revolution, France experienced two major crises during the second part of the nineteenth century: a bloody revolution, the Paris Commune (1871); and, immediately preceding it, a war against the Prussians (1870–1871), which ended with France suffering a humiliating defeat and the regions of Alsace and Lorraine being absorbed by Germany. The building that celebrated the return to order and also expressed national atonement for the uprisings, urging religious renewal, was an overgrown, nondescript, and uninspiring Basilica of the Sacred Heart (Sacré-Cœur) of Paris in Montmartre. It was designed by Paul Abadie, an architect distinguished by his unauthentic restorations, who was known to insert sculptures of his own invention inside ancient buildings. The construction took from 1875 to 1914, by which time the enthusiasm for the project as a monument to conservatism was gone.

The period also witnessed a new interest in regionalist architecture and regionalism as a political cultural movement, a therapeutic reaction to the agonizing political and military events expressing a wish for a return to a quieter, more primeval state of agrarian chivalric order.

In his extremely informative monograph *L'architecture régionaliste: France, 1890–1950* (1994), Jean-Claude Vigato, in a rather exaggerated assertion, claims that 'regionalism is an invention of the contemporary era' and, following Francis Loyer, he identifies the first regionalist project as the city hall of Loos-lez-Lille, built in 1884 and characterized by extensive use of regional motifs.[7] It was designed by Louis-Marie Cordonnier, a graduate of the École des Beaux-Arts in Paris, better known for his design of the Peace Palace in The Hague.

A less narrow and more profound definition of regionalism identifies it as a long-term development of shifting focus and use, as we have done in this book. Within this continuing development, the writings and designs of Viollet-le-Duc mark a distinct phase by leading regionalism towards a modern environmental and functional, rather than formal, direction. However, the generation of architects who succeeded Viollet-le-Duc, while freed from the bondage of the classical canon and promoting regionalism as no other generation in France had done before, compelled themselves to reduce it mostly to a style.

Gustave Umbdenstock, a student of Julien Gaudet, practitioner, teacher, and author, drew from Viollet-le-Duc's books about regionalism but did not carry on his technological analysis and innovative spirit. While Viollet-le-Duc welcomed newness and experimentation, Umbdenstock was an unimaginative opponent of the modernization of building and of the importation of foreign innovations in construction.

As we move toward the end of the century, with the French economy expanding and construction increasing, the question of regional identity and the preservation of traditional local materials and techniques of construction dominate architectural publications for the wider audience of middle-class nouveaux riches, Vigato having made an excellent review of their content: *La Construction moderne*, *L'Art decoratif*, *L'Art nouveau*, *L'Illustration*, *Art et décoration*, *Art et industrie*, *La Vie à la campagne*, *Maisons pour tous*. Most articles in these magazines tend to be rich in passion but thin in new ideas. Many read as postscripts to the ideas of Viollet-le-Duc without necessarily acknowledging the fact. Most speak about the need for a 'regional style' and a 'regionalist engagement'; however, in the end they support a kind of compromise between traditional and new construction technologies.

Nationalist themes were increasingly present in the 1870s and 1880s, understandably so after the humiliation of the Franco-Prussian War and the fear of internationalist subversive ideas following the Paris Commune. The 'regionalist engagement' that architects talked about was the expression of a specific French political strategy, aggressively irredentist in relation to the outside world and within France xenophobic, anti-Jacobin, anti-centralist, and 'federalist'. Much broader than architecture, it covers many facets of French culture, including literature, the most important group leading the movement being the Félibrige.[8] The Félibrige group was founded 'on Saint Estelle's day', in 1854, at the Château de Fint-Ségugne in Vaucluse, by Frédéric Mistral and six other Provençal poets. The aim of the group was to defend the regional language, Occitan, and Provence's regional culture, and to enable the development of the 'meridional' race, traditions, and autonomy. For Mistral, regionalism became not only the focus of his intellectual activities but also a way of life; his wife wore regional dresses.[9]

Mistral's influence grew in French culture, politics, and architecture. In the context of centralization, modernization, and solidification of European states, after the storm of mid-century uprisings, the vacuous and repressive politics that followed, and the incessant threat of the urban 'proletariat', the Félibrige became more than a cultural cause: it assumed the voice of the forgotten rural population, the humiliated 'provincial' man, and became the paradigm for nationalist regionalist decentralization, the only way to regenerate France. But it also emerged as a paradigm for finishing the task of the unfinished reorganization of Europe according to regions. Thus, in the 1870s, the moment of the humiliating defeat of the Franco-Prussian War and the Commune revolt, on the initiative of Mistral, Catalan poets joined the group.

Regionalism as 'Modernism' and Patriotism

The Catalan political and cultural regionalist movement of the 1870s known as the Rebirth (*Renaixença*) was very different from the regionalism of Mistral. The so-called Glorious Revolution of 1868 that eliminated the Bourbon monarchy for six years encouraged extreme Catalan regionalists to demand complete independence. Mistral and his flowers never demanded anything like that. The fact was that Catalonia was the only part of Spain not dependent economically on outside states. Yet some Catalan regionalists were ultra-conservative, such as Josep Torras i Bages, a bishop who was afraid of social and cultural change and perceived regionalism as a return to the traditional order of the 'patriarchic home', or the priest and poet Jacint Verdague, who, like Mistral, wrote in Catalan to advance the regionalist cause. However, others, such as Lluís Domènech i Montaner (1850–1923), who became an architect in 1873 and was known for his Catalan *modernisme* but was a committed regionalist (he was the leader of the Lliga Regionalista), saw no contradiction between regionalism and modernization. Domènech i Montaner, drawing from Arabic and Gothic historical precedents, and Catalan vaulting, used local brick and welcomed technological innovations, as his projects for the World's Fair of 1888 demonstrate. The same can be said of Antoni Gaudí, who was equally devoted to *modernisme* and Catalan regionalism.

In France, the Félibrige retained a more conservative character, and by the end of the century stimulated the creation of other cultural, environmentalist organizations promoting the regionalist cause which continued to emerge in the coming years, among them the Touring Club de France, founded in 1890, and the Société pour la Protection des Paysages et de l'Esthétique de la France, founded in 1901. They combined commercial interests with natural and cultural preservation but also with plain reactionary aims, such as the vicious opposition by the Société in the 1950s to the Unité d'Habitation in Marseille by Le Corbusier – part of the World Architectural Heritage. Initially appearing apolitical, most of these organizations later adopted a strong political agenda.

The Félibrige attracted and inspired young people dissatisfied with the alternatives of the major political parties. It attracted Charles Maurras (1868–1952), a French author and a monarchist interested in regionalist politics who became a member of the Félibrige association. In 1898, Maurras went beyond the benign Féliberge and founded Action Française and in 1905 the Ligue d'Action Française, both royalist and anti-parliamentarian political organizations explicitly hostile to the 1789 'rights of man' which promoted extrajudicial activism to depose the government, believing in *'nationalisme intégral'*, an extreme form of nationalism that places class and individual interests within an 'organic' social whole. Interestingly, Maurras combined the idea of a strong nation with the regionalist/federalist idea of decentralization.

Maurras was joined by Maurice Barrès (1862–1923), also an author and journalist. Barrès held non-monarchist and quasi-socialist views, but, like Maurras, was anti-parliamentarian, anti-internationalist, anti-Semitic, and regionalist. During the Dreyfus affair, in the late 1890s and early 1900s, both Barrès and Maurras were active anti-Dreyfusards. Both of them belonged to a generation that read the Comte de Gobineau's *Essay on the Inequality of the Human Races* referred to above, and both opposed the universalist centralization of France, promoting federalism, a system dividing sovereignty between a central government and the regions. Barrès is credited with having popularized the term 'nationalism', using 'nation' instead of 'people' – *nation* being founded on native soil, history, traditions, and heritage, and *not* on the 'general will' of the people.

However, Barrès made it clear that a precondition for nationalism is 'to have roots'. It is not a question of choice. In his *La Terre et les morts* (1899), he insisted that 'the country is stronger in a spirit with roots than in one which is rootless' and that 'we must root the individuals in the earth and in the dead' – in other words, instill into them a collective memory.[10]

Peculiarly, Maurras, Barrès, and Gobineau have been referred as 'crypto-fascist supporters'. More accurately, they can be characterized as 'proto-fascist'; their ideas were publicized before fascism took over in Italy and Germany, where they became influential in the 1920s and 1930s.

Another member of the Félibrige, with closer connections to regionalist architecture, was Jean Charles-Brun. Basically an organizer and administrator, he played an important role in the promotion of regionalism in combination with tourism. In 1900, he founded the Fédération Régionaliste de France, an organization for carrying out folkloric and ethnographic research, which had 400,000 members before World War II and was contemporary with and very similar to the *Heimat* organizations founded in Germany at about the same time. An admirer of Proudhon, Charles-Brun did not believe in a parliamentarian, centralized state and urged a 'return to the land', promoting a redistributive regionalism.[11]

In the same spirit, in 1912 M. Maignan published in *L'Art decoratif* an influential article with the title 'Économie esthétique'. The 'social question', he claimed in the subtitle of the article, 'will be resolved by aesthetics'. The text, however, indulged in political issues and rather than aestheticism. It warned about the possibility of local revolts that could happen not only as a result of famine but also because of the 'emasculation' of the powerful provinces of the past. Anti-Semitic and anti-capitalist, Maignan believed that the solution to the decline of France lay in 'patriotic' regionalism.

Figure 7.05 Regionalist houses without a region.

Chapter 8

Homelands, World Fairs, Living-Spaces, and the Regional Cottage

The second part of the nineteenth century, when the world was being 'flattened' as never before by a wave of colonialization, saw a new search for a redefinition of regionalism, leading to an array of contradictory agendas.

In Germany, as in France, under several names there was a surge of cultural, environmentalist organizations promoting the regionalist cause. Each one contained as a common component the word and concept *Heimat* (homeland) and they soon constituted a movement. Before long, many European states followed in quick succession.[1]

The *Heimat* movement was a return to regionalism that followed a period of regionalism fatigue, which had in turn resulted from the founding of the German Reich, proclaimed in Versailles in 1871. As we have seen, one of the strongest symbolic acts of the newly created German state, which saw itself as a 'region of regions' made up of the previously fragmented German peoples, was the restoration of the highly symbolic Cologne Cathedral and the recognition of the Gothic as universal expression of the national genius of the German people. Thanks to this massive centralization, the German Reich, with its center in Berlin, had rapidly turned into a cosmopolitan commercial-industrial-military complex, with a navy, and multinational commercial organizations leading a process of menacing internationalization, proletarianization of the German cities, and also physical changes littering the German landscape.

This centralization of Germany was a new reality far removed from Fichte's or Möser's visions of individual regionalist communities. Part of the German population found it hard to identify with the new parliament. They were still attached to the traditional culture and customs of the 'regional homeland', and the regional homeland was now under threat. Reactions soon followed, the most famous being the publication of *Gemeinschaft und Gesellschaft* by Ferdinand Tönnies (1855–1936) in 1871. Tönnies wrote about the phenomenon of *Gemeinschaft* contrasted with *Gesellschaft* (community as opposed to association), which Möser had already analyzed extensively, not as something unique to Germany but as an outcome of the world economic and social developments of modernization.

Out of mistrust, the disenchanted traditionalists did not appeal to the newly founded German parliament, the Reichstag, for help. Instead, they took matters into their own hands and followed the path of establishing private regionally based organizations under different names: Heimatbewegung (regional movement), Heimatkunst (regionalist art), Heimatschutz (Heimat protection), or Heimatarchitektur (regionalist architecture), almost always containing the concept *Heimat* (homeland).

Similarly, emerging regionalist-nationalist tendencies were already responsible for the founding of the first folk museum, the Norsk Folkemuseum of Norway, whose initial version was inaugurated in 1881 and included a series of Norwegian regional buildings built since the Middle Ages, combined with open-air exhibits and conserved woodlands. It was followed by the Skansen museum in Stockholm in 1891, which included real farmsteads.

Initially, the German *Heimat* movements focused on events. Their origin is unclear. A youth movement founded in 1896, the Wandervogel (Migratory Birds), a very German symbol, was probably their earliest predecessor. Its aim was to save German nature from 'Americanization' – industrial and commercial exploitation. An art organization founded in 1902, the Dürerbund, was another forerunner. Named after Albrecht Dürer, it included artists and writers. Its aim was to promote national culture on a broad popular basis, to teach traditional arts (*Heimatkunst*), but also 'the art of living', according to folk tradition.

The Dürerbund operated in Austria and Switzerland in addition to Germany. By 1912, it had 300,000 members. The original *Heimat* organization was founded in March 1904 by Ernst Rudorff, a musician, author, lover of nature, and hater of cities (including Berlin), modern technology, and socialism. In his 1901 book *Heimatschutz*, he protested against the commercialization of German nature, which he saw as depleted and used up, and advocated the creation of large natural reserves. Although they were mostly city-dwellers and lovers of urban life, his supporters campaigned against the 'flattening' of artistic life – centralization. Most of them shared an anti-modernist and anti-Semitic stance.[2]

Influenced by a misreading of Herder, they emphasized the need for having roots in a place, identification with a region, ideas they referred to as feelings of being 'at home' (*Heimatgefühle*), '*das Heimatliche*'. Architecture was seen as a way of restoring the home, which had become lost as a result of modernization, industrialization, commercialization, and the importation of foreign architecture. Jews, who did not possess a home, could not genuinely aspire to a *Heimat*, and for that reason were inferior and to be regarded with suspicion. Richard Wagner had already spelled out this idea in his 1850 text 'Jewishness in Music'. Jews had 'no connection with … natural soil' or 'the genuine spirit of folk'.

However, the *Heimat* movement led to interesting design experiments that were not associated with the increasingly nationalist spirit of the times. One of the important innovations was the development of dense housing in a landscape setting with regional characteristics, a problem with which the British had already dealt in their Garden City experiments, as we shall see. Responding to the British challenge, but also realizing that the rapid economic and technological changes demanded new patterns of residential arrangement, Karl Schmidt, a businessman from Dresden, purchased land from the local farmers and asked the architect Richard Riemerschmid, known for his regionalist tendencies, to design the first German Garden City, Dresden-Hellerau Garden City, as it is known now, founded in 1909.[3]

Involved in the project was Hermann Muthesius (1861–1927), who had just published, in 1904, a three-volume work *Das englische Haus*, the result of six years' study of residential architecture in England, where he demonstrated how regionalist precedents can be recruited in a creative way to solve new problems. Although the point of departure of the project was to create a *Heimat* environment, the outcome was not nostalgic; it did not imitate rural precedents. Several avant-garde artists were attracted by the project, including the Swiss pioneering dance educator Émile Jaques-Dalcroze (1865–1950), who decided to build his workshop, known as the Festspielhaus, in Dresden, commissioning Heinrich Tessenow to carry out the design. However, Tessenow's building was not so well received, and Tessenow was seen as too much of a classical architect, unsuited to a *Heimat* setting.

The Feeling of Being at Home

But the *Heimat* movement had also its dark, uncreative products. One of the most vocal and influential *Heimat* architects was Paul Schultze-Naumburg (1869–1949). His reputation owed less to his mediocre buildings – his most famous regionalist work, Schloss Cecilienhof, was, incongruously, in the English Tudor manner – and more to his writings, which were in a polemical pamphleteering style. In 1902, he launched a book series, *Kulturarbeiten*, that continued until 1917. His first writing, *Gärten* (1902), was an attack on gardens in the classical style and a righteous defense of quaint gardens offering 'feelings of being at home' (*Heimatgefühle*).

Figure 8.01 Richard Riemerschmid, Dresden-Hellerau Garden City, founded in 1909.

Schultze-Naumburg became chairman of the Heimatschutz in 1905, the same year as he published *The Disfigurement of Our Countryside*, focusing on the impact of modernization on the German land. As with Humphry Repton's *Observations on the Theory and Practice of Landscape Gardening* (1803), the success of the publication was due not so much to the writing as to the use of pair-wise juxtapositions of photographs of 'good' and 'bad' cases of buildings, making the effects of commercialization and industrialization easily perceivable. However, the book did not address environmental regional problems. Willy Lange came closer to the idea, using the concept of ecology developed by Ernst Haeckel in 1866.[4]

On the other hand, Lange did not take the idea very far. Like Schultze-Naumburg, he was soon absorbed by nationalist politics. Lange in particular became preoccupied with the idea of authenticity of German 'nature': plants and trees that were 'rooted' in the soil of German regions. Similarly, Schultze-Naumburg in 1927, in an article in *UHU* with the title 'Who Is Right?', denounced Walter Gropius's architecture as 'foreign'.

Subsequently, the analogy between the facade of a building and the character of the human face became one of Schultze-Naumburg's major themes. Using sets of two juxtaposed photographs comparatively, he tried to express the idea of degeneration as it applied to architecture, showing examples of 'flat-' versus 'pitched-roof' architecture intermixed with physiognomic racist populist ideas. In this he was influenced by the racist eugenicist Hans F. K. Günther.

Figure 8.02 Modern art equated with 'degenerate' people. This illustration appeared in Paul Schultze-Naumburg's *Kunst und Rasse* (Art and race) Munich, 1928.

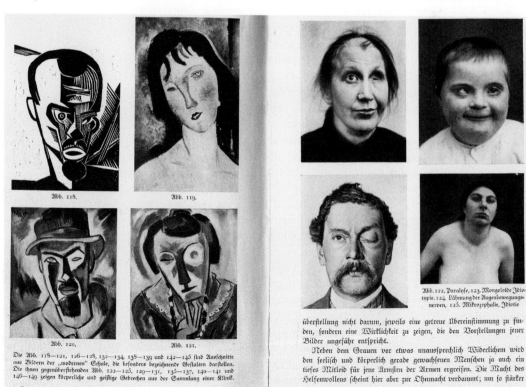

Abb. 118.

Abb. 119.

Abb. 120.

Abb. 121.

Die Abb. 118—121, 126—128, 132—134, 135—139 und 142—145 sind Ausschnitte aus Bildern der „modernen" Schule, die besonders bezeichnende Gestalten darstellen. Die ihnen gegenüberstehenden Abb. 122—125, 129—131, 135—137, 140—141 und 146—149 zeigen körperliche und geistige Gebrechen aus der Sammlung einer Klinik.

106

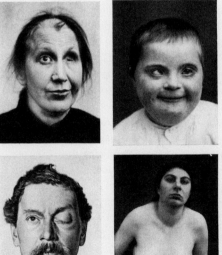

Abb. 122. Paralyse, 123. Mongoloide Idiotopie. 124. Lähmung der Augenbewegungsnerven, 125. Mikrozephalie, Idiotie

überstellung nicht darum, jeweils eine getreue Übereinstimmung zu finden, sondern eine Wirklichkeit zu zeigen, die den Vorstellungen jener Bilder ungefähr entspricht.

Neben dem Grauen vor etwas unaussprechlich Widerlichem wird den seelisch und körperlich gerade gewachsenen Menschen ja auch ein tiefes Mitleid für jene Ärmsten der Armen ergreifen. Die Macht des Helfenwollens scheint hier aber zur Ohnmacht verdammt; um so stärker

107

The idea became clearer in 1928 in his publication *Kunst und Rasse* (Art and race), where the modern is equated with racial degeneration. Part of his evolution was his meeting with Hitler the next year, who visited him in his studio; his publications became part of the Nazi list of recommended books. So did the translation of the Comte de Gobineau's *Essay on the Inequality of the Human Races.*

Schultze-Naumburg's personal interpretation of the regionalist *Heimat* was spelled out in his 1934 article 'Kunst aus Blut und Boden', which declared that 'as the farmer digs the roots of his being in the soil … so must an artist have a *Heimat*, in which he too digs his roots' – 'having roots' being a key point in Lange's writings too. In the 1930s, he became increasingly obsessed with cleanliness and 'hygiene'. Thus, as an administrator in the Hochschule für Handwerk and Baukunst, he 'cleansed' the school, removing from the walls of the building all modern works of art. The next step was to remove thirty teachers, to arrest the spread of 'nigger-culture among the German people'. In 1937, in his book *Nordische Schönheit* (Nordic beauty), he asserted that 'the highest beauty can only arise with racial purity', the regionalist *Heimat* idea having now become a universal doctrine.

If Schultze-Naumburg was more a propagandist than a good architect, other architects, such as Paul Bonatz and Paul Schmitthenner, were successful in developing projects that aspired to the *Heimat* regionalist ideals.

The Region as a 'Way of Life' and as 'Living Space'

One of the important aspects of the *Heimat* movement was that in addition to questions about the regionalist design of buildings, it directed attention to the regional territory, as one can see in the writings of Lange. As a result, there was a new interest in problems whose scale was beyond a garden or a park, problems that could not be handled through common sense.

Jean-Louis Giraud-Soulavie (1751–1813) was a French geologist and geographer who saw himself as a committed revolutionary. He felt the need to define the term 'region' scientifically around the 1780s. Instead of accepting administrative or physical categories, which were in use at that time, Giraud-Soulavie tried to develop categories empirically, 'from the ground up', listening to the way people construed a region in their discussions. The 'people' in this case were the rural population of peasants who inhabited those regions who would say 'this is my country' (*c'est mon pays*). Prefiguring the notion of *Heimat*, Giraud-Soulavie argued that what peasants meant was not that they belonged to a physical parcel of space but that they were part of a community, of a homeland, of a group that shared language, cuisine, festivals, and manners.

In spite of Giraud-Soulavie's work, 'region' continued to be a rather fuzzy term, and most French geographers studying regions continued to use mainly physical, material criteria. On the other hand, there were important developments in the German-speaking world, starting with the astonishing field studies and theoretical work of Alexander von Humbolt (1769–1859). Humbolt tried to introduce quantitative tools to document geographical data and grasp the 'individuality' of the various regions. To understand how the environment consisted of form and function and how they were interlinked, he developed an 'organic', 'physiological' model that looked at a region as a body, coining the term 'biogeography'. Humbolt's contemporary Carl Ritter (1779–1859) shared his 'organic', systemic approach. In a lecture to the Royal Academy of Sciences in Berlin dated December 14, 1826, Ritter presented his Spatial Principle, arguing that in studying any area or region, one has to discover the 'unity that includes climate, production, culture, population, and history', calling for the research to be extended into 'political geography'.

Without doubt, the German obsession with geographical concepts and models had to do with political developments: the reorganization of inherited territorial divisions and the process of unification of the old regions into the German Reich. Continuing Ritter's seminal work, Friedrich Ratzel (1844–1904) tried to study the relationship between natural and cultural – that is, human-made – areas in space (*Raum*). His investigations were published in 1882 and 1891 under the title *Anthropogeographie*, a title in which Ratzel tried to combine Darwinian biological ideas about the struggle of the species with Ernst Haeckel's relatively new concept of ecology. These studies led Ratzel to the creation of a new concept reinterpreting the idea of region, that of *Lebensraum*, 'living space', the space needed for the survival of a species, an idea to become central to Germany's nationalist movement in the twentieth century.

Influenced by these German developments, Paul Vidal de la Blache (1845–1918) in France tried to find criteria to define the identity of a region and the particularity of environmental factors that affect what he called the 'geographical personality' of rural landscapes (*paysages*) and regions. To do so, he introduced concepts such as the environmental setting (*milieu*), and the way people live in it (*genres de vie*). Later, he tried to integrate history, political aspects, and systems of transportation in this analysis, which provided him with an interesting pragmatic conclusion concerning the regionalist question, namely that, within the framework of international competition and given the dynamic evolution of means of transportation and communication, France should be less concerned with control through the centralization of the regions. In 1910, he proposed to restructure the regions of France around a central place, a metropolis. Trying to overcome the bias of environmental determinism, dominant as we have seen since the time of Hippocrates and Vitruvius, Paul Vidal de la Blache created the pregnant concept of 'possibilism', the potential of a region to bring about a certain behavior, which unfortunately he left unexploited in his work.[5]

In addition to influencing Vidal de la Blache and enriching and expanding his idea of region, Ratzel's work was important in the development of the ideas of the German geographer August Meitzen (1822–1910). Meitzen carried out extensive fieldwork and in 1895 he published his results in *Settlement and Agrarian Character of the West and East Germans, of the Celts, Romans, Finns, and Slavs*. His scientific discoveries about the spatial aspects of human-made environment produced a new field of investigation called 'geopolitics', in which regions were thought of as embedded in a larger territorial political setting. The conclusions were immediately politicized, given the climate of nationalist hallucinations about *Lebensraum* prevailing at his time. The work also introduced a theory about the relation between natural landscape, the *Naturlandschaft*, and rural cultural settlements, also constituting a landscape, the *Kulturlandschaft*. Meitzen tried to identify the particularity of the German 'space' (*Raum*), and the deep and unique relation between the German community and the land. The conclusions of Meitzen's work were of particular interest to nationalist, racist politicians who were obsessed with the particularity of German culture because in their view there was not only a need to defend it from outsiders but also a special, global civilizing mission that the Germans had to live up to.

Even more nationalist and political was the work of Karl Haushofer (1869–1946), who carried Meitzen's geopolitical ideas further by studying the morphology of human settlements in the landscape of a region. He looked at their use, their size and typology, and their cultivation as expressions of folk culture. Haushofer founded the Institut für Geopolitik in Munich in 1922 and carried out research in the same direction with his son Albrecht. Four years later, Hans Grimm, a writer, published a best-selling novel with the title *Volk ohne Raum* (People without space), popularizing the idea of *Lebensraum* and thereby intensifying the obsession that the German nation had run out of space.

Walter Christaller's famous regional model, an expansion of von Thünen's idea of an ideal hexagonal 'isolated' region (1826) into a hierarchy of nested hexagonal patterns, which we referred to in the Introduction, was born in this framework and was soon transformed from a fantasy or theory into a realistic plan for organizing the settlements of the new German colonial *Lebensraum* in the vast areas of Poland and Ukraine in the 1940s. Characteristic of these developments in Germany and France was that the *ancien régime* dichotomy between regionalism and universalism, carried over into the nineteenth-century nationalist debates concerning regional particularism and autonomy as opposed to national centralization and standardization, was replaced by more grandiose concerns: the question of how to organize a super-region, a region of regions, such as the new united Germany, and the more ambitious vision of globalization beyond the borders of the nation-state.

Similar ideas were promoted in France, too. The year after the defeat of France by Germany in 1871, Ernest Renan, a French philosopher, in an agonized text, *La Réforme intellectuelle et morale*, about the future of his country, argued that '[c]olonization is a political necessity.... A country that does not colonize irrevocably arrives at socialism, that is, to the war between rich and poor'. Opportunity was knocking at the door, he argued. Countries 'like China are crying aloud for foreign conquest'. Unlike Europeans, the Chinese 'are created a race of workers' and have 'almost no sense of honor'. As for the 'Negroes', they are 'a race of tillers of the soil'.

The conference called *Kongokonferenz* was typical of this development. Called by Otto von Bismark in 1884–1885, its aim was to find out how to organize collectively the 'Race to Africa' by turning the colonization of Africa from an area of fierce competition into one of productive collaboration. Among the participant nations were Belgium, Denmark, France, the United Kingdom, Italy, the Netherlands, Russia, and Spain.

Once the new drive to establish new colonies had yielded results, the next step was to find out how to organize these new territories, whose economies, societies, operating technologies, culture, and demands related to the built environment were so different from those of the colonizers. Hence, the old question of regionalism resurfaced. The alternative was to follow the old formula of colonizing empires that we have already discussed:

disregard differences, regional traditions, and physical environmental constraints and declare the world of the colonizing power universal, and impose its formulas and values, such as classical architecture, on the colonized. Others sought a compromise position.

In 1839, J. M. Derick, an English architect, designed a church in Alexandria on a site donated by Muhamad Ali, about which Benjamin Webb, in his 'Adaptation of Pointed Architecture to Tropical Climates' (referred to on p. 79), remarked that the question was not to fit an English church into the tropics but, given the environment of the tropics, to design an alternative scheme more suited to its environment.

On the other hand, James Wilde in his St Mark's Church in Alexandria (1846) tried to integrate Islamic elements, which he fused with Italian ones. But in a later version, the use of European precedents predominates. The efforts by architects at that juncture in history have several times been misunderstood owing to the use of the term 'eclectic' to characterize their work, implying a freewheeling, playful design thinking behind their work, selecting and mixing 'styles'. The fact is that both architects and clients struggled with important cultural as well as political issues, faced with an unprecedented problem.

In the case of James Wilde's church, it remains unclear whether his attempt to fuse traditions was done 'to conciliate the opinion of the Arab inhabitants', or out of a deeper belief in the reconciliation of cultures.[6] Whatever the intentions, the fact is that this method of trying to fuse architectural motifs, which we will see perpetuated in the twentieth century, remained a highly superficial formal exercise unable to yield creative results that enriched architecture.

French architects and colonial administrators were faced with the same problem as their English counterparts. The fact was that the architects, as a result of their rigorous but narrow architectural education, were confined to the global design norms of the universal classical canon, Viollet-le-Duc's findings not being easily translatable to designing new colonial regions.

The technocrats also brought with them all the biases of French engineering and medicine in construction science and microclimatic physics, based on the latest scientific advances. They were convinced that the French way of life was modern, superior, and progressive. If applied, it would benefit both colonizers and colonized. This was the approach of Joseph-Simon Gallieni (1849–1916), a soldier and colonial administrator, and a republican who believed in science and planning, which he put in use in Indochina and Madagascar.

By contrast, Hubert Lyautey, also from the military and a 'resident-general' of the protectorate of Morocco (1912–1925), paid special attention to regional traditions. Lyautey's behavior was notoriously contradictory and the outcome of contradictory loyalties. His political views were close to those of the growing French fascist movement. In 1934, in the midst of a major political upheaval linked with the Stavisky affair, Lyautey threatened to lead the extreme right forces to forcefully oust his own government. Although he was also on record as opposing the accusations against Captain Dreyfus, and anti-Semitism, he translated Hitler's *Mein Kampf* into French. As a military man, he was shrewd, deceitful, and ruthless. One of his actions was the punitive bombardment of Casablanca in 1907. Yet he believed deeply in the values of Europe, allegedly seeing World War I as a 'civil war … a monumental folly'. Although he was accused by the colonial press of being pro-Muslim because of his promotion of the regional architectural heritage and his resistance to the speculative real estate efforts of the exploiter colonists, it is not completely clear whether this was the result of real respect and admiration for the regional culture or part of his 'pacification' policies to gain the support of the local population.

Lyautey chose as head of urbanism in Morocco Henri Prost (1874–1959), one of the most competent architect-planners of his time. Prost was one of those architects, engineers, and 'urbanists' who chose colonial jobs out of professional ambition, but also in the honest hope of carrying out high-quality and innovative work that would not be possible in France. Prost was a contemporary of Ernest Hébrard, both recipients of the Prix de Rome (in 1902 and 1904 respectively), both, together with Tony Garnier, having struggled to renew the program of the École des Beaux-Arts.[7]

Ernest Hébrard (1875–1933), a French architect who decided to specialize in the new field of urbanism, had worked in French Indochina as an urban designer, paying attention to regional urban traditions in a minor way, but he also worked as an architect concentrating on detailing, trying to identify useful regional precedents to be transferred to contemporary uses. Before going to Indochina, he had been invited by the Greek government to be part of a team to design a new plan for the center of Thessaloniki, recently destroyed by the great fire of 1917. The final plan was mostly his product, providing high-quality urban spaces adapted to the climate of the region. But he disregarded the preexisting settlements and cultural monuments of the Jewish community, which constituted about 60 percent of the population of the city at that time.

Lyautey's fundamental plan, which Prost had to implement, consisted partly in the design of parks and public spaces to make life in the new colonial settlements pleasant and cheerful. In addition, Lyautey required a complete separation between the traditional cities and the new. The idea of such a *cordon sanitaire*, to quote Rabinov, was controversial from the social point of view, reminiscent of British colonial segregation policies. However, there was a strong argument that in so doing, Lyautey made easier the conservation of the regional architectural heritage, as well as the safeguarding of regional culture and customs. In the end, the effect was negative. Functionally, the isolation of the traditional settlements resulted in their overcrowding and the downgrading of their environmental quality.[8]

Certainly, they were also professionals who became involved with the colonies for 'orientalist' reasons. They were attracted by the architectural and landscape particularities of local cities and regions not because they respected or recognized the value of the colonial worlds but because they were driven by a desire to escape the pain, boredom, severity, and lack of sensuality of modern mechanized and bureaucratized Western environments. The colonial worlds appeared hedonistic, permissive, and submissive, available to be grabbed and enjoyed at little or no cost without special permissions and moral controls. Western fiction and poetry are full of realistic or imagined

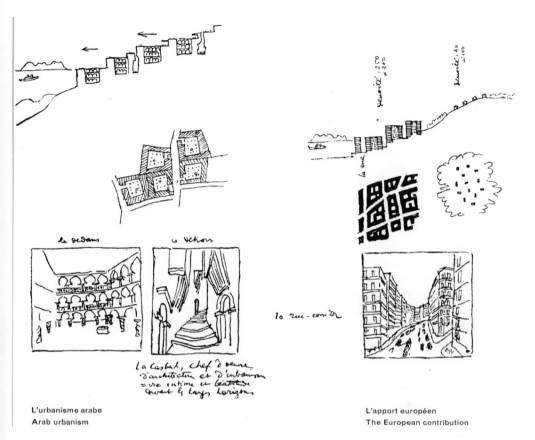

le dedans   u dehors

La Casbah, chef d'oeuvre
d'architecture et d'urbanism
=vie intime et béatitude
quant les larges horizons

lo rue-corridor

L'urbanisme arabe
Arab urbanism

L'apport européen
The European contribution

Figure 8.03 Le Corbusier:
Arab urbanism and the
European contribution.

stories confirming that, and even the travel journals of Le Corbusier reveal elements of this mentality.

Lyautey argued that he could do in Morocco things that no administrator could do in France, owing to the restrictive French laws, regulations, and politics. He used this freedom to institute planning regulations for the existing *medinas* and *villes nouvelles* that to a great extent served the public good and contained the force of private interests.

Regionalism in the World Fairs and the 'Spirit of Commerce'

Part of the dynamic drive toward globalization through colonization was the creation of a new institution and mechanism with the aim of promoting products and prime materials from all over the world as well as bringing together international manufacturers and merchants. The colonial products were about to become objects of mass consumption, and the World Fairs acted as marketing machines.

Interestingly, invited to participate in these celebrations of globalization were exhibits that publicized the products and culture of regions from all over the world. Very limited initially, they increased in number and size as the expositions continued periodically up to 1937.

The first, the Great Exhibition of the Works of Industry of All Nations, took place in London, the capital of a vast global empire, for many the capital of the world. Organized by Prince Albert and Henry Cole, it opened in 1851, just four years after the collapse of British financial markets, thereby demonstrating confidence in the creative future of global industry, communication, and commerce. The exposition was housed in a new, highly innovative building, Joseph Paxton's Crystal Palace in Hyde Park. Although the intention of the event was to stimulate production and commerce in the future, the dominant theme was historical and encyclopedic. The exhibit also included an Ethnological and Natural History Department. It was here that one could see environments of 'exotic' regions represented scientifically rather than for the sake of spectacle.[9]

France followed the Crystal Palace show in 1855 with the Exposition Universelle, housed in the Palais de l'Industrie designed by Jean-Marie Victor Viel. The show was visited by 5,100,000 people. Again in Paris, in 1867, under the direction of Prince Napoleon and Frédéric Le Play, among the designers of the main structure being Jean-Charles Alphand, part of the show was a number of national regional pavilions, some French colonial (including pavilions representing Algeria, Morocco, and Tunisia) but also a Chinese pavilion, an Egyptian garden, and a Bavarian pavilion. The idea of the pavilions was to encourage the participating nations to show off their products in constructions typical of their country.[10]

The Vienna World's Fair of 1873, in the area of the Prater, opened in the midst of a disastrous stock market crash and a cholera epidemic. It contained an international village, a world of regional worlds, among them a Japanese garden, a Turkish coffeehouse, and a North American tepee structure.

The Paris Exposition Universelle of 1878, planned to celebrate the recovery of France from the recent war and the Commune, included the Avenue of the Nations with examples of regional architecture from Asia and Africa: a Moorish tower and a 'Negro village' containing 400 'indigenous' participants living their lives publicly for the sake of the visitors. It was visited by 28 million people. The Paris Exposition Universelle of 1900, attended by 50 million, included national pavilions, among them a Bosnian and Herzegovinian pavilion, together with Finnish, Greek, Italian, Russian, Swiss, and Turkish pavilions, all in a regional idiom designed to produce memorable postcards stressing variety, particularity, and diversity, even if this was achieved through the least authentic means. The Exposition Coloniale Internationale (International Colonial Exposition) held in Paris in 1931 focused on the resources, products, and culture of the French colonies but included other colonial powers: Belgium, Italy, the United Kingdom, and the United States. Once more, a human zoo, in the form of a Senegalese village, was included. The French Communist Party organized a counter-exhibition exposing the practice of forced labor and the crimes associated with colonialism.

World Fairs spread around the world with approximately the same program, advancing globalization while promoting regional commercial products with superficial cultural pretensions. Occasionally, not only the displayed products but also the buildings themselves were expressions of the particularities of regional architecture, occasionally informative about local building techniques but mostly theatrical-like as-if settings of the *genius commercialii*, marketing regional artefacts of the regions.

Figure 8.04 International Colonial Exposition in Paris, in 1931.

One of the most successful examples of this kind of regionalist architecture was the vast Palace of the Arts by Aníbal González Álvarez-Ossorio (1876–1929) for the Exposición Iberoamericana de Sevilla in 1929. In a polychromic tiled amphitheatre-like composition, Gonzales succeeded in integrating and uniting diverse artisan ceramics derived from artifacts from the various regions of Spain, expressing the 'patriotic' idea of political concordance of the regime, representing the nation as a region of regions. Without being vulgar promotion, the project advanced the nationalist dictatorial plans of Primo de Rivera, which had no relation to the emancipative aspirations of the Spanish regions.[11]

A similar populist propaganda display without Aníbal González's power of synthesis and sensuality was the Exposición Internacional in Barcelona, where urban fragments from diverse villages and towns of the regions of Spain were merged into over-familiarized 'as if' settings of an urban kind of theme park.[12]

A Popular Front Regionalism

The 1937 Exposition Universelle in Paris is usually associated with the Soviet Union and the Nazi Germany pavilions confronting each other, as well as Picasso's massive painting *Guernica* in support of Republican Spain, exhibited in a pavilion designed by Josep Lluís Sert and Luis Lacasa.[13] But part of the exposition was also the Regional Center at the International Exposition, which included twenty-seven pavilions, a 'microcosm of France's twenty-seven provinces'. What makes this historical event even more fascinating is that it was organized by the left-wing Popular Front coalition government, traditionally considered hostile to the regionalist movement, its ideas, and even its atmosphere. The reasons are easy to understand, given, as we have seen,

Figure 8.05 Palace of the Arts by Aníbal González Álvarez-Ossorio, Exposición Iberoamericana de Sevilla (1929).

the anti-modern stance of several regions and the pro-fascist and anti-Semitic orientation of many regionalist organizations.

However, the political and cultural situation by the 1930s was very different. On the one hand, there was a traditionalist pro-regionalist approach by the administrators. The exposition's general commissioner, Edmond Labbé, director of regional life, presented it as a humanistic response to mass industrialization and centralization, a unified France of artisans and manual producers. Jean Charles-Brun, one of the main organizers of the exposition, an ideologue of regionalism, attached to it his favorite political theme, 'Unity through Diversity'. By that, he meant to encourage the creative tendencies of the regions, with their becoming 'like a Little France' ('*comme une Petite France*'), a conservative slogan, while the same time strengthening the power of a centralized state.

Next to that, there was the interest of the government in encouraging any activities that would prop up the French economy, which was in severe trouble at that time. Thus, the Burgundian pavilion, the star of the show, designed by Roger Barade and Georges Gendrot, tried to combine a modern free kind of display to present vernacular artifacts and products. The motivation for the choice of Burgundy was clearly commercial, the agricultural products of that region being among the highest-quality and most exportable in France. Whatever the political interests in promoting Burgundian folkloric traditions and identity during the 1937 exposition, the end result was the branding of the region and its products.

The displays in the exposition's regional buildings offered through vivid simulations a view of a way of life in the region concerned, showing artisanal crafts and techniques and demonstrating their modernity. The show terminated with a vast space displaying publicity material, photographs, films, posters, maps, brochures, and guidebooks, several times using advanced media technology to promote tourism of the regions. On the political level, the exposition offered a microcosm of France (*comme une Petite France*) manifesting the diversity and creativity of the regions.

On the other hand, the regionalist question gave an opportunity to deal with studies from below investigating the way of thinking of the people without voice or literature – an area just developing in the Soviet Union at that time. It also gave the chance to explore the nature of pre-modern, pre-capitalist, or 'low-market' communities, very different in structure and mentality from the urban proletarians, even though both might have been on the same economic level. Overcoming the bias of seeing all peasants as backward, less intelligent conservatives, a stigma inherited from peasants' anti-reform attitudes following the revolution, the researchers became interested not in judging but in explaining their behavior. These studies also helped advance the understanding of the popular gains of fascism at that time. The programs that were more open to the public gave the opportunity for politically committed scholars such as Lucien Febvre to warn about the impending Nazi danger. Finally, one should not forget that popular regional artifacts and 'naïve provincial art' fascinated modern artists and their admirers, from Moscow to Munich and Paris. And by 1937 there was a big public that would have enjoyed seeing artifacts brought from the various regions of France. Thus, the 1937 exposition was unique because of the quantity and high quality of the intellectual manifestations that accompany it, arguing for the value of regional culture, French or international, and the significance of regional cultural studies.

Given the novelty and difficulty of the subject, it was commonly agreed that such studies, several times referred to under the term 'folklore' (the Germans, who were ahead in this respect, called it *Volkskultur*), had to be interdisciplinary. In 1937, the Museum of Arts and Popular Traditions under Paul Rivet and Jacques Rivière offered a framework for such work. The program was vast: research, library facilities, a depository of collections of folk art, symposia. The same year, the First International Congress of Folklore was held at the École du Louvre in Paris in August, the event coinciding with the International Exposition's festival involving art activities including singing, dancing, and fireworks.

Involved in these activities related to the redefinition of regionalism was the cream of the new kind of multidisciplinary young French scientist: Marc Bloch, Georges Dumézil, Lucien Febvre, Henri Focillon, Marcel Mauss, the antithesis of the traditional conservatism of official French academic institutions. The congress was followed by a special commission on Folklore in Education, founded in 1939.

Regionalism under the Occupation

With World War II, regionalism became a centerpiece of the Vichy collaborationalist government. But this regionalism under the Nazi occupation had very little of the intellectual character of the 1937 activities. It had regressed back to the regionalism of Maurras and Barrès, whose innocuous, empty nationalism, its anti-cosmopolitanism and loud anti-Semitism, met with approval by the Nazi occupiers. In May 1941, the Vichy government launched a great inquiry into the problem of rural architecture.[14]

This was consistent with the idea that the locomotive of industrialization was to be Germany, while the Vichy government was to direct France toward a 'return to the earth', an approach not very different from Generalissimo Franco's idea, following his takeover of the Spanish government, that the future of Spain, as well as the immediate way to solve the huge unemployment problem of the country after the civil war, lay in agricultural production. Hence Franco's policy of 'regiones devastadas', creating numerous decentralized housing projects recreating the nostalgic idea of an orderly and charming rural-feudal, agrarian society, with an architectural pastiche *genuinamente española* adapted to the 'regional style' while the planning principle was standard: houses built around a 'village square' consisting of an administrative and security building and a church.

For France, despite the support of a large number of professionals, Pétain, and organizations such as the Légion Française des Combattants, it was a fruitless exercise detached from the French reality. In 1943, in his *Entretien avec les étudiants des écoles d'architecture*, Le Corbusier stated that 'regionalism is nothing more but the last move of academicism', 'a means not to think'. And as regionalism stood at that moment, he appeared to have made a shrewd observation.

The Cottage Precedent

Let us cross the Channel and return to the 1860s. The idea of regionalism among a growing number of young British architects was very different from that on the Continent, discussed above. Although still admiring Gothic structures, they felt that all types of 'revivalism' were exhausted. Thus, they began upholding a new movement driven by a desire for new English 'true' architecture, adapted to the reality of the region, the site, the materials, and to a more humane way of life.

Their broader social and moral interests were inspired by contemporary social problems but also by the increasingly polemical essays by Ruskin that dealt with the economy and the environment. *Unto This Last* (1860), published in the monthly journal *Cornhill Magazine*, was, according to Ruskin, 'very violently criticized', forcing the publisher to stop its periodic publication. It was finally published as a book in May 1862.

In his *Crown of Wild Olive: Three Lectures on Work, Traffic and War* (1866), a later text, he asserted with bitter irony that the 'political supremacy of Great Britain' lay in its control over power resources, the 'cheapness and abundance of our coal', which he saw as bringing about not only social disaster but also environmental catastrophe, 'carbonic acid' leading to 'the sky black' and 'ashes to ashes'. His last publications, published with his own money during the 1870s, were a series of pamphlets called *Fors Clavigera* aimed at the 'working men of England'. Ruskin did now succeed as a political pamphleteer; however, his impact on architects during the second part of the nineteenth century, as we will see later, was enormous. Even more significantly, he succeeded in shaping twentieth-century ideas about ecology, critical regionalism, and sustainability.

Moreover, architects still had in mind the ideas published in Ruskin's first book on humble cottages as examples of successful architecture that fitted their environment and region. As was mentioned on p. 79, John Claudius Loudon, interested in the long-term future of London's green spaces and in large-scale residential projects for people of limited financial means, published *The Encyclopedia of Cottage, Farm, Villa Architecture* (1834), which included a long list of cottage types based on vernacular precedents, not all from England;

their lack of authenticity was criticized by Pugin. But Loudon was a pragmatist, and the cottage types he chose met certain basic functional, technical, and economic requirements. As in an earlier book, *A Treatise* (1806), he promoted the Gothic for England because it could facilitate functions better, and was more appropriate for the English climate.

What motivated Loudon to write his book was the rising need for affordable houses on the part of a group of newcomers to London. The booming commercial construction for this group on the periphery of London, controlled by the tastes and interests of the 'speculative builder', which generated an 'obvious perversion of true architecture', was the topic also of John B. Papworth's book *Rural Residences: A Series of Designs for Cottages, Decorated Cottages, Small Villas* (1818). Like Loudon, he searched for precedents for cottages for laborers, 'habitations of the laboring poor'. Papworth's precedents originated closer home. He looked into the tradition of regional farmhouses, which he thought had been built by local masters 'imitating' or 'adopting' elements from local high-class buildings, expecting the future builder to match them with the local sites.

By the 1860s, the need for good-quality efficient and effective 'cottages' adapted to the new functional needs and construction possibilities, overcoming hurdles of commercialism, was even bigger, and the idea of learning from local traditions and knowledge of building by studying regional vernacular structures and even working closely with local craftsmen was even more appealing.

George Devey (1820–1886) was one of the first architects to design cottages employing construction elements and materials from local vernaculars. In the summer of 1861, together with Norman Shaw and William Eden Nesfield, he traveled in Yorkshire, documenting vernacular structures. Many other tours followed in other parts of England, and they immediately affected the projects that followed.[15]

In 1884, William Richard Lethaby (1857–1931), architect, writer, and civil servant, founded the Arts Workers Guild, together with Edward Prior and other members of the office of Richard Norman Shaw (1831–1912). In support of their efforts, William Morris joined the guild. It organized discussion evenings but it also arranged travels to interesting vernacular buildings all over the country following the example of Shaw, who, together with his partner William Eden Nesfield (1835–1888), went on sketching tours studying old rustic vernacular residential communities.

Soon afterwards, there emerged a number of small-scale cottages designed and built by young architects and drawing from vernacular precedents. They supplied high-quality innovative solutions, as in the remarkable Farmer's House in Fortingall, Perthshire, built in 1889 by James MacLaren; and in the lodging houses and the Lost Sailor Hotel at West Bay, Dorset, and House in Dorset (*c.*1885) designed by Edward Schroeder Prior (1852–1932), the plans growing out of the site as if spontaneously, following the method learned from the study of rural structures. The use of vernacular knowledge is evident in the inventive plan and volume for the Barn, Exmouth, Devon (1896–1897), the Club Promenade Baths (1890s), and House in Dorset by Edward Schroeder Prior; in Ernest Gimson's Soneywell Cottage in Leicestershire (1898–1899); and in James MacLaren's Glenlyon House in Fortingall, Perthshire (1889). They used

Figure 8.06 Edward Schroeder Prior: study for a cottage.

local materials but also created a highly innovative configuration of the building volumes, fitting the site and reflecting an equally original functional plan drawn from the lesson of vernacular local tradition.

Equally pioneering and successful were the projects by Philip Webb (1831–1915), one of the leaders of the movement. For him, local building traditions had a pragmatic value. They consisted of tested ways of construction that achieved good results when reused. In 1877, Webb joined Morris's radical Socialist League, becoming its treasurer, and in 1877 he founded the Society for the Protection of Ancient Buildings, referred to on p. 84. Among his projects was the Red House – 'red' because of its 'deep red color' – at Bexleyheath in Kent in 1859 for William Morris. The house became at the same time a studio where a group of artists and designers worked together, forming a firm aimed at reviving the medieval 'brotherhood', stressing the belief in craftsmanship and expressing Morris's distaste for 'reform in art based on individualism'. The design reused 'thirteenth-century' elements, and they were not exclusively English.

Charles Francis Annesley Voysey (1857–1941) designed every detail of his houses, including the furniture. His houses drew from English vernacular sources of the sixteenth and early seventeenth centuries, featuring white roughcast walls with horizontal ribbon windows and huge pitched roofs, and used rough plaster and other materials typical of English farmhouses. Functionally, his plans reflected a new way of life away from the formality and servant-based public spaces of houses of the nobility and the bourgeoisie. They included a 'living and work' room that had its origins in the multi-task spaces of rural houses.

One of his earlier projects, Tigbourne Court, a cottage near Godalming, Surrey (1899), was designed by Sir Edwin Lutyens (1869–1944) for Gertrude Jekyll (1843–1932), a leading garden designer and collaborator of Lutyens. Jekyll remarked, four years after the completion of the house, in *Old West Surrey* (1904), that 'the local tradition in building is crystallization of local need, material, and ingenuity ... when adaptation of means to ends is so satisfactory that it has held good for a long time', 'it becomes a style', meaning 'fixed'. Lutyens used traditional local materials and regional seventeenth-century classical elements, rather than elements from the 'international' classical canon, and equally successfully integrated the building into its site and surroundings. Yet after 1900 he turned to classicism from above, his commitment to regionalism not being very lasting.

However, the vernacular regionalist movement was far from exhausted. In 1901, *The Art of Building a Home* by Barry Parker (1867–1947) and Raymond Unwin (1863–1941) contained examples of houses still based on regional vernacular precedents. The basic concern of the authors was to demonstrate new ways of construction through which the cost of houses for the working class could be radically reduced without sacrificing quality, and they claimed that they found in vernacular buildings valuable guidance. Parker and Unwin were equally concerned with the renewal of the plan of the contemporary house. Drawing from the arrangement of the English vernacular traditional 'great hall', like Voysey they proposed an open plan, multifunctional but also satisfying the 'gathering instinct', enabling communal interaction, an idea to be traced to William Morris in an encounter with Yeats, when he had asserted that 'the house that would please me would be some great room where one talked to one's friends in one corner, and ate in another, and slept in another, and worked in another'.[16]

Thirty years after Morris's death, in a lecture delivered at Columbia University in 1936, Unwin referred to the 'English single-room dwelling' of the early days of the 'free' Saxons, where there was minimal distinction between servant and master. In recommending the study of regional structures to develop successful techniques of site planning, he commented: '[D]oes not the old building seem almost to grow out of the ground on which it stands? Built on local stone; roofed with material common to the district – thatch, stone, shingles ... harmonizing in color with the rocks and soil ... appropriate to the soil on which it rests.'

Unwin was more than a generation younger than most of the architects who were part of the vernacular regionalist movement. Like Morris, Webb, and other members of the movement, he was a committed social reformer. Belonging to a different generation made him realize that to pursue his goals, the right domain was neither regionalist artifact design nor regionalist buildings but design on a larger scale, what came to be known as regional planning. At about the same time, inspired by the book *Garden Cities of Tomorrow* (1898, 1902) by Ebenezer Howard, there emerged the Garden City movement. In 1905, Parker and Unwin were asked to plan a new suburb at Hampstead, London. The 'regional' in these ideas and projects was the overriding planning principle of applying decentralized independent settlement units interwoven with nature. The new regionalist idea circulated around the world, and in 1922 Unwin was invited to advise on the Regional Plan for New York. In 1929, he became technical adviser to the Greater London Regional Planning Committee. He was invited back to New York during the Great Depression and consulted the New Deal teams on issues of legislation, housing, slum clearance, greenbelt towns, and regional development in the United States. In this manner, he contributed to the mutation of regionalism from architectural and landscape design into regional planning.[17]

Chapter 9

International Style versus Regionalism

The Regional Planning Association of America (RPAA), the body that had invited Unwin to the United States, was formed in 1923. It was a small group of architects, developers, and planners but they were linked with important friends such as Eleanor Roosevelt and the Russell Sage Foundation. They were concerned with the mounting post-World War I urban crisis and believed the future of the cities depended less on the excellence of isolated buildings than on the quality of the urban fabric made up of built wholes. They also believed that these built wholes should be decentralized into the regions of the country. Among the key initiators of the group were Clarence Samuel Stein, an architect, Benton MacKaye, a forester, and Lewis Mumford, an author.

The first major project of the RPAA was one proposed by an RPAA member, Benton MacKaye (1879–1975). The idea he presented in his 1921 article 'An Appalachian Trail: A Project in Regional Planning' was the Appalachian Trail. It was what we would refer to today as a greenway. The idea had first appeared in an article with the same title that he had published in the *Journal of the American Institute of Architects* two years earlier. The trail was planned as a footpath extending from Maine to Georgia. Its purpose was to 'lead civilization to the wilderness'. It was not implemented by the RPAA, but in part the RPAA was successful in promoting it to various groups of mountain clubs. As a result, most of the trail was completed by the mid-1930s. The RPAA also became involved in 'the preservation of large areas of the natural environment, including parts of the wilderness, as a green matrix for shaping a "regional city" and for serving its various-sized, spatially well-defined, specialized communities'.

Mumford was initially involved with English writings and experiments about the regionalism developed at the end of nineteenth century. His ideas were influenced by the writings of the Scottish biologist, planner, and regionalist advocate Patrick Geddes, who in turn had been influenced by the works of the French regionalist geographers and administrators that we discussed in the previous chapter, without much regard for their political beliefs and activities. By the beginning of the 1920s, Mumford had become increasingly absorbed by architecture.

A year after the founding of the RPAA, Mumford published *Sticks and Stones: American Architecture and Civilization* (1924), in which he used regionalism as a framework through which to present the first history of American architecture. Many of the ideas were taken from the writings of Viollet-le-Duc and Ruskin. The very title of the book alluded to Ruskin's *The Stones of Venice* and Ruskin's commitment to the social responsibility of the architect. Mumford juxtaposed regionalism to the 'imperial' Beaux-Arts architecture, very successful in the United States at that time. He condemned Beaux-Arts architecture as 'conspicuous waste', as 'icing on a birthday cake', as 'putting in a pleasing front upon a scrappy building, upon the monotonous streets and the mean houses', and as 'new slums in the districts behind the grand avenues'. He complained that it 'placed a premium upon the mask', upon the 'imperial facade', upon 'the very cloak and costume'. The Beaux-Arts tradition did nothing but apply an 'imperialist approach to the environment', encouraging 'a negligence of the earth', using the land for 'profitable speculation' rather than 'home'. It led to the 'depletion and impoverishment' of nature. Instead of this, 'achievements in science' and 'experiments in democracy' should be harnessed to 'serve economically' the 'capital city'.[1]

The Museum of Modern Art's 1932 International Exhibition

By the end of the 1920s, Mumford was considered the leading architectural critic in the United States. That is why, in the early 1930s, he, together with the unknown Philip Johnson and Henry-Russell Hitchcock, was asked by the director of the Museum of Modern Art (MoMA) in New York, Alfred Barr, to organize an exhibition under the title 'Modern Architecture: International Exhibition'. The exhibition opened in 1932. In the introduction to the catalog, Barr suggested the term 'International Style', arguing that while the exhibited architects came from various countries, 'it would be difficult to find in their work any national characteristics'. In his part of the exhibition, Mumford did not touch on the question of regionalism. He preferred to focus on the social and functional aspects of housing included in the show.

Simultaneously with the show, Hitchcock and Johnson published a book titled *The International Style*, in which they amplified their position that a new, universal modern architecture had come about.

In spite of Johnson's sudden departure in 1934 as curator of architecture at MoMA, just two years following the exhibition[2] (he became busy very actively in pro-Nazi political activities), the hold of the International Style on MoMA was assured, partly by Hitchcock, who stayed on. Ernestine Fantl, a former Wellesley College-educated art history student of Barr, replaced Johnson as director between 1935 and 1937 and proved to be an efficient keeper of the flame. Under her directorship, several other manifesto-like books and exhibitions took place that remained faithful to the International Style spirit. She mounted 'Town of Tomorrow' in 1937, an International Style-inspired protest against the New York World's Fair, which had presented a more mainstream, mediocre exhibition under the same title, and 'What Is Modern Architecture?', an exhibition of the problems and principles of the new architecture prepared especially for schools and illustrated with examples of work in the International Style in the United States and abroad.[3]

During this time, Hitchcock mounted two major shows that were equally true to the International Style theme. One was devoted to the architecture of H. H. Richardson in 1936. As opposed to Lewis Mumford, who had already written about Richardson in his *Sticks and Stones* and *The Brown Decades* (1931), and his *The South in Architecture* (1941),[4] and who praised Richardson for being the first 'regional' and 'romantic architect', he made no mention of it. The second exhibition was his 'Modern Architecture in England' in 1937. In the catalog, Hitchcock heaped praise on British architects or architects working in Britain such as William Lescaze, Wells Coates, Erich Mendelsohn, and Serge Chermayeff, who had, he intimated, fallen into line with the International Style's prerogatives within the five years since the original show.

Meanwhile, in 1934, Mumford was publishing his magisterial *Techniques and Civilization*, which established him as a cultural critic in addition to his reputation as an architectural one. The book presented a large-scale synthesis bringing in a historical and a sociological dimension in discussing the human-made environment and the problem of regionalism, beyond the framework of the writings of Geddes and the French geographers. It was a synthesis very much in line with the economic and political situation in the world and in the United States.

In 1938, Mumford took a break from his hectic activities in New York to become involved with a consulting 'design' project: planning a garden city in the tropics. The product, *Report on Honolulu*, was published after World War II, in 1945, having been prepared during a consulting trip to Hawaii.[5] It raised farsighted ecological or sustainability issues. Mumford saw Honolulu as a 'great park' made up of 'tropic foliage, with the pepper red of the Poinciana, the brilliant yellow of the golden shower, the feathery greens of the palms, the dark tones of the banyan trees'.[6] He suggested widening and planting the major thoroughfare, Bishop Street, the provision of a parking area, and the wiping away of the collection of miscellaneous buildings marring the view of the mountains. But he was also critical of the fact the present parks were restricted to 'recreation zones'[7] and proposed that they be used in a more integrated way in urban life, first as a potential cooling device capable of 'renewing the air, tempering the heat of the sun, reducing glare and strain, providing visual delight for play and relaxation and supplying one of the most sanative of all modes of work – the care of plants itself'.[8]

In 1937, the US economy had changed for the worse. The Great Depression had gone into a double dip. It was spread all over the country. However, certain regions suffered significantly more, as John Steinbeck's *Of Mice and Men* and Margaret Bourke-White's photographs demonstrated. The Roosevelt administration focused on regional inequality, undertaking a number of projects all over the country, the most famous being the Tennessee Valley Authority development program.

Within the framework of these developments, International Style seemed out of step. For the next decade, MoMA became a bastion of regionalism.[9] Regionalism not only took root there but came to virtually dominate its architectural exhibition program. The person who oversaw this changing of the guard was John McAndrew, a Renaissance scholar whose interest in contemporary architecture was mainly focused on regionalism, as evidenced in his *Guide to Modern Architecture, Northeast States* (1940).[10] He took over as director (1937–1941), followed by Janet Henrich and Alice Carson (1941–1943), and then Elizabeth Mock (1943–1947).

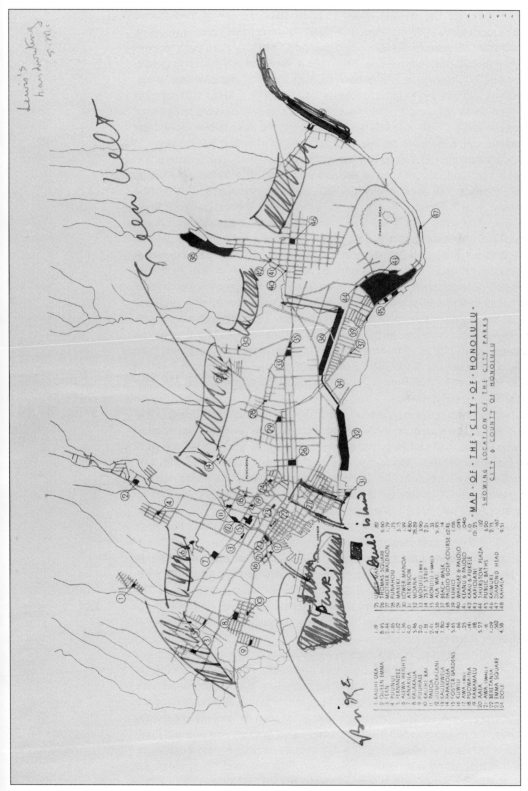

Figure 9.01 Lewis Mumford, urban plan for Honolulu (1938), bordered by a green belt to impede sprawl in the direction of the mountain.

During this decade, from 1937 to 1947, no fewer than twelve MoMA architectural exhibitions put forth a regionalist message. And, remarkably, they were a resounding success, attracting a much greater public than had the 'International Style' show, and without resorting to sensationalist controversy – lest it be forgotten that the 'International Style' exhibition had opened to street protests.[11] 'International Style' had had only fourteen showings outside the Museum. 'Modern Architecture in England' had even fewer, just ten. On the other hand, the first show McAndrew organized, an exhibition on Frank Lloyd Wright's house Fallingwater in 1938, in which he celebrated the 'warm humanitarian approach apparent in its soft light and pleasant surfaces' and its providing a 'romantic escape' from 'machine-age functionalism', had eighteen showings outside the museum.

The same year, there was another show, on Aino and Alvar Aalto. Alvar Aalto was an architect known for his distancing from the International Style and his adherence to regionalism. Aalto did not have an innovative agenda for his architecture and preferred to stay with an almost Ruskinian definition of regionalism. However, in terms of real design implementation – expressed in terms of selection of materials, adaptation to the site, and relation of the profile of the building to the landscape – the projects were highly innovative, and consistent to the 'millimeter', as Aalto would have said. The exhibition had fifteen showings outside the museum. An exhibition on Swedish regionalism, 'Stockholm Builds', with photos by E. Kidder Smith in 1941, had twenty showings outside the museum, and the 'The Wooden House in America' thirty-nine.

Although the exhibition entitled 'TVA Architecture and Design', prepared by the Tennessee Valley Authority in collaboration with the Department of Architecture, had just five, two shows organized by Elizabeth Mock were especially successful. Mock had worked her way up from temporary employee in the Department of Architecture and Industrial Design in 1937 to the position of acting curator of the Department of Architecture and Design between 1943 and 1947.[12] She was Catherine Bauer's sister;[13] and she was apprenticed under Frank Lloyd Wright at Taliesin in Wisconsin, and had close links with the American Regional Planning Association.

Both shows were held in 1941 and both had a regionalist slant. In the first, 'American Architecture', Mock presented, among other exhibits, 'Dymaxion Deployment Unit' by Buckminster Fuller for the first time. Fuller was a confirmed regionalist, as we shall see. The second was 'Regional Building in America', on the influence of climate and locally available materials. It had fifteen showings.

The interest in regionalism was mounting. The same year, April 1941, Mumford delivered 'The South in Architecture', a Dancy Lecture at Alabama College. World War II had already started, but United States was debating whether or not to participate. Mumford was for 'striking at once the Axis powers – striking *first*'. 'If we are to triumph as a democracy in the days to come, we must know what we are living for as well as what we are fighting for.' Interestingly, Mumford chose architecture as his subject for this occasion. It is fascinating that he decided to be critical and challenging about the state of affairs in America in relation to this topic.[14]

What was most significant in Mumford's text was that he reworked the idea of regionalism in a *critical* framework, taking apart the commercial and chauvinistic components built into it during the second part of the nineteenth century and the first part of the twentieth, reframing it in a new context that related it to the economic, environmental, and social problems of the twentieth century. Mumford developed his definition of regionalism in confrontation to the one by the Nazis in the 'deification of *Heimatsarchitektur*', which by then, together with the classical monumentality of Speer, was blooming in Germany, used in the Nazi youth camps and in Wehrmacht facilities such as the renowned Bad Reichenhall, north of Berchtesgaden, designed between 1934 and 1936 for mountain artillery troops, called the Ritter-von-Tutschek-Kaserne.

Mumford tried to define what regionalism meant in the present day. He warned that it was not a return to the traditional picturesque or Romantic regionalism in search of the 'rough', the 'primitive', the 'purely local', the 'aboriginal', 'the self-contained'. Neither was it in conflict with the 'universal'. He argued that regionalist architecture has to overcome the 'deep unbridgeable gulf between the peoples of the earth', which *Heimatsarchitektur* – that is, nationalist regionalism – is in fact deepening. Regionalism, Mumford argued, has to help people come to terms with 'the actual conditions of life' and make them 'feel at home'. 'Regional insight' has to be used to defend us from the 'international style', the absurdities of present technology, and the 'despotism' of 'the mechanical order'. They all fail to give 'form and order to a democratic civilization'. 'The brotherhood of the machine', argued Mumford, 'is not a substitute for the brotherhood' of people. The problem therefore lies not with science or technology but with society, institutions, and morality failures.

A string of regionalist exhibitions were shown at MoMA. Especially successful was Mock's 'Planning the Modern House', put up the next year, in 1942. It was a small show on the architecture of John Funk of the San Francisco Bay Region School, and had seventeen showings. In 1944, there was 'Look at Your Neighbor', an exhibition on regionalist neighborhood planning principles, and the same year saw a show prepared by Mary Cooke and by Catherine Bauer, who had been a prominent member of the Regional Planning Association and part of the TVA project. Bauer went on to become a professor at the University of California Berkeley College of Environmental Design.

'America Builds' (1944) was a show with a section on housing and a special section on regional and city planning[15] prepared by G. Holmes Perkins. It contained sections on Richardson, Sullivan, and Wright, 'Housing in War and Peace', and 'Planning in the USA' (typified by Chicago and the Tennessee Valley). Part of that exhibition, entitled 'Buildings of the Past Ten Years', was a runaway success and became a separate travelling exhibition renamed 'Built in USA since 1932', accompanied by a catalog, in 1945.[16]

In 'Built in USA', Mock was highly critical of the 'International Style' exhibition of 1932, which she called an example of 'badly assimilated European modernism',[17] pointing out the highly biased selection of architects as well as the eliminating of structural innovations, the social democratic program, urban planning, and regionalism.[18]

Mock's definition of modern architecture did have a distinctly regionalist slant. As a response to what she reported to be the American reaction to the fact that 'there has never been an architectural movement more deeply distrusted by the public' than that presented in 1932 at the 'International Style' exhibition, she went on to point out that since then, architecture, sadly in need of 'humanization', had managed to 'stimulate our minds', but 'only in conjunction with two other factors'. The first was 'a strong interest in Frank Lloyd Wright'. The second was 'a re-evaluation of that very dark horse – traditional vernacular architecture'.

So it was that 'Americans looked again at the stone and wood barns of Pennsylvania, the white clapboard walls of New England, the low rambling ranch houses of the West, and found them good'. They were interested in these buildings for their 'picturesque detail' but also because of their straightforward use of material and their subtle adaptation to climate and topography. Here was 'local encouragement for the growing international movement towards a friendlier, more differentiated contemporary architecture'.

She singled out California, which had been 'enjoying a continuous but seriously unpublished tradition in this new sense', as the most active of the regionalist centers in the United States, citing Berkeley's redwood houses from the office of Maybeck and his contemporaries. 'Shamefully little research has been done on these important regional developments,' she complained, citing the work of William Wurster (her brother-in-law-to-be) in the San Francisco area, Frank Lloyd Wright's Fallingwater (or Bear Run House) in Pennsylvania, and the work of Richard Neutra in Los Angeles.

An early proponent of sound, sustainable building, she argued that architecture must adapt to regional climate. 'Life in Puerto Rico is tolerable in a building that faces into the wind for its entire length, different from that in San Francisco where strong north winds must be avoided,' she writes, suggesting the 'brilliant example' of Brazil in its 'imaginative use of sun breaks' in its buildings. Closer to home, she urges architects to follow the example of George Fred Keck's 'solar' houses near Chicago that used double glazing, unlike Mies's Illinois Institute of Technology architecture department building, to avoid heat loss in the Chicago winters.

A contextual sensitivity to site also concerned Mock. She faulted buildings like Le Corbusier's Villa Savoye, which maintained 'a proud independence from its surroundings', as opposed to the organic approach of Wright, and included in her criticism the Sears Roebuck department store of 1939 and the storage dam and powerhouse of 1936 by the Tennessee Valley Authority.

Mock's regionalist inclination was not confined to the American scene. 'America Builds' had been the second blockbusting exhibition at MoMA under Elizabeth Mock's stewardship that was positive about regionalism. It had been preceded by 'Brazil Builds' in 1943, whose catalog was edited by Philip Goodwin, an architect, along with Edward Durrell Stone of MoMA (1938–1939).[19] His collaborators were also regionalists. Bernard Rudofsky, an Austrian post-*Anschluss* expatriate architect settled in São Paulo, who had won a Latin American architecture prize from MoMA for 'Organic Design' in 1941 and would go on to write one of the most influential regionalist manifestos of the post-war period, *Architecture without Architects*, supplied the drawings.[20] The remarkable photographs of the catalog were by G. E. Kidder Smith, who soon afterwards, during the 1950s, wrote a series of books called *Italy Builds*, *Switzerland Builds*, and *Sweden Builds*, describing the particular regionalist identity of the architecture of different countries.[21]

Since the outbreak of World War II in Europe, the United States had tried to cultivate alliances with Latin America, with which relations were at a low ebb. It was especially important to repair the rift with Brazil. By 1940, it was unclear how far its president, Getúlio Vargas, was going in his pro-fascist and pro-Nazi leanings. Nelson Rockefeller, whom FDR had named coordinator of inter-American affairs, saw the enhancement of cultural exchange, along with economic aid in the form of favorable loans for industrial development by the American Development Bank, as part of Roosevelt's so-called Good Neighbor policy.[22]

The aim of this cultural policy was to make Latin American culture in general attractive to North Americans. In 1942, Walt Disney was commissioned to shoot *Saludos Amigos*, an animated film set in Peru, Argentina, Chile, and Brazil, with Jo Carioca, a Brazilian parrot, singing 'Brazil' to Donald Duck. It was followed in 1944 by *Three Caballeros*, featuring a Mexican hero, Panchito Pistoles, and Donald Duck falling in love with various Latin American dancing women.

MoMA was a natural venue for an exhibition praising Brazilian architecture. Rockefeller was its president. In his introduction to the catalog, Goodwin repeatedly praised the Brazilian designs of the 1940s and 1950s for succeeding where North American architecture had failed: in adapting to the realities of the region.

> North America has blandly ignored the entire question [of climate]. Faced with summer's fierce western sun, the average office building is like a hot-house, its double-hung windows half closed and unprotected. The miserable office workers either roast or hide behind airless awnings or depend on the feeble protection of Venetian blinds.

Goodwin praises the Ministry of Education and Public Health by Lucio Costa, Oscar Niemeyer, Affonso Reidy, and others, with Le Corbusier as consultant (1937–1943). As opposed to possessing 'skin-deep beauty', this building was a 'fresh and careful study of the complicated problems of the modern office building'. He reserves his greatest praise for the arch-regionalist Oscar Niemeyer, but the book embraces Brazilian architecture in general as a model.[23] How positive Goodwin was about Brazil is obvious from the photograph of himself in his introduction to the catalog, in his pin-striped suit surrounded by lush, exotic tropical foliage.

An indication of the lasting appeal of the exhibition among the architectural establishment is that when the Graduate School of Design was contemplating who its next dean would be in 1953, Oscar Niemeyer was the first choice of the department, with the Europeans Ernesto Rogers and Josep Lluís Sert running second and third respectively. According to the future chairman Jerzy Soltan, Niemeyer was ultimately turned down for political reasons. He was a Brazilian communist and this was the McCarthy period.[24]

By 1947, after a decade-long series of successful exhibitions devoted the topic, it was now the future of regionalism that seemed assured at MoMA. But two events occurred that same year. First, Philip Johnson, apparently forgiven for his pre-war pro-Nazi escapades, reclaimed his position at MoMA, eliminating Elizabeth Mock.[25] Second, Lewis Mumford resumed his pre-war architectural column called 'Skyline' in the *New Yorker*, his campaign for regionalist architecture not diminished. In one of his first articles, he declared that the little-known so-called San Francisco Bay Region school of architecture, from Bernard Maybeck to William Wurster, was superior to the International Style.[26] A 'product of the meeting of Oriental and Occidental architectural traditions' was a 'far more universal style than the so-called International Style of the nineteen thirties, since it permits regional adaptations and modifications'.[27]

Regionalism Debated

The coincidence of these two events was explosive. Under Johnson's renewed and reinvigorated leadership, MoMA lost no time in retaliating against Lewis Mumford's article, which it saw as blasphemous. On February 11, 1948, barely three months following its publication, Alfred Barr, by then director of collections at MoMA, took the unprecedented step of organizing a public roundtable in order to respond. The title of the roundtable, 'What Is Happening to Modern Architecture?', sounded a note of alarm. In spite of the short notice, much of the East Coast architectural establishment came out en masse to be part of the panel. The panel was a 'who's who' of post-war architecture: Marcel Breuer, Walter Gropius, Edgar J. Kaufmann, George Nelson, Matthew Nowicki, Eero Saarinen, Peter Blake, Vincent Scully, and Edward Durrell Stone. Among the people who came to attend as part of the audience and commented from the floor were Serge Chermayeff, Talbot Hamlin, Gerhard Kallmann, and Isamu Noguchi.

The battle lines were drawn. Alfred Barr opened the meeting with a smear. He decried the Bay Region Style as a mere 'cottage style', appropriate for quaint domestic architecture in only the most provincial backwater. Worse yet, he deemed it to be redolent of '*Neue Gemütlichkeit*', insinuating by his use of the German term that there might perhaps be even a tinge of Nazi *Heimat* sympathy to Mumford's position. *Gemütlichkeit* was after all one of the epithets that the ultra-Nazi Paul Schultze-Naumburg upheld against the modernism of the Bauhaus, and in particular Walter Gropius.[28] Hitchcock spoke next, and in much the same condescending vein. His talk, aimed mostly at praising Frank Lloyd Wright and criticizing the present Corbusian solutions for the United Nations Headquarters, also dismissed regionalism as a 'cottage style' embodying a backward-looking 'reaction' to modern architecture, which was 'synonymous' with the phrase 'International Style'.

A number of participants from the major schools of architecture stepped up to defend the International Style. Not surprisingly, Gropius took the floor and defended the functionalism of the Bauhaus, presenting it as something open-ended and non-dogmatic. He went on to claim that the International Style had actually been 'regional in character, developing out of the surrounding conditions', as opposed to Mumford's regionalism, which was based on 'chauvinistic sentimental national prejudice'. For George Nelson, the regionalist roots of contemporary English cult of regionalism, the so-called 'new empiricism', was 'an ostrich-like and historically insignificant reaction to the impact of modern architecture'. Marcel Breuer defended the modernism of Le Corbusier. Peter Blake lashed out against regionalism for trying to 'delay' the 'industrial revolution in building' that was finally taking place in America.[29] As for Edgar Kaufmann Jr, he was caught in the middle. A close member of MoMA's inner sanctum but also a student of Wright and heir to Wright's Fallingwater, built for his parents, chose the noted California *Journal Arts and Architecture* to attempt a conciliatory position that gave both the International Style and the Bay Region their places according to varying sites and demands.[30] The London-based *Architectural Review* supported Mumford, saying that Bay Region architecture was 'modern although local in origin'.[31]

The architectural historian Sigfried Giedion, the first secretary-general of the Congrès International d'Architecture (CIAM) and an impresario of the 1920s and 1930s, had already brought his position to bear. The introduction to his *A Decade of New Architecture*, also published in 1947, had criticized the current regionalist trends in architecture in Sweden, the Netherlands, and Switzerland, which he referred to as 'lifeless eclecticism' that 'slowed down and even twisted backwards' the development of modern architecture.[32] This was consistent with his immensely popular textbook published in 1941, *Space, Time and Architecture*, which had omitted any mention of one of the major architects of Europe, Alvar Aalto, because he was a regionalist.

The reason MoMA and the East Coast establishment attempted to retaliate against Mumford's article is that his regionalist declarations had not fallen on deaf ears. They had, actually, struck a deep chord, particularly with the younger generation in attendance. In fact, this generation was closer to Mumford's sensitivity than to that of the older generation. Gerhardt Kallmann, the recently immigrated young German architect who was teaching at the Harvard Graduate School of Design, for example, distinguished post-war regionalism from 'folkloristic revivalism' and saw it as an attempt to overcome the 'over-schematic and blatant solutions in earlier phases of modern architecture'.[33] He went so far as to declare that architects had 'more to learn from the work of Frank Lloyd Wright and Alvar Aalto', two regionalists, than from what he saw as the detached, vacuous 'form world' of Le Corbusier.[34] Christopher Tunnard, a young assistant professor of city planning at Yale, was also present. He was pointedly critical with regard to MoMA. Indeed, he launched into an *ad hominem* attack on Johnson and Hitchcock. He declared that 'we were brought up in the school of modern architecture, we were bred on the *Architectural Review* and Mr. Johnson's and Mr. Hitchcock's book, and we have gone through a period of modern building, and it seems there are limitations'.[35]

Another member of the MoMA audience that day who was sympathetic to Mumford was the American architect Ralph T. Walker (1889–1973). He spoke out at length against the whole idea of an international style, ill-adapted to local conditions:

> I have been around South America recently and I have just come back from Europe, and I find everywhere that modern architecture means a slab on pillars. It means the same thing in the United

States because you pick up the architectural magazines and prac-
tically every issue has as its leading number a slab on pillars...
Functionalism of materials has blazed our thinking around the world
because you will find that the building in Rio for the Education Ministry looks exactly like a building that was designed for a giraffe in
the London Zoo, and it looks exactly like the building that has been
designed for the United Nations. In other words, you have a cover
of unthinking uncritical acceptance of things.[36]

The battle had just begun. In spite of the apparent regionalist sympathies of
the younger, post-war American generation of architects, there followed a
decade of unrelenting anti-regionalist campaigning by the powerful, media-
savvy MoMA and the CIAM-dominated architectural establishment both in the
United States and elsewhere. In 1943, Giedion, with Josep Lluís Sert and
Fernand Leger, had already written a manifesto. 'Nine Points on Monumentality' was a repackaging of pre-war CIAM members such as Le Corbusier,
Gropius, and Sert for post-war consumption.

Now that we no longer adhere to a creed of production for production's sake, the civilization that is now in the making draws closer to
the mental outlook that is shared by primitive man and Eastern man.
We are in the West are again becoming conscious of something that
they never forgot: that the continuity of human experience always
exists alongside and in contrast to our day-to-day existence.

It was Giedion's attempt to reassert his position as top theoretician after his
star had been eclipsed by Johnson and Hitchcock's formulation of International Style. Now, in 1948, Giedion got the London-based *Architectural Review*
to provide a forum entitled 'In Search of a New Monumentality: A Sympo-
sium'. The issue, entitled 'The Need for a New Monumentality', included
Giedion, Sert, and Leger's original article along with contributions by Gregor
Paulsson, Hitchcock, William Holford, Gropius, Lucio Costa, and Alfred Roth.
    Even within the ranks of the faithful, there was a rumble of dissent.
One of the participants, Paulsson, resisted the call to a new monumentality,
relying on his reading of modern architecture as fundamentally allied with
democracy. He advocated instead of formalism a range of issues that modern
architecture must address: psychology, sociology, and, especially, ecology (in
the sense of human and urban ecology), echoing regionalists such as Elizabeth Mock, Catherine Bauer, and Lewis Mumford.[37]
    Paulsson's article appeared in *Progressive Architecture* in Decem-
ber 1948, and there were many regionalist respondents, notably from among
the Bay Region architects such as Gardner Dailey and Ernest Kump. William
Wurster and Robert Woods Kennedy, both from MIT, wrote in support, while
Christopher Tunnard, Carroll Meeks of Yale, Talbot Hamlin of Columbia, and
Philip Johnson, Hitchcock, and Peter Blake voiced their opposition.
    The battle raged on. MoMA meant business, because the stakes
were high in 1947. Among other things, the commission for the United
Nations Headquarters building hung in the balance. Niemeyer had been one
of the competitors and posed a serious threat to the International Style

architectural firm Harrison & Abramovitz, the first choice of MoMA and Wallace Harrison's brother-in-law, Nelson Rockefeller. Not only was Rockefeller president of MoMA, but he owned the land the United Nations Headquarters was to be built on. This meant that the credibility of both MoMA and the International Style now hinged on the success of the UN building. The campaign paid off. Harrison & Abramovitz got the job that same year.[38]

But even after the commission was awarded to its first choice, MoMA remained on the offensive. It spent nearly a decade in relentless pursuit of its anti-regionalist campaign. In 1951, Hitchcock took advantage of the twenty-fifth anniversary of his and Johnson's exhibition in an article entitled 'The International Style Twenty Years After' to attack Mumford's *New Yorker* article of 1947 once again.[39] Taking aim at Mumford's fellow regionalist William Wurster, he wrote that

> the architects of the San Francisco Bay Region, whom some critics have wished to build up as the protagonists of a more humanistic school opposed to the international style, have also frequently followed its principles almost down to the point of parody – although admittedly not in their best and most characteristic country house work.[40]

By 1952, the campaign was still going strong. Back at headquarters, Hitchcock and Arthur Drexler, the new curator of architectural exhibits at MoMA, organized a new exhibition in which they actually hijacked the title that Mock had used six years earlier, that is, 'Built in USA'. They also enlisted Philip Johnson to preface the catalog.

It was as if Mock's original 'Built in USA' had never existed. In a ringing paean to both himself and Hitchcock, Johnson boasted:

> [T]he battle of modern architecture has long been won. Twenty years ago the Museum of Modern Art was in the thick of the fight, but now our exhibitions and catalogues take part in that unending campaign described as simply the continuous, conscientious, resolute distinction of quality from mediocrity – the discovery and proclamation of excellence. To make this proclamation from time to time is the prime function of the Department of Architecture and Design ... [as a judge] we chose Professor Henry-Russell Hitchcock of Smith College, the leading historian of modern architecture in this country. With me, Mr. Hitchcock was responsible for our first international exhibition of modern architecture exactly twenty years ago.[41]

There was nothing but the International Style in American architecture, according to him. 'If we should think back twenty years to the 1932 exhibition, the change is ... striking,' he declared.

> The International Style ... [has] spread and [has] been absorbed by the wide stream of historical progress. Every building in this book would look different if it had not been for the International Style. With the mid-century modern architecture has come of age.[42]

As for Hitchcock's contribution to the catalog, it was as anti-regionalist as Mock had been pro-regionalist in her own, 1944 version of 'Built in USA'. 'Today there is no further need to underline the obvious fact that what used to be called "traditional" architecture is dead if not buried,' he declared.

In defending the International Style to such an extreme, Hitchcock's sights, like Johnson's and MoMA's in general, were set on issues above and beyond the UN building. They involved geopolitics. Just as FDR's policies, based on the Good Neighbor approach to Latin America and New Deal public housing programs at home, had shaped Elizabeth Mock's exhibition program, so the Cold War and the Truman Doctrine, initiated in 1947, now made their own presence felt. What MoMA saw as good about an 'international' stance in architecture also had a lot to do with what its president, Standard Oil's Nelson Rockefeller, saw as good cultural diplomacy for the increasingly interventionist United States on the rapidly expanding stage of globalizing geopolitics. In the aftermath of America's victorious military feats in World War II, the country had what Mumford once called an 'imperial facade' to project.[43] Rockefeller, who had been both head of the governmental International Office of Foreign Affairs under Franklin D. Roosevelt and president of MoMA from 1939 to 1948, had great faith in the arts and architecture. Famously, he was to describe Jackson Pollock's paintings, for example, as 'free enterprise painting'.[44] To him and MoMA, the International Style appeared to be a diplomatic calling card, or rather a branding device for selling the image of a powerful, modern, free American nation to a growing global audience of consumers.

As a tool of nation branding[45] in an expanding, globalizing world, the 'International Style' was made to order – or so it seemed to Johnson and Hitchcock in the early 1950s. Its role, and in particular that of the architectural and design section, in US expansionism, thanks mainly to funding by Porter A. McCray and the Rockefeller brothers, has been documented. McCray, who during the war had worked in American intelligence under President Roosevelt with Eero Saarinen, Charles Eames, and Buckminster Fuller, was appointed director of the Rockefeller-financed Department Exhibition Program at MoMA after the war.[46] Twenty-two of the first twenty-five exhibitions prepared under him traveled outside the United States.[47] In the specific case of 'Built in USA', the catalog was distributed on an international scale and translated into many languages, thanks to a Rockefeller brothers fund that made possible a five-year project, the International Circulating Exhibition Program. The scope of the museum's traveling exhibitions was in this way expanded to include Europe, Latin America, and India,[48] and formed an important chapter in the history of the way private capital was starting to shape American Cold War cultural politics in combination with official governmental agencies.

An anonymous article in *Arts and Architecture* in 1953, in referring to American buildings abroad as the 'architectural calling cards' of the US government, had quoted Hitchcock as saying that 'by the middle of the twentieth century American architecture has come to occupy a position of special prominence in the world'.[49] This had been a quotation from his introduction to 'Built in USA', where he had claimed, furthermore, that 'in architecture, as in many other things, we are the heirs of Western civilization'.[50]

To some extent, the International Style might have been a truly judicious choice of calling card – notably in post-war Germany. The so-called America House information center program in post-war Germany is a case in point. Started by the American Military Authority and continued by the United States Information Agency after 1953 under the Eisenhower administration, it comprised seven information centers in different German cities, all designed by Gordon Bunshaft. The Nazis had condemned Bauhaus modernism in Germany, in particular the ultra-Nazi architectural ideologue Paul Schultze-Naumburg, who had referred to the modernist buildings at Weissenhof in 1927 as 'foreign', but now it returned via the United States.[51] 'The use of the Bauhaus idiom, transformed into an American icon', was 'a fitting goodwill gesture toward Germany'.[52]

This goodwill campaign would have resounded with the old student of the Social Democratic Bauhaus, Max Bill, the founding director of the Ulm Design School in 1953, particularly the idea that it had inherited the mantle from the Bauhaus. Because of regionalism's pre-history in Weimar Germany, linked to *Heimatschutz* and Schultze-Naumburg, together with his follower Martin Heidegger, anti-regionalism was almost a part of Max Bill's mindset as a designer. This besieged mentality on the part of a former Bauhaus-trained architect explains why, at the Biennale in São Paulo in 1953, he went on the offensive and attacked Niemeyer for his regionalism, to the consternation of the Biennale hosts.[53]

But ultimately the International Style had inherent shortcomings as a diplomatic calling card or national branding device. Hitchcock's introduction to MoMA's 1955 catalog for the exhibition by the same name, *Modern Architecture in Latin America since 1945*, revealed how deep these could be.[54] Hitchcock's introduction to the catalog opens with some laudatory sentences about Latin American architecture. First he declared that his exhibition would

> be found, I believe, to exceed that exhibition ['Built in USA' by himself and Johnson] in a variety of interest and at least to equal it in the average level of the work included. In certain fields, notably university cities and public housing, the United States in recent years has had little to offer as extensive in scope or as brilliant in design as the best Latin American work.

He expressed great admiration about Latin American cities: 'because the quantity of Latin American building exceeds our own, the appearance there of "modern" cities gves us the opportunity to observe effects which we ourselves only anticipate'.[55]

But compliments like these were offset by the derogatory tenor of many of Hitchcock's other remarks. Oscar Niemeyer, for example, was dismissed as a charlatan. Although Hitchcock conceded that 'Niemeyer is certainly the architect whose fame is justifiably greatest', Brazilian modern architecture, he said, 'cannot stand or fall by the work of the man Gropius has called its "bird of paradise"'. He even quips, when describing Niemeyer's Banco Boavista, that 'built relatively early, the bank set a pace for Latin American business buildings that has not always been successfully kept up even by Niemeyer himself'.[56] About Barragan, Hitchcock starts off by saying that his buildings have 'no façade', adding that Barragan was 'not trained as an architect', indeed had 'no technical training at all'. Needless to say, Barragan's degree was in engineering. As for Lina Bo Bardi's house in São Paulo (1950) and Matthias Goeritz's masterful El Eco (1953) in Mexico City, they are not even mentioned.

International Style diehard that he was, Hitchcock preferred the work of Moreira, Bratke, and Bernardes. The reason was that it was a 'quieter and more disciplined elegance, related ultimately to the work of Mies'. As for the Caribe Hilton by Toro Ferrer & Torregrossa, it is mentioned as 'the most successful of the resort hotels in Latin America' because, 'despite the skillful adaptation to a near tropical climate', it looked 'very North American'.

The lion's share of praise went to North American architects who had built in Latin America in the International Style. He singled out Edward Stone's El Panama Hotel in Panama and his hospital in Lima, still under construction, Holabird & Root's Tequendama Hotel in Bogotá, and Lathrop Douglas's Creole Oil building in Caracas. Henry Klumb receives kudos as 'the only Wright discipline of North America working in Latin America'. Equally kind words were heaped on Don Hatch, an American working in Venezuela. But the highest encomium was reserved for Harrison & Abramovitz's American embassy in Rio and, particularly, the one in Havana because it avoided 'the usual Latin American devices for sun control' and had instead 'all-over sheathing with imported travertine', thus assuring its 'cool and untropical look'.

From a position of assumed architectural superiority, Hitchcock declared that 'the major contribution of the United States' had been of a 'different and less direct order' than providing just buildings for Latin America. It simply consisted in educating Latin American architects to design in the style of North American ones. As a result, 'a very considerable proportion of the best Latin American architects, particularly those under forty', owed 'at least the final stages of their professional education to the architectural schools of the United States'. His attitude bordered on bullying. 'Considering the very large numbers of Latin American architects who have at least completed their professional education in the United States,' he declared, 'it is surprising that there is not more influence from the United States.'

Intimating that Anglo-Saxons were naturally better endowed as architects, certainly more global than their regional Latino counterparts, he mentioned that 'the visitor from the north cannot help being struck by the fact that a leading Argentinian architect is named Williams and a leading Uruguayan is named Jones'. Another proof of this superiority was that 'Chile and Uruguay have relatively less new architecture than Peru but the design standards are higher' because, 'as has been said', both countries have excellent architecture schools, naturally 'run by architects trained in the US'. It is

> a tribute to our schools that they have given to Latin Americans a training so broad that it could readily be applied under different local conditions.... In a sense there is in present day Latin America – outside Brazil and Mexico at least – something approaching Gropius's ideal of an impersonal anonymous architecture.

Hitchcock's comments lacked the subtlety and artfulness required of good branding. He passed around his calling card with a heavy hand. He made it all too clear that the main reason for Latin America's architectural weakness was its regionalism. The worst offenders were Brazil and Mexico. The main brunt of his condescension was targeted at the very regionalist features of their architecture that had been so highly praised by Philip Goodwin in 'Brazil Builds': that is, the brise-soleil, the vault engineering, and the collaboration with prominent artists in the fabric of the building. Colombia and Venezuela fared far better because they conformed to the International Style. In fact, he went so far as to assert that Brazil 'might profitably learn something of the sounder building techniques from Colombia or Venezuela', which have 'something more than a few clichés of brises-soleil, shell vaults and azulejos to offer the rest of the world'. Modern architecture had 'grown by following the leaders – Le Corbusier, Gropius, Mies, Frank Lloyd Wright',[57] he warned, the implication being that Brazil and Mexico should relinquish their misguided regionalist attachment to national identity and fall into line with the lead of their neighbor to the north.

Remarkably, it never occurred to him that the finest Latin American architecture was at least the equal to the finest North American. 'The forty six buildings that follow should prove that modern architecture in Latin America has indeed, in this decade, come of age even if they include no Johnson Wax

Figure 9.02 Ludwig Mies van der Rohe with the collaboration of Philip Johnson, the Seagram Building (1957).

tower and no Lake Shore Drive apartments.'[58] It is as if masterpieces such as Felix Candela's Cayoacan Market Hall, Carlos Villanueva's Ciudad Universaria, or Juan O'Gorman's library at the University of Mexico simply had not registered.

However, the most forceful counterattack against the regionalist point of view and in favor of a resurrection of the International Style was once more through an exhibition on Mies van der Rohe, in 1953 at MoMA.[59] The curator was Philip Johnson. The next year, Mies received the commission for the building of his life, the Seagram Tower (1954–1958), with Philip Johnson as his collaborator. The impact of the show was tremendous, inside the United States and all over the world. Through Mies, it established a new global classical canon for years to come. But it was not instantly felt. For the moment, regionalism was rising once more.

Chapter 10

Regionalism Rising

By the early 1950s, the International Style was fighting a losing battle both at home and abroad. Johnson's and Hitchcock's triumphal pronouncements had been a far cry from reality. They take on a decidedly hollow ring when one takes a close look at their 'Built in USA' of 1952. Here one finds that only half the projects fit the definition of International Style. Among these were Mies's Farnsworth House and Lake Shore Drive apartment houses, Eero Saarinen's General Motors technical center, Marcel Breuer's Caesar Cottage, Aalto's Senior Dormitory, Gropius's Harvard Graduate Center, Philip Johnson's glass house in New Canaan, and Pietro Belluschi's Equitable Savings and Loans building prominently displayed. But, in addition, among the buildings selected as International Style were buildings that have become classics of regionalism: Neutra's Tremaine House, Paul Rudolph's Healy House, Harwell Hamilton Harris's Johnson House, Lloyd Wright's Wayfarer's Chapel, Frank Lloyd Wright's house for Herbert Jacobs, Eliel and Eero Saarinen's Opera Shed for Berkshire Music Center, and Paolo Soleri's Desert House. What the book established is very different from what it claimed to be the case: good projects carried out in the International Style were slim pickings.

International Style architecture was not faring well at all. Public and professional sentiment at home had already massively turned against it by the time *Built in USA* was published, in 1952, and the main reason for this was, precisely, the UN building. As Jane Loeffler points out in *The Architecture of Diplomacy*, it was a public relations disaster, and received massive negative coverage in the press. Lewis Mumford, for one, blasted it in the *New Yorker* of December 1952.[1] Among the architects who followed suit and expressed dismay at the building were Rudolph Schindler, Bruce Goff, and Pietro Belluschi.[2] Paul Rudolph, in particular, condemned it for bringing 'the so-called International Style close to bankruptcy'.[3]

One project that would indeed have brought not only the International Style but also New Monumentality close to bankruptcy if it had been built was the 1955–1958 project for a new urban plan for Havana and new residence for the Cuban dictator Fulgencia Batista by Paul Lester Wiener and by Josep Lluís Sert, who had not only been one of the founding members of the Congrès International d'Architecture (CIAM) but also one of the main representatives of the International Style and the co-author of the New

Monumentality movement (he had co-authored 'Nine Points on Monumentality' in 1947 with Giedion). In Havana, Sert was bent on overturning the very
'humanistic' precepts that he had himself put forth in his *The Heart of the City*
in 1952: that is, to 'respect the customs of people and their quality of life'.

Sert and Wiener's plan for Havana was to raze most of the historic center of the town, Habana Vieja, a World Heritage Site since 1982,
full of seventeenth- and eighteenth-century buildings with the most expansive extent of covered porticos in the world, and turn it into a business
center.[4] In the words of historian Roberto Segre, this would have been to
'erase the architectural typologies that constituted the social memory of its
community' and to destroy 'the historic center of Havana exalted in her
streets by the co-existence of modest dwellings and pretentious eclectic
buildings and the taste picked up from its piazze'[5] by uprooting its population into housing on the periphery. The plan also included plans for a new
presidential palace across the strait from the old city and constructing an
underwater tunnel linking it to the new business center. The third part of
the plan was to create a new island in the bay facing the famous seaside
promenade of the Malecón. The island was to become the 'Latin Las Vegas'
and was supported by the government but also by Meyer Lansky, the
founder of the National Crime Syndicate and one of the United States' top
ten racketeers, along with fellow Mafia mobsters 'Lucky' Luciano and Santo
Traficante Jr.[6]

The plans came to an abrupt end with the Cuban Revolution. The
public relations disaster that would have ensued was averted. But it is telling
of Sert's moral compass that his partner, Lester, wrote on January 13, 1959,
a few days after Castro's takeover:

> [N]aturally, I have many friends in Cuba who belong to the Castro
> party and hope to meet the new president in the next few months
> to fill him in on the work we have been doing in Cuba ... I have
> heard the project office is intact. Only the dictator is different. It
> would be a great shame if the new project were not built.[7]

An additional setback to old mainstream architecture was the reception of the
Pan Am Building (1958–1963) by Gropius and Pietro Belluschi. The main critique pointed to the environmental impact of the building and its incongruence
with the surrounding urban architecture. Ada Louise Huxtable, the *New York
Times* critic, called it a flagrant example of private interests riding roughshod
over public concerns.[8]

Beyond MoMA's walls, regionalism was becoming an increasingly
attractive alternative, not least in the major American architecture schools. In
1944, Paul Zucker published a book entitled *New Architecture and City Planning* based on the proceedings from a seminar he had organized with contributions by many of the major Ivy League educators of the time: Serge
Chermayeff, Louis Kahn, Charles Abrams, Richard Neutra, Josep Lluís Sert,
Oscar Stonorov, George Boas, Albert Mayer, George Boas, Sigfried Giedion,
George Nelson, Carroll L. V. Meeks, László Moholy-Nagy, Josef Albers. It was
intended to map out the curricula of the architecture schools of the time.
Thirty percent of the content was devoted to regional planning.

Regional planning was an important part of the curriculum in architecture schools in the 1940s and 1950s. The reason is that the major government planning had been carried out since the Progressive Era by landscape designers. Many of the first metropolitan and regional plans in the late nineteenth century were developed for park systems that integrated recreation, transportation, storm drainage and flood control, and wastewater management, and that created a framework for future urban development. Frederick Law Olmsted and his sons, John Charles Olmsted and Frederick Law Olmsted Jr, Charles Eliot, and John Nolen were not only landscape architects but devised plans for entire new communities, like Forest Hill Gardens.[9] They were among the founders, in 1909, and first presidents of the National Conference on City Planning. The first course in city planning at an American university was initiated in 1909 at Harvard University's School of Landscape Architecture. By 1923, the school offered a degree in regional planning.

By the mid-1940s, many American universities were eager to emulate Harvard and incorporate the 'region' into their curricula. In 1943, Lewis Mumford was hired by Stanford University to found the humanities department, which would be the basis for a broadly based, multidisciplinary regional planning program.[10] During the mid-1950s, he was professor of city and regional planning at the University of Pennsylvania. The Illinois Institute of Technology in Chicago found a convert to regionalism in the German immigrant Ludwig Hilberseimer, who had been one of the early adherents of Le Corbusier's CIAM but who tried to adopt the stance of Mumford and Stein's Regional Plan Association in his teaching and writing, notably in his *New Regional Pattern* in 1949.[11] At around this time, two major universities became centers of environmental design. William Wurster founded the College of Environmental Design at Berkeley. In the landscape department at the University of Philadelphia, Walter Isard founded the Regional Science Association in the mid-1950s.

But the most cutting-edge regionalist American school of architecture in the late 1940s and early 1950s was probably North Carolina State College, founded in 1947 under the deanship of Henry L. Kamphoefer. The school was a veritable powerhouse. Kamphoefer created strict admissions policies for the new architecture department and instituted a distinguished visitors program from architecture, planning, engineering, sculpture, art, and landscape architecture, as well as cultural critics and systems theorists. Among these were Alexander Archipenko, Rudolph Arnheim, Pietro Belluschi, Marcel Breuer, Roberto Burle-Marx, Félix Candela, Serge Chermayeff, Thomas Church, Arthur C. Clarke, Willem Dudok, Charles Eames, Gerrett Eckbo, James Marston Fitch, Yona Friedman, Buckminster Fuller, Naum Gabo, Charles E. Gauss, Clement Greenberg, Walter Gropius, Lawrence Halprin, Douglas Haskell, Joseph Hudnut, John Johansen, Louis Kahn, Richard Kelly, Dan Kiley, Robert Le Ricolais, Eric Mendelsohn, Ludwig Mies van der Rohe, George Nelson, Pier Luigi Nervi, Richard Neutra, Cedric Price, Ad Reinhardt, Paul Rudolph, Eero Saarinen, Mario Salvadori, Hideo Sasaki, Edward Sekler, Josep Lluís Sert, Raphael Soriano, Clarence Stein, James Stirling, Raymond Stites, Eduardo Torroja, Heinz von Foerster, H. Th. Wijdeveld (who was a visiting professor), and Frank Lloyd Wright.[12]

The direction of the department was preeminently to exploit modern structural engineering to serve regionalist development in the South. One of the first appointments was Lewis Mumford. He joined the faculty in 1947 and stayed for four years.[13] It was on the recommendation of Mumford that Matthew Nowicki, who in spite of his young age had been chosen as one of the contestants for the new UN building, along with Niemeyer, Le Corbusier, and Harrison & Abramowitz among others, was invited to join the school. Nowicki was appointed acting head of the Department of Architecture, beginning with the fall 1948 session. As the planner and chief architect of Chandigarh, drawn up after the regionalist plan of Albert Mayer, his goal as the head of the architecture department was naturally to introduce regionalism into the architectural curriculum as part of his effort to shape the requirements of a scientific and technical approach.[14] Unfortunately, Nowicki tragically died in a plane crash over Egypt in 1950 while flying back to the United States from Chandigarh at the age of forty, to be replaced as the new town's chief architect by Le Corbusier.[15]

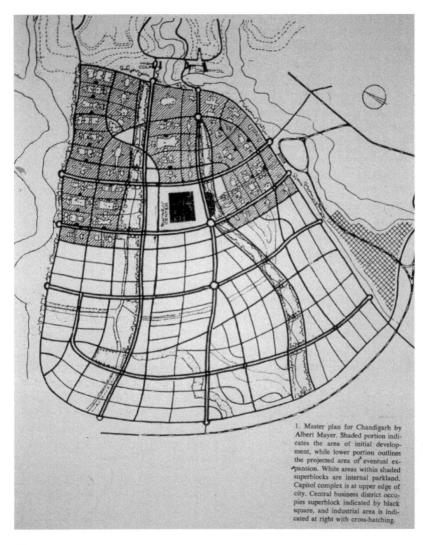

1. Master plan for Chandigarh by Albert Mayer. Shaded portion indicates the area of initial development, while lower portion outlines the projected area of eventual expansion. White areas within shaded superblocks are internal parkland. Capitol complex is at upper edge of city. Central business district occupies superblock indicated by black square, and industrial area is indicated at right with cross-hatching.

Figure 10.01 Albert Mayer and Andrew Nowicki, plan for Chandigarh, showing the differentiation of traffic that Le Corbusier would later introduce into his own plan for Chandigarh.

In addition to curriculum development, Kamphoefer was working on the regional development of the South. In 1948, he asked Nowicki to produce a series of studies for the development of a variety of facilities for the North Carolina State Fair, including the Raleigh Arena, a very advanced engineering project.[16] Nowicki was succeeded by the Argentine architect and engineer Eduardo Catalano (1951–1956), whose own house in Raleigh, a structural feat, was an interesting experiment in using modern technology to serve needs created by the regional particularity of the humid subtropical climate of North Carolina: the roof, covered by a canopy of trees, was a square-plan interior sheathed entirely in glass and open to the cooling breeze.

Another avant-garde building from the North Carolina school whose scheme was created to fit the regional reality of the South was Buckminster Fuller's geodesic dome. In developing it, Fuller took advantage of the experimental laboratory spirit encouraged by Kamphoefer working with faculty and students.[17] On April 6, 1952, the *Journal and Sentinel*, the newspaper of Winston-Salem, featured an article about the school with the headline 'True Regional Architecture Is Goal Of State College School of Design'.

During the early 1950s, regionalism was also on the agenda at the American Institute of Architects. It threw its support behind a traveling exhibition by Mary Mix in 1951,[18] 'American Architecture since 1947', also supported by the State Department, starting off from where Elizabeth Mock had ended.

Mix in her introduction stated that regionalism was one of the three primary features of American architecture, the other two being eclecticism and industrialization. For her, regionalism consists in a freedom to adapt to climate without being tied to historical formal prototypes, and to use local materials, the main example being the shingle-style Cape Cod House, a regional architecture whose merits Vincent Scully praised in his masterful *The Shingle Style* (1955). She included more regionalists than Mock had done: Neutra's public schools and hospitals for Puerto Rico, Raphael Soriano and

Figure 10.02 Front page of the *Journal and Sentinel*, the newspaper of Winston-Salem, North Carolina, April 6, 1952, presenting Buckminster Fuller's design for a cotton mill in the form of a geodesic dome as a regionalist project.

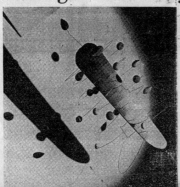

JOURNAL AND SENTINEL

WINSTON-SALEM, N. C., SUNDAY MORNING, APRIL 6, 1952   SECTION C

True Regional Architecture Is Goal Of State College School of Design

By Chester S. Davis

A textile mill (above) designed by State College students uses tensile strength and new materials to escape the vast investment in massive walls and roofing that is typical in traditional building. The factory would be covered with translucent plastic. This design seeks efficiency in operation and economy in construction.

Quincy Jones in Los Angeles, and Harwell Hamilton Harris from the Bay Region in San Francisco. The most remarkable regionalist building in the catalog is Antonin Raymond's school in Pondicherry for the students of Sri Aurobindo Ghose, one the first modern tropical buildings, built in 1936.[19]

Richard Neutra, of course, had been consumed since his early years by the question of fitting a building into its site and region. In 1946–1947, he designed the Kaufmann Desert House, Palm Springs, California. The building was commissioned by Edgar Kaufmann, who also commissioned Frank Lloyd Wright's Fallingwater (1935–1939), both twentieth-century icons for their harmonious response to the region. 'Try to understand the character and particularities of your site. Heighten and intensify what it may offer,' Neutra wrote in his *Mystery and Realities of Site* (Scarsdale, 1951).

There is a basic difference between Wright and Neutra, however. Wright's notion of a building fitting into its site was Ruskinian. The fit was in the eye of the outside onlooker. Neutra's house is not merely meant to be seen as an architectural object framed in a landscape from the outside. As compared with Wright's house, the boundaries between the dwelling and the landscape are reduced to a minimum. There is no difference between inside and outside. The aim here is to create such an interpenetration of both that the true walls to this living space seem to be the hills in the distance, beyond the huge sheets of polished plate glass. The 'only visible division between outdoors and indoors' is the 'subtle sheen' of the glass, unhindered by constructional posts, to quote Neutra once again. Taking his cue from 'hypaethral spaces in classical Greek temples', he writes that just 'as the building may

Figure 10.03 An example of tropical architecture: Richard Neutra's designs for houses in Puerto Rico (1944).

root itself in nature by outward reaching tentacles, so the site may be tied into the building by pleasant infiltrations'.

Neutra was not involved in the regionalism polemics of the time, but a young practicing architect, the Southerner Paul Rudolph, was. He embarked on a one-man anti-International Style, pro-regionalist campaign in parallel to his hectic regionalist design activities in Florida.[20] In 1949, Rudolph had already written:

> We have today sufficiently clarified our minds to know that respect for tradition does not mean complacent toleration of elements which have been a matter of fortuitous chance or simple imitation of bygone esthetic forms. We have become aware that tradition in design has always meant the preservation of essential character-istics which have resulted from eternal habits of people.[21]

In 1954, he read a paper to the American Institute of Architects in which he said:

> [W]e need desperately to relearn [from traditional architectures] the art of disposing of buildings to create different kinds of space; the quiet, enclosed, isolated, shaded space; the hustling, bustling space pungent with vitality; the paved, dignified, vast, sumptuous, even awe-inspiring space; the mysterious space; the transition space which defines, separates and yet joins spaces of contrasting character.

During the second part of the 1940s, Rudolph was working with his partner, Ralph Twitchell, in Sarasota, Florida, designing the light timber structure for the so-called Cocoon House of 1948–1950, a single rectangle with a platform

Figure 10.04 Paul Rudolph, the 'Cocoon' house for the Healy family in Siesta Key, Florida, 1950.

THE COCOON HOUSE

SIESTA KEY
1950

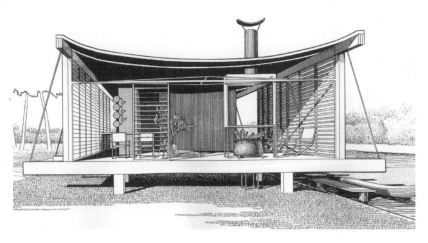

floor above grade extending into the lagoon. Although extremely modest in scale, it created a sensation when it was built because of the new lightweight wartime materials it experimented with in order to create a building well adapted to the climate conditions of the Florida Keys.[22]

His regionalist theoretical position was published in 1957 in *Perspecta*, the journal of the Yale School of Architecture. Like Neutra's, many of Rudolph's ideas had their origins in Frank Lloyd Wright's beliefs about the relation between building and site. In *Perspecta*, he complained that the architectural output of current times is 'probably lower than mankind has ever seen' because, 'with brilliant exceptions, we seem content with merely making it work and meeting the budget'. He suggested to his readers that

> you pay close attention to what we regard as untutored people and how they approach their problems.... Of course, I mean vernacular architecture. I think quite often people do things when left to their own devices, do things very well, and solve an awful lot of problems that architects tend to forget.[23]

For him, 'regionalism is one way toward that richness in architecture which other movements have enjoyed and which is so lacking today'. In the text, Rudolph attacked Mies's Lakeshore Drive buildings for having treated all facades identically, regardless of orientation, even though the building was not air-conditioned. He preferred the brises-soleil solution of Le Corbusier and, still more, Niemeyer's Ministry of Education and Health, which 'treats every facade according to its orientation'. The building is magnificently adapted to a warm climate and its monumentality is fittingly Latin, he said. The play of clear light and deep shadow on the clean, sharp lines of the sunny side give it an additional dimension which is possible only in such light. In Boston, where the light is soft and often misty, such treatment would appear crude. He compared Lever House in New York to 'cellophane-wrapped packages ... as American as canned soup'. He concluded that 'unlike containers, our buildings have to be adapted to local conditions'.

Two years before this article, participating in the Gulf States Conference in Biloxi, Mississippi, organized by the American Institute of Architects, he declared that 'regional characteristics are a part of all good architecture and should be accepted without resistance or overemphasis'. Neutra and Tunnard participated in the conference. Rudolph warned against 'monumental anonymity' and, describing his own practice, which was becoming increasingly tropical, declared that 'the splendidly integrated cultures and the great architecture of antiquity were originally subtropical, and man himself was a Southerner'.[24]

At another important professional meeting, at the Northwest Regional Council in 1956, Harwell Hamilton Harris, a southern Californian architect, distinguished between 'regionalism of restriction' and 'regionalism of liberation'. Referring to the case of the French Quarter in New Orleans, he wrote:

> This regionalism is the result of standing still while the rest of the world changes ... It cares more for preserving an obscure dialect

than for expressing a new idea. It is anti-cosmopolitan and anti-progressive. Such regionalism becomes a cloak for the misplaced pride of the region and serves to build-in ignorance and inferiority. Let's call this type of regionalism the Regionalism of Restriction.

Opposed to the regionalism of Restriction is ... the Regionalism of Liberation. This is the manifestation of a region that is especially in tune with the emerging thought of the time. We call such a manifestation 'regional' only because it has not yet emerged elsewhere. It is the genius of this region to be more than ordinarily aware and more than ordinarily free. Its virtue is that its manifestation has significance for the world outside itself.[25]

An interesting case of a defender of regionalism in the early 1950s was J. B. Jackson, writing in a magazine that he had founded, *Landscape*, devoted to the way of life and geography of the American Southwest. Because of his almost mystical attachment to the geography and topography of the desert, the art critic Lucy Lippard has referred to him as 'the lure of the local',[26] placing him at the origins of land artists such as Walter de Maria, Robert Smithson, and James Turrell.[27] Jackson targeted Johnson and Hitchcock's 'Built in USA' for ignoring the vitality of vernacular American architecture and preferring to exhibit 'buildings ... [that have] not been obliged to adapt themselves to their immediate surroundings'.[28] For Jackson, the main villain was the 'Bauhaus', which he attacked with an almost xenophobic zeal.

In 1949, Mumford, continuing to defend regionalism, presented an exhibition entitled 'Domestic Architecture of the San Francisco Bay Region', which ran from September 16 to October 30 at the Museum of Civic Art of San Francisco. The Bay Region style, he argued, had only been used as a contrast to 'the restrictive and void formulas of the so-called International Style, tied to tags and clichés.' It was a reaffirmation of a truly modern movement and a defence against post-war fakes. The same argument was taken up by

Figure 10.05 William Wurster, Schuckl Canning Co. office building for the Cooperative of California Canners and Growers, Sunnyvale, California (1942).

Wurster himself in his own exposition in the same catalogue. And in the April 1954 issue of *California Monthly*, Wurster affirmed that 'architecture is a social art' and that 'buildings cannot and should not conjure up life in any terms but those of their own era'.

Branding Regionalism[29]

By the mid-1950s, the disenchantment with the International Style was running so deep within the profession and among the general public that even the diehards who had so polemically defended it at the original regionalism-bashing MoMA meeting in 1947 began to waver. It was not long before even some of the most establishment old boys were changing their tune – or at least trying to.

Surprisingly, Sigfried Giedion was the first. It took merely six years for him to morph from chief zealot of neo-monumentality (1948) into a devout regionalist. In 1954, he published 'The Regional Approach', in which he castigated the very movement he had helped to create; he turned against the International Style because, in his words,

> the word 'style' when used for contemporary architecture is often combined with another password label. This is the epithet 'international.' It is quite true that for a short period in the twenties the term international was 'international.' But then it quickly became harmful and constantly shot back like a boomerang. 'International' architecture – 'the International Style' – so went the argument, is something that hovers in mid-air, with no roots anywhere.[30]

Giedion also went to some length in the same article to establish that he had been a regionalist as far back as 1951, when he had attended a conference of art critics in Amsterdam. There he had made the claim that De Stijl was regionalist in the way it represented the polders. He presented himself as a defender of this regionalist view against Gerrit Rietveld, who 'was in the audience and sprung to his feet and sharply protested'.[31]

Giedion, the same person who had been preaching in favor of a transcendent, almost heroic New Monumentality in contrast to banal day-to-day architecture was now celebrating what he called the 'new regional approach'. One of the projects he singled out in this light was his old comrade Sert's housing project of 1953 in Havana, which, as we have seen, flew in the face of the regional character of the city.

And in 1956, Giedion even went on to take the opposite tack from the one Hitchcock had just taken the year before in his exhibition on Latin American architecture at MoMA. He wrote the introduction to *Modern Architecture in Brazil* by the Brazilian architect Enrique Mindlin, conceived as the continuation of Goodwin's *Brazil Builds*. In it, Giedion praised the fact that 'there is something irrational about the development of Brazilian architecture'.[32] In spite of what Giedion saw as the explosive economic growth, the relentless pace of real estate speculation, and the absence of planning policy, which were detrimental to good architecture, 'Brazilian architecture is growing like a tropical plant'. Brazil compared favorably with the United States in his view because it had assumed its 'own architectural expression with a surprising rapidity'. What he admiringly referred to as the 'Brazilian phenomenon' was exemplary from his point of view.

As for Pietro Belluschi, whose International Style Equitable Savings and Loans building in Portland, Oregon, had featured prominently in Johnson's and Hitchcock's 'Built in USA' of 1953, he too soon started to backpedal. By 1955, he could not have been more regionalist-sounding. It was then that he published 'The Meaning of Regionalism in Architecture', complaining that 'in America we often think of "regionalism" as a naïve and rather soft-headed variation of our architectural mainstream'. In an apologetic tone, he confessed that he had thought of regionalism

> with particularly deep feelings during my frequent trips in foreign lands where examples of regional architecture are more obvious against the very drab and substandardized background of the straight, no nonsense type of architecture which is being built with appalling sameness all over the world. No one who has travelled abroad can fail to speculate on the causes which had given such unity and beauty and a sense of fitness to almost all the old cities, and on the reasons why modern man seemed to have lost this ability to impart character and meaning to his environment.[33]

The article ends with Belluschi waxing almost poetic about regionalism:

> One may well speculate on the relationship between the unfolding of this era of human civilization, and the shortcomings which many people feel in our architectural forms and certainly in our squalid environment. The old forms which constitute what we call regionalism express the more serene times of the past. It is certain that in our tumultuous times it cannot be revived. It would be impossible for us to retreat or escape from a word in evolution, but somehow we must believe that a society of men gain in wisdom by seeking again the things that man can understand and love.... These are my utopian thoughts as I was revisiting recently the exquisite little villages of the Aegean and the Tyrrhenian Sea Islands, of Brittany and the Tyrol, and remembered how my generation was once somewhat ashamed to admit the delight in their simple spontaneous architecture lest it be tagged romantic.[34]

The Embassy Program

There was more to Belluschi's, and Giedion's, change of heart than romance. It was also prompted by, once again, geopolitics, more precisely the geopolitics behind one of the three biggest international building programs of the time. The one that concerned Belluschi in particular was the State Department's Embassy program under the direction of Foreign Buildings Operations. Another was the Hilton Hotels program for Puerto Rico, Havana, Jerusalem, Athens, Cairo, and Istanbul. The third was the government of Iraq's call to modernize Baghdad and the country in general. In all three cases, architects responded by interpreting their briefs in a regional manner. Architects had everything to gain by embracing the cause they had tried to suppress.

The increasingly contentious course of the Cold War was a considerable factor in tipping the scales in favor of regionalism. With the decline of colonial powers, numerous new nations had been formed. Between 1947 and 1964, nearly fifty new ones were created. The embassy building was seen as an important way for the United States to counterbalance Soviet influence in the Third World. The government's Foreign Buildings Operations, which had been in charge of embassy buildings from the mid-1940s onwards, underwent a change of policy in 1954. The International Style-inspired buildings were judged to be insufficiently insensitive to local cultures. When Harrison & Abramovitz presented their designs for the embassies in Havana and Rio, Congress objected, comparing them to the United Nations tower in New York, pointing out how the buildings shunned their surroundings.[35] The Cold War balance of power, it was felt, required a new, more diplomatic kind of embassy building.

Pietro Belluschi was a central figure in this change. By now dean of architecture at MIT, he was named director of the newly founded Architectural Advisory Board (AAB). There was a growing awareness of the need for the United States to project a positive image abroad through its embassies. Secretary John Foster Dulles himself invited each of the members to join the board. In 1954, an anonymous article in *Arts and Architecture* declared that '[t]he United States Government is making modern American architecture one of its most convincing demonstrations of the vitality of American culture. The credit for this accomplishment goes to FBO – the State Department Foreign Buildings Operations program'.

Under Belluschi, an architectural advisory panel was set up to assist the Foreign Buildings Operation of the State Department in the selection of architects and the evaluation of their designs. The potential rewards for converting to regionalism were considerable for American architects with an eye to getting commissions for foreign buildings. Architects had no trouble understanding the potentials for their practices. Josep Lluís Sert, for one, who was to receive the commission for the Baghdad embassy, wrote in his notes that

> every project takes into account in the preliminary phase was based on the state department's request to the architect of the country in question to examine the site, know the materials, the resources and artisanal of the place and to acquire a knowledge of the culture, climate and population ... [because] it is a program of cultural exchange and reciprocal practical advantages.[36]

Between 1954 and 1956, the AAB met regularly, handing out fifty new design projects.[37] Unbuilt were Paul Rudolph's design of 1957 for the embassy in Amman, Jordan, Mies's design for the consulate in São Paulo in 1958, Louis Kahn's consulate in Luanda, Angola, in 1960 and John Carl Warnecke's embassy in Bangkok. But Edward Durrell Stone did build the embassy in New Delhi, Walter Gropius the embassy in Athens, John Johansen the one in Dublin, Harry Weese the one in Accra in Ghana, Ralph Rapson and John van der Meulen that in Copenhagen, Hugh Stubbins the consulate in Tangiers, Richard Neutra the embassy in Karachi, Marcel Breuer the one in The Hague, Eero Saarinen the one in London, and Josep Lluís Sert got the commission for Baghdad, Iraq.

Figure 10.06 Edward
Durrell Stone, US
embassy, New Delhi
(1959).

Figure 10.06 Edward Durrell Stone, US embassy, New Delhi (1959).

Belluschi was clear about the role regionalism should play as a branding device in American expansionism. Writing in 1955, he emphasized that

> the point of evaluating the architectural characteristics of a region became more than an academic question when the State department through its Foreign Buildings Operations asked Henry Shepley and me to go to India, Pakistan and Iraq to discover the elements of a style which would be appropriate for the embassies to be built in those regions.

The establishment of the AAB was considered important enough for the American Institute of Architects to organize a meeting about it in 1954. In May 1955, *Architectural Forum* magazine had already come up with an article entitled 'US Architecture Abroad. Modern Design at Its Best Now Presents This Country in Foreign Lands'. Illustrated with Office of Foreign Buildings Operations (FBO) projects around the world, the message was that the American century was transferred into an American journal. 'Whether consciously or not, the US government has now made US architecture a vehicle for our cultural leadership.'[38] 'Embassy Buildings' was another long article that appeared in *Architectural Record* in June 1956.

> Rarely have American architects been challenged as in the program of building embassies abroad by the State Department. Architects commissioned to plan the various buildings are asked for designs which will 1) represent American architecture abroad, and 2) adapt themselves to local conditions and cultures so deftly that they are welcomed, not criticized by their hosts. Architecture is asked to undertake a highly important diplomatic mission.

As Jane Loeffler points out, the regionalist embassies were often at odds with the realities of the regions in which these buildings were constructed. In her view, projects like Stone's for the US embassy in New Delhi, Walter Gropius's for Athens, and Josep Lluís Sert's for Baghdad, resulting from efforts to flatter local sensibilities, led to contrived explanations, and sometimes also to contrived designs.[39] But the weakness of the designs was actually the result of the superficiality of the knowledge on the part of the architects of the regional cultures in which the buildings were implanted and the naïveté to think it didn't matter. A whole series of fantasies – orientalist, tropicalist, Gaelicist, Africanist – led to an inevitable trivialization of local motifs, according to Ron Robin.[40]

In trying to justify their projects in terms of local identity, most architects used the most kitsch, irresponsible analogies. Gropius, for example, declared that he had based the design of his Athens embassy (1959–1961) on the Parthenon. John Johansen, for his design for the Irish embassy in Dublin, compared its facade to the braid pattern in an Irish sweater. Harry Weese claimed that the tapered concrete peers on the facade of his embassy for Accra in Ghana were inspired by African spears, and John Carl Warnecke made his unbuilt embassy in Bangkok resemble a Thai pagoda.

Belluschi may well have made sure to the best of his abilities that the embassy program was based on what Sandy Isenstadt has referred to as 'faith in a better future'.[41] Defending the choice of Edward Durrell Stone's Indian embassy (1954–1959), for example, he would say that

> it so happened that the design which Ed Stone conceived for the New Delhi Embassy had been looked upon with disfavor by the State Department because it did not look sufficiently 'Indian.' If one should have the patience and fortitude to read all that has been written by critics, kibitzers, social moralists, and by professional geniuses with a gift for arrogance, one would be thoroughly confused.

He was only interested in the possible influence of the style of building:

> It is also with a deep thrill that we perceived how sensitively Stone had understood the real essence of India, how subtly he had included in his design for the embassy the things which really belong to the region…. He did not copy but brought his sympathy and his understanding to bear upon his creative powers. Finely perforated grills, roof overhangs, water pools, serene proportions, exquisite materials…. Indeed we could report back that the Stone design was really suitable for India…. I felt great elation to think of the possible influence which such design might have on the local architects. I met with many of them and with the students of the school in Delhi. I saw their works and heard their words and felt they were anxious to find native expressions, but Western influences were too strong and too disrupting, and few had the wisdom or maturity to break through with work which would reflect their new status as an independent nation, a synthesis of their old culture, and of all that they had so far learned of new ways and techniques.[42]

Yet in spite of Belluschi's pitch to the State Department in defense of the Indianness of Stone's embassy, the building was unsuited to its context. Stone claimed to have been inspired for his New Delhi embassy by the Taj Mahal, to which it bore not the slightest resemblance. In addition, Loeffler points out that it was a microclimatic disaster, totally disregarding the realities of the local climate. The double-layered umbrella roof he placed on top of the building to reduce heat gain only increased it. The glazed walls surrounded by a screen facade proved impossible to clean and a further source of heat excess.[43]

Four diplomatic buildings would have been low on pastiche and exceptions to the rule. The first is Mies's consulate for São Paulo (1957–1962). It might have been free of kitsch, but it would have been ill-adapted to the tropical climate with its steel-framed glazed building of two and one half stories supported by a columnar grid, rectangularly symmetrical plan, four bays wide, and seven bays long.[44] But it was never built.

Second is Paul Rudolph's embassy for Amman, Jordan (1954–1956). Thanks to his successful and extensive experience in designing climate-responsive architecture in Florida in the 1940s, his building, on the other hand, with its double-layered roof allowing for the circulation of cooling air, was ideally suited to its context. It is interesting that Rudoph's regionalist scheme, high on know-how, low on pastiche, failed to impress the AAC members and was turned down.

Third was Richard Neutra's Karachi embassy in Pakistan (1955–1956). Neutra was knowledgeable about the tropics and had published widely on India, Guam, and Brazil, among others. His building was a stark slab building perfectly adapted to the tropical climate, responding to the hot Karachi climate thanks to the detailing of the narrow horizontal, strip windows, the use of vertical adjustable louvers, and the use of water in the landscaping. But because it also ran counter to the contemporary sensitivity among the architectural community, Neutra's partner, Robert Alexander, while on a trip to the site, without adding what Neutra had already dismissed as the 'pretty' aspects of the other embassies, discovered cylindrical molds for casting concrete vaults and proceeded to top the building with a series of pseudo-vernacular vaults as a means of decorating the facade of the rear warehouses and roof of the main administration building.[45]

Fourth, in 1961, was Louis Kahn's design proposal for a US consulate in Luanda, Angola.[46] It would probably have been a regionalist masterpiece if he had not lost the commission. Upon visiting Luanda, he observed that, as a result of the 'marked glare in the atmosphere' in the equatorial region of Angola, people working outside tended to look at nearby walls and not at the sky. 'Looking at a window', Kahn said, 'was unbearable because of the glare. The dark walls framing the brilliant light outside made you very uncomfortable.' Kahn sought to develop an architectural response to this situation and found it, not surprisingly, in the everyday behavior of Luandans, which he described as follows:

> I ... noticed that when people worked in the sun – and many of them did—the native population ... usually faced the wall and not

the open country or the open street. Indoors, they would turn their chair toward the wall and do whatever they were doing by getting the light indirectly from the wall.[47]

This observation led Kahn to consider making walls whose primary purpose would be to receive daylight, in order to diffuse and redistribute it. He recalled: 'That gave me the thought of a wall a small distance in front of every window.... One doesn't feel like having the view cut away, so I thought of placing openings in the wall.'[48] As a result, he designed an additional layer of walled space around the building to protect inhabitants from intense sunlight – 'wrapping buildings with ruins', as he put it, intended to catch sun and day-light and reflect it inward. He proposed a concrete wrapping wall whose finely textured, light-gray surface would have absorbed maybe half of the incoming light and reflected the remaining half, diffusing it toward the interior. Inside, people would see softened light on that wall as it was reflected toward their eyes and they would live or work in spaces illuminated in the resulting more comfortable light. And even if, according to Kahn, inhabitants saw a piece of the bright sky or sun, the softly lighted adjacent wall surface would minimize the glare that results when a very bright source, the sky or sun, is seen imme-diately next to a dark surface, without any mediation.

Besides enhancing a particular spatial experience of light and space, he believed that this solution was superior to the knee-jerk grillwork solution endorsed by his professional contemporary Edward Durrell Stone in his New Delhi embassy:

> Some of the buildings used piece work, grillwork ... in front of windows ... [the grillwork] was dark against the light; it gave you just a multiple pattern of glare ... little pinpoints ... of glare against the dark ribs of the grillwork. And that tended to be unsatisfactory.[49]

In his design for the consulate, Kahn proposed a 'sun roof', in his words, in the shape of a trellis-textured parasol suspended above the 'rain roof', the real roof structure. The resulting interception of the direct sun by the sun roof and the air passing through the interstitial space not only was functional but also would have helped the interior of the consulate buildings to effectively avoid a substantial amount of heat, of course. But behind the design would also been a sense of respect for the local culture and a real attempt to com-municate, nurtured by the time it takes to observe and learn.

> I feel that in bringing the rain roof and the sun roof away from each other, I was telling the man on the street his way of life. I was explaining the atmospheric conditions of wind, the conditions of light, the conditions of sun and glare to him. If I use a device – a clever kind of device – it would only seem like a design to him – something pretty. I didn't want anything pretty. I wanted to have a clear statement of a way of life.[50]

The second massive architectural branding commission that elicited regionalist architectural response was that for the Hilton hotels for Cairo, Athens,

Istanbul, Puerto Rico, and Jerusalem. Conrad Hilton was an entrepreneur who took American geopolitics into his own hands. In his autobiography, *Be My Guest*, he 'explicitly represented his international hotels as ideological, in the popular sense of ideology as propaganda', as Annabel Jane Wharton points out.[51] He repeatedly stated that Hilton hotels were constructed not only to produce a profit, but to make a political impact on host countries. He was in the foreign policy business. He writes:

> Now why is Hilton building hotels in all these key spots around the world? Because there is a job to be done there. And I will tell you frankly, satellites and H-bombs will not get the job done. I do not disparage the West's armament program; we must keep our defense superior to the Communist world ... but a far higher dividend is likely to follow from industrial assistance in Asia, Africa and the Middle East, than from military aid.[52]

He added: 'Each of our hotels is a "little America".'[53]

In 1951, Hilton and the Turkish government announced their plan to build a new hotel in Istanbul.[54] It was inaugurated in June 1955. The Turkish architect Sedad H. Eldem collaborated with Gordon Bundshaft of SOM on the design. Nathaniel Owings writes in his memoirs that 'like a meteor in the sky came an *Arabian Nights* job: the Istanbul Hilton ... The result is a salubrious blend of strong Turkish architecture and American plumbing and heating'.[55] It harbored its share of pastiche elements, such as the painted vaults in the main lobby designed by Eldem, and the canopy at the entrance was dubbed the flying carpet because of its billowing forms.[56] And the hotel came equipped with teak *mashrabiyah* (traditional wooden screens against the sun) and ornamental tiles recalling Ottoman architecture, as well as a tulip room reserved exclusively for women, as in a harem. But the structure was sensitively tucked into the famed rolling hills of Istanbul and less disruptive of the panorama than current hotels in that city.

The Cairo Hilton was finished in 1953. By then, King Farouk had been overthrown and US influence in the area was beginning to decline. The hotel, however, was left intact and its decoration continued to be associated with the Pharaonic past. The entrance lobby bore a massive reproduction from the Egyptian Museum: a colossal Pharaoh hunting the wildlife of the Nile. In the guest rooms, the brass lamp stands were inspired by the lotus, and the draperies were hand-blocked with a stylized version of the same lotus flower.

The last Hilton in this series, the Athens one, was constructed between 1957 and 1963. The advertising emphasized that it was 'entered through a series of descending stairs in ancient Greek Amphitheater style, classic lobbies, gallery terraces, gardens, superb swimming pool, health club, garden rooms. Interior courts in the manner of Greek atria, surrounded by fascinating shops'.

The project benefited from a special royal decree that permitted it to exceed considerably the height of any building in the city. The new regulation was arranged, scandalously, by one of the Greek co-designers of the project who was at the same time a high-ranking employee of the Ministry of

Figure 10.07 Istanbul Hilton advertisement (1956).

Public Works, which controlled building heights. The exemption opened the way for more tall buildings to appear in the future, disfiguring the character of the historic landscape.

An influential Greek journalist celebrated the globalist identity of the building with the words 'Yes, here is ... the most perfect American product, the shining Cadillac ... coupled with the added luxury of European taste and Greek marble', to be enjoyed 'with the moonlight, a little music, the evening breeze, a glass of wine', while at the same time the building was incongruous with the environmental conditions of the region.[57] The only critic who confronted the banality and environmental hostility of the project was Vincent Scully. He argued that the project was what today would be called 'unsustainable' and it was going to add to the 'smog that now hangs over Athens', about which few complained at that time and even fewer perceived its long-term implications. 'The effect', he concluded, 'can most accurately be described as obscene.'[58]

Greater Baghdad

The government of Iraq launched the third massive architectural commission of the time that was met at least partly with a regionalist response on the part of the architectural profession. The Greek architect Constantine Doxiadis (who incidentally had also objected to the irregularities of the architecture of the Hilton) was the first to be hired. Since 1945, he had maintained very close contacts with the US authorities in charge of the reconstruction program in Greece, funded by the Marshall Plan and Truman Doctrine. By 1955, he was working on the National Housing Program of Iraq, a job he received from the Development Board, created in 1950 by the prime minister of Iraq, Nuri al-Said, but with the help of the highly influential planning consultant Jacob Crane.[59]

Doxiadis was initially asked to draw up a five-year plan for nothing less than the entire country by King Faisal II's administration. In 1958, he was also asked to create a master plan for Baghdad. The master plan stressed two things: housing for all and a foundation for long-term urban and regional growth. Doxiadis made it a point to distinguish his regionalist approach to planning from that of Lucio Costa's Brasília and Le Corbusier's Chandigarh, whom he compared to 'magician planners' who had all the solutions up their sleeves and pulled them out 'like rabbits'.[60] He promised he would 'diagnose' each site's specific local, regional needs and potentials rather than applying universal norms and standards. He hired a group of interdisciplinary collaborators, unique in that it included architects and planners as well as archaeologists and sociologists. He worked with local architects such as Rifat Chadjiri and Mohamed Makiya. He invited Hassan Fathy, who had built New Gourna in 1945–1949, to join the project.

Doxiadis drew up a plan for 3 million inhabitants, three times more than lived in the actual city at the time. The plan retained the historic souk but did not try to reproduce its patterns for the newly planned residential districts. It broke down the new residential areas into a polycentric network of 'neighborhood units' or sectors modeled on the British post-war new towns, favoring pedestrian movement. Hassan Fathy suggested accommodating local social habits and public spaces. One such gesture was the so-called gossip square for every grouping of ten or fifteen houses. Doxiadis also called for the inclusion of hammams and mosques in each sector,[61] and the occasional covered market. He included reinforced concrete version of the traditional wooden window screens.[62]

A series of smaller commissions followed. In 1957, the architect Nizar Ali Jawdat, a graduate of the Harvard Graduate School of Design, persuaded his father, who was then the prime minister of Iraq under King Faisal II, to engage some of the world's most internationally renowned architects to build major buildings in Baghdad. Six major commissions were handed out. Le Corbusier was asked to design a sports complex to support Baghdad's bid to host the 1960s Olymic Games (It was not actually built until 1981, when it was renamed the Saddam Hussein Stadium.) Alvar Aalto was given a post office and a museum to design, neither of which was actually built. Gio Ponti was given the Development Board Headquarters. Walter Gropius's office, TAC (The Artists' Collaborative), received the commission for the new university outside the city, and Frank Lloyd Wright proposed a master plan for

Greater Baghdad, only part which was to see the light of day – not in Iraq but at the University of Arizona in 1964, as the renamed Gammage Concert Hall.[63]

Of the six projects, those of Gropius and Wright were the ones that most clearly attempted to interpret their brief in an orientalizing regionalist manner. The site of the university that Gropius and TAC designed was an age-old palm grove in a bend of the Tigris River on the outskirts of Baghdad. Only a few dozen of the buildings were actually Gropius's, but the original comprised 273 buildings. Around the same time as Gropius was making regionalist claims with regard to his design for the US embassy in Athens (1959–1961), he was designing his campus for the University of Baghdad. As opposed to the Athens embassy, however, this project was highly praised by the regionalist Ernesto Rogers for 'setting aside' Gropius's 'Bauhaus purity' to 'make room for liberties of the vernacular',[64] thereby 'avoid[ing] too much Americanism'.[65] Indeed, the project incorporated the by then commonplace concrete versions of *mashrabiya*, and it placed vaults on top of skyscrapers. It also created a mosque in the form of a gigantic concrete dome supported on three points surrounded by a circular pool of water.

However, it also uprooted 500 palm trees to line the streets for vehicular traffic in a gesture of monumentality, while chopping down thousands of others on a campus that is now planted with grass with almost no availability of outdoor shaded area in a hot, dry desert climate that often reaches 50°C.

Decidedly fabulist in its embrace of Iraqi culture was Frank Lloyd Wright's thinking at this time. Obviously making no distinction between Iran and Iraq, he wrote to the Iraqi government that '[t]o me this opportunity to assist Persia is like a story to a boy fascinated by the Arabian Nights Entertainment as I was', and went on to explain that he had been enthralled by *A Thousand and One Nights* as a boy.[66] Although he had initially been commissioned

Figure 10.08 Walter Gropius on the site of the sixteenth-century Al Kadhimain Mosque, Baghdad, Iraq, 1958.

Figure 10.09 Design by TAC and Walter Gropius for the mosque of the University of Baghdad.

to design a combined theater and opera house, he visited Baghdad in order to convince the government development board that he should be commissioned to design a master plan for a new Baghdad. King Faisal II, who was twenty-one at the time, decided that Wright should be responsible for a large portion of the reconstruction of the city, which included an opera house, a theme park called the Garden of Eden, a national museum, a post and telegraph office, botanical gardens, parking garages, an art gallery, the university, an island in the Tigris with a civic auditorium, a landscape park with pools, a planetarium, a bazaar, botanical gardens, a zoo, a monument to the eighth-century caliph Harun al-Rashid, a casino, a heliport, and radio and television towers – all related in a constellation of spirals and ziggurats.

Wright's orientalist vision of reconstructing Baghdad on the basis of his boyhood fantasies, along with Doxiadis's more pragmatic urban plans for Greater Baghdad, came to an abrupt end in 1958 with the coup against King Faisal II and his subsequent assassination by General Abdul Karim Qassim. Of all the projects that had been commissioned by Faisal II, the general retained only Gropius to continue working on the university.

Chapter 11

Regionalism Redefined

While the contest between regionalism and International Style was taking place in the United States after World War II, the interest in regionalism did not die out in Europe despite regionalism's entanglement with chauvinist and racist politics in Nazi Germany and Vichy France before and during the war. On the contrary.

In Germany, in spite of the de-Nazification program and the efforts by the allies to promote 'Bauhaus' modern architecture, the respect for *Heimat* architects did not diminish. While Schultze-Naumburg kept busy with his publications until his death in 1949, Paul Bonatz continued to design prestigious pastiche projects in Ankara and Addis Ababa until 1948, and Paul Schmitthenner produced an abundant body of work fusing *Heimat* and classical styles until the end of the 1960s.

In France, there were still strong sympathies for regionalism, as the success of the writings of René Closier shows. But, as opposed to Germany, where *Heimat* was still at the heart of regionalism, here the idea of regionalism went hand in hand with a warning against the possible effects, cultural and ecological, of the excesses of industrialization and mass production needed for the post-World War II reconstruction. The overall tendency was not to return to older forms of regionalism but to redefine and renew it.

Among the leading architecture of the post-World War II period, not only did Le Corbusier's have regionalist origins – his first projects were all in the regionalist mould, consistent with the Arts and Crafts school he attended in Chaux-le-Fond – but despite his periodic rhetorical denouncements of regionalism, his thinking remained deeply attached to the environmental and cultural particularity of the regions he built in.

Before the war, in 1933, he had designed a scheme for the Durand Housing Estate in Qued-Ouchaia, and in 1934 he proposed the urbanization of Nemours, a town in Algeria with a population of 50,000. Both schemes were driven by the recognition of the particularity of the region, the site, and the 'topography'. He called the Nemours project 'the new Casbah of Algiers made out of steel and cement', and he asserted that the old casbah had better architecture than the colonial settlements. And in 1930, inspired by the rustic sheds he noticed in the often rain-drenched countryside overlooking the Pacific in Chile, he designed there the (unbuilt) Errazuris country residence, with the vernacular roof made of two adjacent gables sloping inward toward the middle, perfectly adapted to heavy rainfall. In so doing, he inadvertently invented the so-called butterfly roof that was to become a craze in the architecture of the mid-century all over the world. Undoubtedly the first architect to plagiarize it was the most interesting. This was Antonin Raymond, and he did so in a regionalist spirit. In a remarkable example of transnational aptness, he made the mental leap of adopting it for his own rustic country house in an equally rainy Japan in 1934.

After the war, Le Corbusier conceived Roq and Rob (1948–1950), a low-profile hotel facility in the Mediterranean for 'post-war' people, which, in contrast to the aggression and arrogance of the Hilton Hotels, responded to the regional cultural and historical environment, recruiting spatial ideas from vernacular Mediterranean precedents.

For Alvar Aalto, Le Corbusier was too much of a technocratic globalist as well as International Style formalist. Aalto avoided any attachment to universal systems of architecture. Though a great admirer of classical architecture and culture, he never saw it as a canon; the same with modern architecture. Even prior to World War II, Aalto was not so popular among the propagandists of International Style, who had dismissed his regionalist approach as overly subjective. As we have seen, Giedion was even to exclude him from his canon of modern architecture in *Space, Time and Architecture* on the grounds of his regionalism. Aalto's concern with the identity of a site, materials, microclimate, and the way of life of a region was in conflict with mainstream globalist US architects. Neither did Aalto have much to do with the Scandinavian nationalist regionalism and its imitations of folk architecture, both strong tendencies in pre-war Finnish architecture.

While respecting the idea of the region, across the dimensions referred to above, Aalto kept a *critical* distance, and remained a *stranger* to their bygone precedents, a stance that ultimately, as we mentioned in the beginning of this book, goes back to the critical philosophy of the Enlightenment, and the writings of Immanuel Kant[1] and the Frankfurt School.[2]

Aalto's critical approach is demonstrated in his 1948–1952 town hall for Säynätsalo, a town growing around a plywood factory in a forest fought fiercely over and greatly damaged by both German and Soviet troops during World War II, where Aalto tried to achieve a sense of belonging and community. The result is a scheme with unique characteristics emerging out of the particularities of the site and the program. The various buildings forming the complex are planned round a courtyard artificially raised above the surrounding wooded countryside. Gaps between the buildings allow access to the courtyard and also allow views toward distant lakes, and penetration of the low northern sun. The materials, not unlike the buildings of the region, are naked: dark red brick, wood and copper, and abruptly varied roof shapes.

As for Latin America, Henry-Russell Hitchcock had been right. The main inspiration for the best buildings of the time was overwhelmingly and explicitly regionalist, particularly in Brazil, with its roots in the broadly based anti-colonial, quasi-Dadaist, avant-garde cultural movement Antropofagia, founded by Oswald de Andrade in 1928 with his *Manifesto antropófago*. The movement brought together great artists, writers, actors, sculptors, and musicians – Heitor Villa-Lobos, Carmen Miranda, Emiliano da Cavalcanti,

Figure 11.01 Alvar Aalto, Säynätsalo Town Hall, Säynätsalo, Finland (1948–1952).

Geraldo de Barros – and led eventually to the architecture of Gregori War-chavchik, Rino Levi, Affonso Reidy, Roberto Burle Marx, and Oscar Niemeyer, among others.[3] By 1944, the identity of the avant-garde had morphed. From the ideal of an all-inclusive Brazilian culture constituted by a voracious inges-tion of European and native Brazilian elements, it assumed a more purely Bra-zilian identity. Now it was events like the first Brazilian Congress of Regionalists, organized by Gilberto Freire, that brought them together.[4]

Greatly admired for his opposition to classicist or modern universal systems was the young '*antropófago*' Oscar Niemeyer, the Oscar Niemeyer of the period before Brasilia. As was mentioned in the previous chapter, his work was shown at MoMA during World War II together with the work of other Brazilian architects and was received enthusiastically. What impressed the audience were his ingenious innovations fused with the tropical regional culture and environment. The new approach was born with Le Corbusier's role in the collaborative design of the offices of the Ministry of National Edu-cation and Public Health in Rio de Janeiro in 1938, where Le Corbusier intro-duced the *brise soleil*, a regionalist response to the tropical conditions. Among his collaborators were Lucio Costa, Oscar Niemeyer, and Affonso Reidy.

Figure 11.02 Lucio Costa, detail of the facade of the Bristol Building, Rio de Janeiro (1950).

The project had a liberating effect for the Brazilian architects. It made them feel able to redefine 'Brazilianness'. Le Corbusier did not give them a solution. Even the innovation of the *brise-soleil* was not meant as a standard solution; it was a way of thinking, a case of regionalist thinking. Like Aalto, Niemeyer's and his generation's regionalism did not mimic colonial and folk traditions. They recruited solutions from these precedents while keeping a *critical* distance, like *strangers* to that era. Among this architecture, the 1930s and 1940s work of Affonso Reidy, Lucio Costa, and Rino Levi is most characteristic. Of special interest is Lina Bo Bardi's work, part of the Bahia

Figure 11.03 Affonso Reidy, Pedregulho Housing Project (1950–1952). This social housing project built on the site of a slum was distinguished by its highly innovative program. It was unique, worldwide, for its mixing of races. It included a school, covered playground, laundry facility, daycare center, swimming pool, and gymnasium.

regionalist movement. Her houses marked a new departure, incorporating Brazilian foliage into the walls of her buildings, as in her Chame Chame house in Salvador in Bahia (1958).[5] The house, built around an ancient tree, was covered with pebbles, vegetation, shells, and ceramic fragments evoking the past life of the site, which had been inhabited by ex-African slaves.

A unique contribution to the Brazilian regionalist architecture, as well as a unique contribution to the world architecture of this time, was the landscape projects of Robert Burle Marx, landscape architect and painter (1909–1994). Marx studied with Lucio Costa and later worked with him. He collaborated with Niemeyer on several projects, including the Pampulha complex in 1942, both experimenting with the reinterpretation of the agility and movement of the Brazilian baroque together with Brazilian dances.

Pampulha was an upper-class satellite town on the banks of a picturesquely landscaped artificial lake in 1940, when the prefect of the region, Juscelino Kubitschek, invited the thirty-year-old Oscar Niemeyer to present plans for the design of the monumental buildings there. One of the products of this project was the Dance Hall (1942). Once more, the influence of Le Corbusier's 'law of the meander', the sweeping embrace of sinuous, organic contours (*Precisions*, 1930), is evident. But at the same time, the building draws from a much broader regionalist long-term current in Brazilian culture expressed through rhythm and geometry, interrelating body movement and the environment.

The Dance Hall in Belo Horizonte, Minas Gerais, which Pampulha devoted to the samba, seems itself to be caught up in the gently swaying motions of that quintessentially Brazilian dance. The Dance Hall dates from 1942, a year before the Church of St Francis of Assisi (1943), where Niemeyer launched the icon that was to become the most celebrated hallmark of all Brazilian architecture to follow: the sensual, rippling curve. In 1956, Kubitschek,

Figure 11.04 Lina Bo Bardi, Chame Chame House, Salvador, Bahia, Brazil (1958). The neighborhood contained many 'Candomblé' houses owned by former African slaves. The house was covered with pebbles and vegetation and shells, and bits of dolls and toys, and ceramic fragments – a way of evoking the past life of the site.

Figure 11.05 Roberto Burle Marx, garden of the Capela da Jaqueira, Perambuco, 1954.

now president of Brazil, once more called on Niemeyer to design the more ambitious, if less successful and certainly not regionalist, development of Brasilia.

In comparison to the enthusiastic reception of Brazilian architecture in the United States in the 1940s, Mexican did not attract much attention. During the time of the Depression, in the 1930s, Mexican regionalist realist 'muralist' painters such as José Siqueiros, Diego Rivera, and José Orozco took the United States by storm, but their Marxist politics raised problems, and further promotion of Mexican artists might have been seen as most unwanted.

The person who created the 'muralist' movement had been the minister of education in the 1920s, José Vasconcelos Calderón (1882–1959), who invited painters to create murals about Mexico in public buildings, the murals being aimed at constructing a national social identity for the masses. Although he argued in his writings for the desirability of mixing people to create a cosmic race, his cultural programs unleashed a wave of creative regionalist works, and the Chicano regionalist movement drew from his writings in the 1970s.

In 1931–1932, Juan O'Gorman designed a double house-studio for Diego Rivera and Frida Kahlo. It consists of two boxes on a lot fenced off in a typically Mexican way by cactuses and, although the scheme draws from Le Corbusier's Maison Ozenfant, its use of vivid blue and terra cotta color and the arrangement of spaces fitted the culture and the microclimate of the region. Although inspired by internationalist ideas of socialism, the regionalist movement in Mexico continued to grow during and after the war, with a strong regionalist/nationalist bent. One of the reasons for its nationalist tenor was the unending antagonism and fear of globalization sponsored by United States as well as the still remembered oppression of the country, political and cultural, by the Spanish Empire. The National Autonomous University of

155

Figure 11.06 Oscar Niemeyer, Dance Hall, Pampulha, Belo Horizonte, Minas Gerais, Brazil (1942).

Mexico, planned by Mario Pani and designed with the participation of over 110 Mexican artists, is an example of this. Especially striking are the Central Library, designed by Juan O'Gorman, Gustavo Saavedra and Juan Martínez de Velasco (1952); the university stadium, with a gigantic mural by Diego Rivera; and the extensive use of murals in the campus, blending architecture and art, offering a particular *mexicanidad* identity to the whole project.

A unique regionalist synthesis of art and architecture was tried by Mathías Goeritz, a German historian and artist refugee, in his El Eco in Mexico City in 1953, one of the most significant although mostly overlooked architectural works of the century. Goeritz's intention was to design an experimental museum rooted in the Mexican environmental and cultural environment. For the opening, Luis Buñuel choreographed a special show. The building owes a debt to the bareness and purposeful poverty of O'Gorman's Rivera–Kahlo house-studio. It consists of two linked prismatic rooms connected through a spiral movement and a court enclosed by high walls, leaving only the sky visible, containing a zigzag 'dragon' crawling on the floor. Goeritz chose the colors of this abstract composition to interact with each other and with the outside sky in the way colors interact in a painting of Joseph Albers – who, like Goeritz, had taught at the Bauhaus. Yet walls of contrasting colors are also a powerful highly charged abstract representation of simple regional Mexican people's spaces. The influence of Goeritz was decisive for the transformation of

Figure 11.07 Juan O'Gorman, library, University of Mexico (1952–1953): the mosaic-clad façade, done in collaboration with Gustavo Saavedra and Juan Martínez de Velasco.

Luis Barragán's architecture from Corbusian imitation to his better-known mini-malist, intensely polychromic works, such as his own house, Las Arboledas, and Los Clubes. Goeritz and Barragán would later collaborate in the monumen-tal Towers of Satellite City, a remarkable and novel fusing of the intense Mexican vernacular colors with abstract sculptural forms (1957).

The regionalist experiments by Goeritz, O'Gorman, Burle Marx, and of course Le Corbusier all drew from precedents of regionalist vernacular culture, a method that went back to the turn to the vernacular by the English architects of the second half of the nineteenth century and ranged from the not so distant rural vernacular to 'primitive art', an approach expressing their political ideals, the cultural 'power of the people' as opposed to the globalist International Style and its neo-monumental epigones.

The same idea, of turning to the vernacular, also bore fruit in 1950s Europe in the work of a younger generation of regionalist architects. In an art-icle entitled 'Regionalism and Modern Architecture' published in the 1957 *Architect's Yearbook*,[6] James Stirling ironically called regionalism an English 'minor movement' in 'reaction to another English minor movement … neo-Palladianism'. By neo-Palladianism he meant the esoteric post-war impact of Rudolf Wittkower's book *Architectural Principles in the Age of Humanism* (1949, 1952) via the First International Congress of Proportion in Milan in 1951, at the Ninth Triennale, as well as through the impact of International Style mixed with the 'neo-monumentality' and neo-historicism predominant in the United States in the 1950s, as we saw in the previous chapter. Stirling might have also been irritated by the Royal Institute of British Architects (RIBA) debate in London on 'proportions' that year (1957). His reaction was that 'today', for his generation, 'Stonehenge is more significant than the archi-tecture of Sir Christopher Wren'.

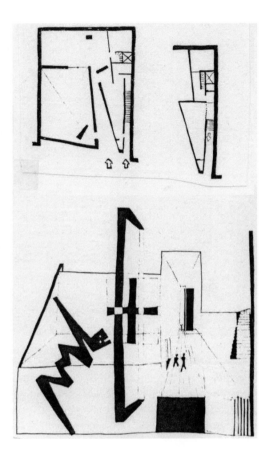

Figure 11.08 Mathias Goeritz, diagrammatic sketch for his El Eco Experimental Museum, Mexico City (1953).

This was an updated version of Goethe's regionalist-nationalist text. But the rest of Stirling's article is written in a different tone. 'In this country,' he goes on, 'the decline of technology, particularly in building and civil engineering is forcing architects away from the radical or science fiction outlook.'[7] The 'new traditionalism' therefore is backed by economic and practical arguments as well as by policy statements. Stirling's diagnosis is that material needs rather than nationalist or sentimental ones required that Europeans engage in 'a re-assessment of indigenous and usually anonymous building' and a 're-evaluation of ... the use of traditional methods and materials'. He also refers favorably to MoMA's G. E. Kidder Smith's *Italy Builds* (1950), a publication that avoided Renaissance and Mussolini-type architecture, taking a stance sympathetic to regionalism.

The end of the article repeats the point Mumford had raised in the *New Yorker* in 1947 and in the 1948 MoMA gathering, that modern architecture was in real danger of being taken over by a neoconservative wave of reaction. As a defense against this threat, Stirling's article formulates an argument for a new regionalism. His designs for the Village Project (1955), and even more for the Preston Infill Housing (1957–1959), are the expression of this newly defined regionalism.

Stirling was not associated with any group at that time. Most of the young architects interested in renewing the debate of regionalism were

Figure 11.09 James Stirling's sketch of an imagined vernacular building in the landscape (*c*.1957).

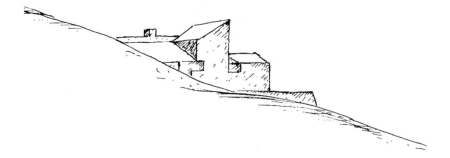

associated with CIAM, having read Mumford's books as students. According to Jerzy Soltan, a Le Corbusier collaborator and later Harvard professor, Mumford's books were read even in concentration camps in Poland during the war.[8]

Similarly driven by the post-war reaction against the wave of globalization and neo-monumentalism, and in an effort to restore region and nature, Jørn Utzon (1918–2000) built his state-funded Kingo Houses in Elsinore (1956–1958) for low-income workers, just before Stirling started work in Leicester. Utzon, who had studied with Steen Eiler Rasmussen, a regionalist with a special concern for site and materials, chose the low-profile courthouse type in order to provide intimacy and privacy, while orienting the courts to offer the best view, shelter from the wind, and sunlight. The houses were assembled to fit to the contours of the site and clustered to form small communities, an idea rooted in Danish rural traditions.

Figure 11.10 Jørn Utzon, site plan of the Kingo houses in Elsinore (1956–1958).

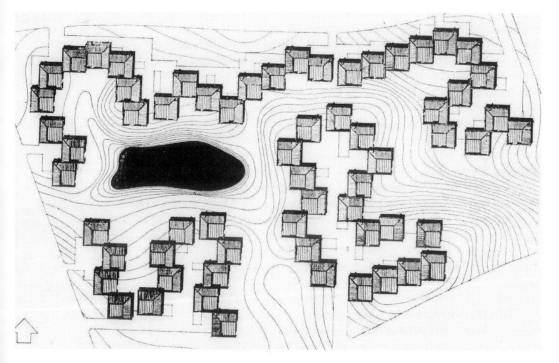

Many other European architects of the same generation followed the same approach in the 1950s in order to enrich the effort to produce a better modern environment. They achieved remarkable results. Among them were José Antonio Coderch and Manuel Valls in Barcelona, and Aris Konstantinidis in Greece.

But the movement was truly global. A similar approach was taken by Minnette de Silva, a Sri Lankan architect. Like that of Lina Bo Bardi of Brazil, her work was unknown outside her local circles until she took it upon herself to write and publish a monograph at her own expense.[9] De Silva studied in the 1940s at the Architectural Association in London, one of the few centers of education and research into post-World War II African and Asian architecture in the world during the 1940s and 1950s. In contrast to her European regionalist colleagues of her generation, who drew from a well-researched corpus of the European vernacular, e Silva had to rely on the regional tropical studies by her one-time teacher Otto Koenigsberger, a most important tropical architect of the post-war period not only in India but in Pakistan, Latin America and Singapore,[10] along with her friends Jane Drew and Maxwell Fry.

Drew and Maxwell Fry worked in Ghana in the early 1950s before Nkrumah declared Ghana 'free for ever', and in Nigeria and Ghana during the late 1950s before the declaration of the country's independence in 1960. They published several books on tropical architecture in which social and cultural issues played a secondary role; the books focused on regional aspects seen primarily from an environmental, microclimatic point of view. Thanks to them, the *brise soleil* or louver – originally created by Stamo Papadaki, and subsequently employed by Le Corbusier and by Antonin Raymond in his Golconde Ashram[11] – was introduced to Africa through their design and the publication of their now classic book *Tropical Architecture*.[12] Their work, however, never matched the technological excellence and practicality of the portable Maison Tropicale (1949–1951) designed by Jean Prouvé for the French colonies of West Africa. Its naturally ventilated interior was always cooler than the outside and never needed to be air-conditioned, as was attested by one of the former owners of the one in Brazzaville, Mireille Ngatse, filmed in Manthia Diawara's documentary film about the fate of the sites of the original Maisons Tropicales after the houses had been bought and eventually resold at Christie's in 2007 for around $5 million.[13]

De Silva's father had been a leading figure in the anti-colonial movement of what was then called Ceylon and in the post-colonial government after 1948. Her mother, an early Ceylonese suffragette, campaigned actively for the preservation of the traditional Sinhalese arts and crafts. Equally engaged was her sister Anil, founder of the post-colonial magazine *Marg*. For De Silva, the architecture of the tropics had to be more than just a form of microclimatic control. It had to be linked to broader political and cultural questions.

As early as 1950, Minnette de Silva, conscious of her responsibility, coined the phrase 'modern regional architecture in the tropics'. Ceylon, she wrote,

> like much of the East, emerged after the Second World War from a feudal-cum-Victorian past and was exposed to new technological influences from the West. A veneer of modernism was acquired

Figure 11.11 Antonin
Raymond, Golconde
Ashram, Pondicherry,
India (1936).

second hand, ill-digested and bearing no relationship to Ceylon's traditions or to the region.... It is essential for us to absorb what we absolutely need from the modern West, and to learn to keep the best of our own traditional forms. We have to think understandably in order to develop an indigenous contemporary architecture, and not to lose the best of the old that has meaning and value.

She went on to say that 'accepting the need to synthesize our past with present technology, we need to examine our own roots and understand them before achieving a creative life in literature, music, painting, education, society, and architecture'.

In her first project, the Karunaratne House of 1949–1951, in an open-plan interior living area she articulated movable Japanese screens, 'an ancient Japanese feature now taken over into Modern Architecture', with the traditional Sri Lankan veranda.[14] Her second project, the Red Cross Hall of 1950, had none of the trappings of traditional Sri Lankan architecture. In its defense, she stated:

As an architect, I cannot subscribe to copying the architecture of an era that is long past ... I believe in building to suit our living needs

Figure 11.12 Jean Prouvé, Maison Tropicale, first prototype published, *Architecture d'Aujourd'hui* (December 1949).

Aspect de la maison métallique Jean Prouvé, type Tropique (avec véranda et brise-soleil). — View of the Tropique type of metal house, by Jean Prouvé. — Aspecto de la casa metalica Jean Prouvé, tipo Trópico.

LES MAISONS PRÉFABRIQUÉES A L'EXPOSITION POUR L'ÉQUIPEMENT DE L'UNION FRANÇAISE

in a living way, utilizing the most suitable modern and progressive means at our disposal, and in adopting these sound and fundamental principles of building of the past, which are as authentic today as before.... The era of the Kandyan style roof is dead. It was achieved in a feudal era with feudal means.[15]

In her work she retained regional inventions, such as traditional rammed earth for low-cost housing, as long as they were combined with modern construction techniques,[16] and the veranda and the *midula* (vernacular garden), and fused them with modern innovations or findings from other regions, calling the method 'trans-regionalism'.

In her Senanayake Flats (1954–1957) in Colombo, she used Le Corbusier's Unité d'Habitation elements, the pilotis and the roof garden, but to maximize ventilation through breeze circulation she used the regional facade verandas and the *midula*.

In her *Cost Effective Housing Studies* (1954–1955), she wrote: '[W]e must re-orient our ideas for living comfortably in congested towns ... where we no longer have expansive acres of garden and spacious pillared halls of the pre Second World War days.' And she asked: 'How can we create this comfortable atmosphere in small restricted sites?' 'I considered the movement of air within the house as one of the primary concerns and was to achieve this with the utilization of split-levels, midulas and stairwells situated in the centre of the plan', allowing drafts to be 'able to move horizontally and vertically through the house, a feature not normally accommodated in small town houses.'

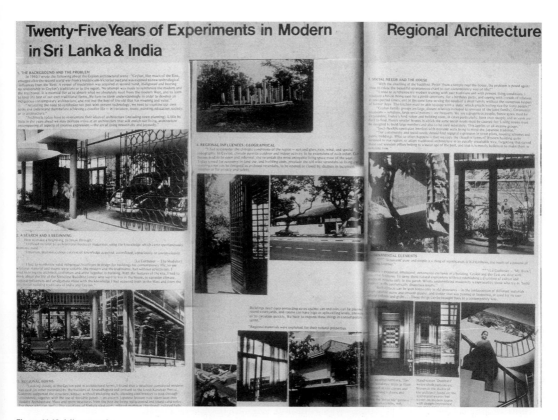

Twenty-Five Years of Experiments in Modern Regional Architecture in Sri Lanka & India

Figure 11.13 Minnette de Silva, pages from her article on her modern regional architecture.

Similar regionalist concerns steered the work of Laurie Baker and Charles Correa, yet each took a very different direction. Laurie Baker (1917–2007) practiced mostly in Kerala, India. Inspired by Gandhi, he committed himself to a regional approach, employing vernacular precedents and avoiding energy-intensive materials and wastage. He used strategically perforated brick screens to permit airflow and diffuse light, and he often employed recycled materials. Preoccupied with the uniqueness of the site, he preferred to conceive his schemes during construction rather than preparing them in advance.[17]

Similarly, Charles Correa, renowned for his masterful Gandhi Memorial in Shangrahalaya (1958–1963), has famously drawn throughout most of his career from vernacular precedents and integrated them in new ways into his structures. During the 1960s, he went through a less well-known phase where he experimented in highly innovative ways with contemporary technology in order to design buildings suited to the regional tropical Indian climate. For the Hindustan Lever Pavilion, part of the Industrial Fair in Delhi of 1961, for example, he employed a randomly 'folded' reinforced concrete structure, sprayed under pressure *in situ*, with top-lit 'cannon' openings that allowed the hot air to flow out and to cool the interior through convection currents – an ingenious reinvention of the traditional air scoops on some of the regional architecture of India. He transferred the same idea to the Tube House or Ramkrishna House in Ahmedabad (1962–1964) and, transnationally, in his design for low-cost houses in the massive UN-funded Previ housing complex in Lima, Peru, in 1969.[18]

Figure 11.14 Minnette de Silva, Senanayake Flats (housing), Gregory's Road, Colombo, Sri Lanka (1954–1957).

The Generation of 1956

In Europe, many of the young regionalists were attracted by the organization of CIAM, although it was becoming clear that most of its older members, with the exception of Le Corbusier, had lost contact with the new realities of the post-war world. These young architects had already formed an underground caucus within the tenth post-war CIAM meeting in Dubrovnik in 1956, the so-called CIAM X meeting, and prepared to take over the next CIAM meeting, in Otterlo in the Netherlands, in 1959. This meeting was to be CIAM's last. Although this group of young architects called themselves Team X or Team Ten, they were part of a broader group of architects who were rebelling against CIAM. Le Corbusier addressed a letter to them in which he called them the 'generation of 1956' One of the main focuses of this generation was the question of regionalism.

As with the Le Corbusier of Roq and Rob, the Aalto of Säynätsalo, and the Niemeyer of Pampulha, the regionalist architecture of the generation of 1956 was not a regression to the pre-war one, which had been caught in the trappings of nationalism and racism. Its members kept a *critical* distance from its seductive irrational emotionalism and make-believe settings. They tried to overcome the destructive forces of globalization that the universal, centralized design models of post-war mainstream architecture promoted, standing for the values of environment, cultural heritage, and human community.

One could see this in the housing of the architect of the INA-Casa, Ludovico Quaroni, in Martella, near Matera in southern Italy (1949), supported by the American Economic Cooperation Administration (ECA), which helped to rebuild post-war Europe, and in Giancarlo de Carlo's apartment buildings with shops in Spina Bianche in Matera (1956–1957).

Quaroni and de Carlo belonged to a broader movement in post-war Italy that also included Mario Ridolfi and Carlo Aymonino. They saw them-selves as reacting to the hallucinatory, violent monumentalist culture of *ventennio*, the twenty years of the Fascist regime that had adopted a 'post-Roman' monumental idiom with universal pretensions as its 'imperial style'. By contrast, they favored an anti-monumental culture, a society of

Figure 11.15 Charles Correa, study model for his Hindustan Lever Pavilion, New Delhi (1961).

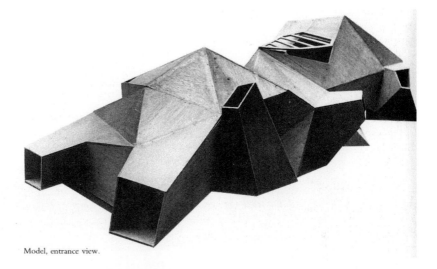

Model, entrance view.

caring, and a return to 'reality', the reality of everyday Italy emerging out of the war ruined and poor, a program shared by the a large number of non-Fascist Italian intellectuals, especially in the field of literature and cinema, that came to be known as 'Neorealism'. They hardly used the term 'regionalism', but presupposed in the idea of Neorealism was the recognition of the particular needs and aspirations of the Italian people, the understanding of their natural and social environment that is the reality of the region. They also kept a distance from the Mediterranean vernacular and its associations with *mediterranismo*, a trend promoted by some pro-Mussolini architects.

However, the idea of realism was not so clear. Looking more closely at Quaroni's drawings of the Tiburtino project in La Martella, one sees a vision of urban life and the space containing it that resembles the Franco-era visions for the restored *devastadas*, a not so realist return to a regional pastoral center dominated by the Church and the priest; the only difference here is a couple of smoking 'English' tourists in the forefront of the picture.

By contrast, the project that de Carlo presented at the CIAM meeting in 1959, while 'departing from the architectural background of the area' and respecting 'the custom of the people in this area', also took into account that 'the people who moved' into new quarters that reproduced the conditions of the past 'did not find them suitable'. The presentation was followed by a controversy because of the use of regionalist 'picturesque' elements such as the overhanging roof, resembling local peasant structures. But de Carlo took great care to use these familiar elements in a 'defamiliarized' way; as in the projects of Le Corbusier, Aalto, Niemeyer, or Burle Marx, the regional elements were used not to create a hallucinatory past but to aid the creation of new solutions fit for the real conditions of the present and future. In addition, the use of traditional regional elements inside a new modern technological and cultural framework, according to de Carlo, was intended to give 'the people ... the consciousness of their rights ... against the background of their lack of rights'. In this way, de Carlo succeeded in redefining the role of regionalism in the post-World War II reality through the demonstration of a concrete experimental case.

Figure 11.16 Giancarlo de Carlo, housing project for Matera, Italy (1957–1958).

Even more ambiguous was the regionalism in another Italian project debated in the CIAM 1959 meeting: Ernesto Nathan Rogers' Torre Velasca (1950–1958). In stark opposition to the other contemporary tower built in Milan, the mainstream modernist Torre Pirelli by Gio Ponti, Rogers' tower tried to respect existing characteristics and tendencies. Rogers cited in his defense Alvar Aalto's exclamation upon seeing it: 'It is very Milanese.' Rogers argued that his building was

> a skyscraper in the very centre of Milan, five hundred metres from the Cathedral ... and we found it necessary that our building breathe the atmosphere of the place.... The attitude of the fathers of modern architecture was anti-historical. But ... it was necessary that the first premise of our culture be a new attitude to history.

This new attitude he called 'continuity'. Gerhard Kallman wrote in *Architectural Forum* (February 1958) that 'it is not a self-sufficient structure that could be located anywhere, instead it is a valiant essay in the neglected art of fitting modern architecture into a historic continuity'.

Behind Torre Velasca there was a whole theory that Rogers developed as an alternative to globalist modernization. In 'Our Responsibility towards Tradition', published in *Casabella* (August 1954), he attacked dogmatism and 'neo-Arcadian populism' as being 'anachronistic if not hypocritical or downright demagogic lying', both tendencies being in fact anti-modern in their lack of a realistic, socially responsible approach to the architectural problems of the day. A later article by Rogers, also in *Casabella*, 'The Existing Environment and the Practical Content of Contemporary Architecture' (February

Figure 11.17 Ernesto Rogers and BBRP, Torre Velasca, Milan (1950–1958).

1955), again attacks the 'autonomous visions' of the 'frozen', 'a priori thinking' of 'so-called modern' architecture. He called for an 'extension of the Modern Movement' true to the original spirit of functionalism and for an architecture which, while innovative, considered the 'environment'. This 'environment', as in Mumford's case, is the natural context inside which a new project had to be inserted, but it also means the 'cultural' one, the 'historical setting'. 'To consider the environment means to consider history.'

Another important project bringing together historical and vernacular regional elements in a non-mimetic, non-pastiche, critical way at that time was the School of Plastic Arts in Havana, Cuba (1961–1965). In January 1960, two years after Fidel Castro's overthrow of the Batista dictatorship,[19] Castro decided to turn the unused Havana Country Club site into a facility for promoting art and culture for the people. The program included a complex of national arts schools, including a School of Modern Dance, the School of Plastic Arts, a School of Music, and a School of Ballet. Ricardo Porro, a well-educated and well-traveled revolutionary young Cuban architect, designed the first of these.[20] Porro chose brick and tiled Catalan vaulting for his building. It was a choice in direct reaction to the mainstream American International Style of the time and in contrast to the architecture of other communist countries at that time. However, it was very much in the regionalist spirit of the generation of 1956. As with de Carlo's project in Matera, Castro saw in the choice of material and geometry of space a manifestation of '[people's] consciousness of their rights ... against the background of their lack of rights', a celebration of *cubanidad*, a synthesis of Spanish colonial and Afro-Cuban forms reminiscent of the way Niemeyer and Burle Marx used regional elements to find and redefine their 'Brazilianness'. In this, Porro's exploration of female sexuality through the curved outlines of the vagina-like passageways and the breast-shaped cupolas as well as the inclusion of the papaya and phallus fountain in the middle of the complex was very similar to Niemeyer's sexual geometric meditations in the Pampulha Dance Hall. As the Cold War intensified, Castro aligned himself more closely with other communist countries. This change coincided with Porro's decision in 1966 to flee the country. France offered him a home. In 2001, however, the Cuban government commissioned Porro to return to Cuba and restore the building.

Some of the architects of the 'generation of 1956', such as De Carlo, while anxious to design within the framework of the regionalist reality, found vernacular architecture uninteresting. Similarly, George Candilis, Alexis Josic, and Shadrach Woods, who had worked for Le Corbusier during the seminal period of the design and construction of the Unité d'Habitation in Marseille but since 1955 had faced as an independent firm the problem in North Africa of providing housing for the 'greater number' (*le plus grand nombre*), not as a theoretical hypothesis but as a programmatic requirement, found no help in vernacular architecture.

However, in 1949, Josic, Candilis, and Woods joined ATBAT (the Atelier des Bâtisseurs) to design the 'Nids d'abeille' (beehives) in the Quartier

Figure 11.18 Ricardo Porro, *School of Plastic Arts*, Havana, Cuba, 1961–1965.

Figure 11.19 George
Candilis, Alexis Josic and
Shadrach Woods, 'Nids
d'abeille', Quartier des
Carrières, Casablanca
(1949).

Figure 11.19 George Candilis, Alexis Josic and Shadrach Woods, 'Nids d'abeille', Quartier des Carrières, Casablanca (1949).

des Carrières. Concerned with the question of local microclimatic environmental constraints and particularities of way of life of homeless urban people in Casablanca, they developed a new residential type fusing the super-high-density Casbah plan with the high-rise, industrially produced slab. In so doing, they attempted to recreate the Mediterranean atrium as an enclosed balcony up in the air, a misguided enterprise that unfortunately was ineffectual.

In their attempts to enhance the sense of community through their buildings, Candilis, Josic, and Woods were reacting to the formalist architecture of the highest quality in North Africa at that time, the best being by Jean-François Zevaco, a French-Moroccan architect educated at the École des Beaux-Arts who began practicing in Casablanca in 1947. Zevaco believed in the synthesis of the arts and his work tried to move away from the skin-deep colonial interpretation of environmental and cultural regionalism of the Lyautey and Prost era.[21] The results – the center of reeducation Tit Mellil and the service station at Marrakech – were sculptural and photogenic, interpreting the light and lines of the Moroccan desert landscape. But apart from their striking visual effect, they had very little to do with the region.

Figure 11.20 Jean Zevaco, service station, Marrakech (1950).

Behind this anti-formalism was the original attempt of Candilis, Josic, and Woods to free themselves from the idea of architecture as a 'plastic art', promoted since the 1930s by Sigfried Giedion. In their explorations to redefine the idea of a socially enhancing 'architectural space', their guide was the French urban geographer Chombart de Lauwe, who had researched and written about the 'ecology of the city', in turn extending theories of Giraud-Soulavie and Paul Vidal de la Blahe. Woods, the theoretician of the group, developed and presented the concept of *stem* in *Carre Bleu* (no. 3, 1961), a small-circulation review founded by Andre Schimmerling that played an enormous role in promoting the new anti-formalist new ideas of architects of the 'generation of 1956'.[22]

According to Woods, in addition to 'space' the architectural invention of the 'stem' captured 'time', 'movement', and 'human interaction,' all three making up the reality of buildings and cities as mechanisms for sustaining human community. Woods tried to show what the theory could do by presenting a real urban project, Toulouse-Le Mirail, recently designed by his firm. Woods published the plan of Fort Lamy in Chad, creating a new settlement according to the *stem* principles, interweaving a European colonial quarter and the dense African casbah in the hope that architecture would make the two populations interact. But it did not happen. Woods, like many members of Team X and many architects before, fell prey to so-called environmental determinism: untested wishful thinking that the environment can control with certainty the behavior of people.

In the same spirit as Woods, the Nigerian-born Oluwole Olumuyiwa, trained in England in the 1950s and having worked for Team X members the Smithsons and Jacob Bakema, designed a cultural centre in Lagos (1960) as a multifunctional complex of low and high buildings linked through a network of pedestrian paths conceived as 'stems'. Clearly, the ideas of Team X about the social use of circulation networks had an international impact, redefining regionalism not only as a microclimatic endeavor but also as concerned with communication and community.[23]

Figure 11.21 Shadrach Woods, urban extension for Fort Lamy, Chad (1962), between the colonial settlement and the casbah.

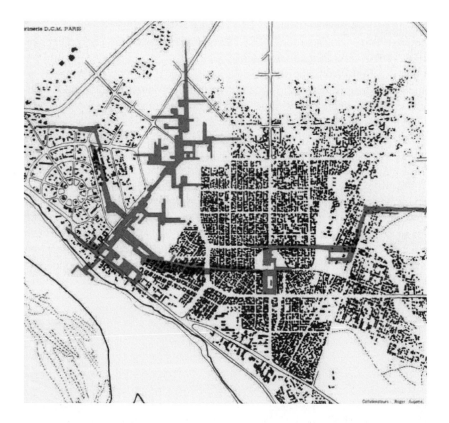

The projects we have just seen occurred in former colonies. Ceylon became independent in 1947. The French colonial administration in Indochina ended in 1954. In 1956, Morocco gained its independence, followed by Nigeria in 1960 and Algeria in 1962. In 1963, Singapore declared independence. And in December 1964, Che Guevara delivered his United Nations speech declaring that 'the final hour of colonialism has struck ... millions ... rise to meet a new life and demand ... self-determination'.

The conditions of the post-colonial states were not uniform, neither were the goals of their architecture. Most of the former colonial countries were located in the tropical or semi-tropical Vitruvian 'region' facing common environmental problems, and, as we have already seen, architects developed a regionalist approach, focusing on controlling the microclimate by recruiting local precedents.

The exception was Singapore. It chose another path from the rest. Its founding premier, Lee Kuan Yew, made a famous statement that the air conditioner was the best invention of the twentieth century.[24] This echoed Mumford's own statement in 1931 that 'mechanical air conditioning might be a useful auxiliary to nature under special conditions such as the work place'.[25] Lee Kuan Yew had a clear vision for independent Singapore developing as an affluent, global modern garden city using cutting-edge technologies to overcome tropical environmental inconveniences. In line with this vision, ten years after the declaration of independence Tay Kheng Soon and William Lim designed the Golden Mile Complex, or Woh Hup (1973),[26] one of the most ambitious and original post-war, post-colonial projects, preceded by another, equally large development, the Singapore's People's Park Complex (1967–1970), also designed by them.

Both Woh Hup and the People's Park projects may be taken as aggressive megastructures imposed on the environmental and lifestyle particularities of the region. In fact, they were the product of patient research to find a solution fit into the natural and social setting of the new nation-capital. As in the traditional urban settlements of the region, both projects are mixed-use housing and commercial centers, an arrangement that permitted people to work and to have a family and leisure life without having to use transportation. There were also ecological concerns for the high-density solution. It 'protected the agriculture plain' of land-scarce Singapore. At Woh Hup, the residential tower block was designed so as to catch the sea breeze, eliminating the need for air conditioning. Drawing from Louis Kahn's 1953, Team X's, and perhaps Neutra's Rush City Reformed ideas, the organization of movement generated the plan.[27] The circulation formed the basis for a cityscape of interconnected internal cool spaces as well as the external sheltered urban and communal

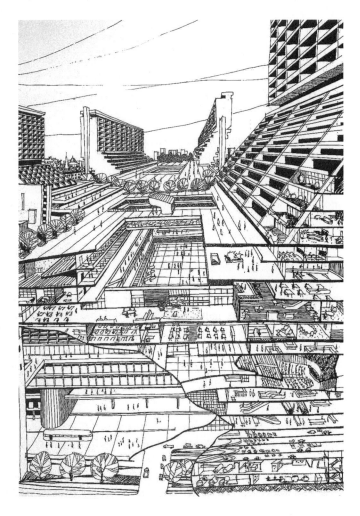

Figure 11.22 Tay Kheng Soon and William Lim, perspective section of Wo Hup (Golden Mile) Complex, Singapore (1972).

spaces that the architects envisaged would serve as platforms for mass rapid transit stations, bus stops, and activity nodes. 'Two dimensional planning on the horizontal should give way to planning in four dimensions, introducing ... height and ... time [in transportation and programming of areas for building],' Kheng Soon insisted.[28] 'A true city is a congested city – congestion not of cars but of people drawn close together by a multitude of related activities.'[29] He continued, quoting Lewis Mumford, by saying that the ideal he had in mind was a city where 'work and leisure, theory and practice, private life and public life were in rhythmic interplay ... [where] one part of life flowed into another. No phase was segregated, monopolized, set apart'.[30]

In contrast to Singapore's mixed economy and strong planning, balancing globalization with regionalist requirements, post-World War II Greece followed a different path of development, allowing chaotic, freewheeling growth open to the forces of globalization. Soon, as we have seen already in reference to the construction of the Hilton Hotel, the cultural, social, and ecological environment of its historic capital, Athens, was under threat.

It was a Japanese architect, Kisho Kurokawa (1934–2007), who pointed out the significance of the path up the Acropolis and the Philopappos Hill in Athens (1953–1957) as an exemplary project expressing with the utmost clarity and intelligence the ideals of the 1956 generation about process, movement, interaction in a regional context.[31] Dimitri Pikionis, the architect of the path, was born in 1887, studied in Munich and Paris at the end of the nineteenth century, and had designed very little before the path. Yet in designing it, he was conscious that he was creating a critical project of international significance commenting on the destructive forces of mindless globalization.

Pikionis had been preoccupied with the phenomenology of movement in the landscape since he was a child climbing the seaside hills in Piraeus. As a young architect fascinated with traditional folk architecture in Greece, he studied the design of vernacular countryside footpaths in the Greek landscape. In the 1930s, studying the plan of the Acropolis in relation to the landscape of Attica, he began developing a theory that linked the geometry and surface of a path to the environment of the region. Echoing Rousseau's *Rêveries du promeneur solitaire*,[32] Pikionis used the term 'sentimental topography' to describe his system.

A testimony to this inquiry was published by Erich Mendelsohn in the *Berliner Tageblatt* in May 1931 when Mendelsohn visited the Acropolis with Pikionis as guide. Later, Mendelson, the master of the poetics of mechanical movement in Berlin, in the design for the Weizmann Mansion of Rehoboth in Israel (1936–1937) introduced a serpentine landscaped pathway up the hill very similar to the one suggested for the Parthenon by Pikionis and later applied to the Philopappos Hill.

Despite the extensive use of motifs and real fragments of folk art and architecture, Pikionis believed that the path was not a sentimental regionalist spectacle but a critical response – technical but also 'aesthetic' – to the globalization of Greece that was destroying the ecology and memory of the landscape as well as human community. He felt that the work 'read into the souls of simple people and appreciate[d] their unerring judgment'[33] while at the same time had the reflective density of what came to be known as 'land art'.

Figure 11.23 Dimitris Pikionis, view of the part of the path leading up Philopappus Hill, Athens (1953–1957).

The leading Israeli regionalist architect and planner Artur Glikson, struggling to apply regionalist principles in his fast-growing country at that time, visited the path and found in it recognition of 'land as a community to which we belong',[34] arguing that the project was another version of the famous Appalachian trail by Benton MacKaye.[35] Pikionis showed Mumford the path in 1960. Mumford recognized the value of the project immediately and included it in his masterpiece *The City in History*.[36] But it was the article by Kisho Kurokawa, an avant-garde 'metabolist', that stimulated the curiosity of younger architects about the path.

Not surprisingly, Kurokawa had been a student of Kenzo Tange and a member of the 'metabolist' group created around Tange, who was himself intensely preoccupied with movement and 'process', and sympathetic to the ideas of Team X. Tange had participated to the CIAM meeting in Otterlo in 1959, presenting his Kagawa Prefectural Office of 1956. Ernesto Rogers welcomed the building but Tange's response was guarded, opposing any misinterpretation of his use of regional elements. 'I cannot accept the concept of *total* regionalism,' he asserted, adding that 'tradition can be developed through *challenging* its own shortcomings, implying the same for regionalism', a real definition of *critical regionalism*: that is, a regionalism that is self-examining and self-questioning.

Years before this public presentation, in fact since the end of the nineteenth century, generations of Japanese people, including architects, had

Figure 11.24 Kenzo Tange,
City Hall, Kagawa
Prefecture, Japan
(1955–1958).

been trying to discover what is 'Japan-ness', the identity of Japanese architecture. Indicative of the Japanese perplexity during the Meiji period is a masterpiece of modern Japanese literature, *I Am a Cat* (1905–1906), about the Japanese (a cat) confronting Westerners (the humans), the cat being unable to communicate with the people. The story ends tragically with the destruction of the cat by humans.

Western architecture dominated Japan at the turn of the twentieth century, before the popular success of the Japanese pavilion at the Columbia World Fair in Chicago in 1893, a copy of the O-Ho-Den Pavilion that revealed to the Japanese the appeal of their architecture abroad.

The late 1920s and 1930s saw various attempts to assert the regionalist Japanese character in architecture, not unrelated to regionalist anthropologist studies in France and Germany about regionalist and ethnic identity at that time. The fascinating research and writings of Wajiro Kon, published in his *Modernology* (1930),[37] were part of this investigation exploring the Japanese urban environment. An important first step was the so-called *teikan* (meaning 'imperial crown' in Japanese) style, which consisted in designing a traditional Japanese roof to cover in a crow-like manner a low-rise modern, functional building, epitomized in Jun Watanabe's Tokyo Imperial Museum in 1937. To this monumental architecture, which expressed the nationalist vision of imperial Japan, several architects offered different alternatives. In 1926, Sutemi Horiguchi designed a house that was an art deco structure surmounted by a thatched roof typical of country tea houses.[38] The influence of the German Bauhaus architect Bruno Taut, who had moved to Japan in 1933 to escape the Nazis, was overwhelming in shaping the regionalist architecture for the rest of the century. A leading international authority in the eyes of the Japanese, he singled out the minimalist imperial Katsura Palace and the Ise Shrine as the models. A series of buildings followed that were incongruous collages of Japanese and modern elements, such as Horiguchi's Okada Residence in Tokyo in 1934, which had a Japanese roof with half the house being a pastiche of the imperial Katsura Palace and the other half a Western house. The Fujiyama Mansion of 1932–1933 was actually two buildings, a Tudor revival stone building complete with half-timbered gables and carved stone ornaments, the other a copy of the O-Ho-Den pavilion of 1893. Mamoru Yamada's House of T in Tokyo (1931–1932) incorporated a traditional Japanese house already on the site into a larger modern one. The vacation house in Nagano Prefecture, designed by Antonin Raymond, a Czech-American architect living in Japan, combined Le Corbusier's Arrazuris House, with its butterfly roof inspired by regional Chilean architecture, with a Japanese farmhouse.[39] According to his one-time assistant Arata Isozaki, it is Kenzo Tange who defined Japan-ness in the most compelling way, overcoming the contradictions between the Japanese and Western architectural elements through their total fusion into one coherent whole.[40]

Tange achieved this after World War II with his design for the Hiroshima Memorial Peace Center in 1949–1955. Here, as Isozaki intriguingly argues, Tange deployed 'pilotis, a flat roof, flowing space, exposed structure, and transparency in full'. The result was that '[a]t the same time, points of reference to traditional Japanese architecture – the plan of O-Ho-Den and column ratios based on Katsura – were unmistakable'.[41]

Throughout the 1960s, regionalist themes played a guiding role in Tange's buildings, such as the National Olympic Stadium (1961–1964) with its gigantic suspended, highly technological roof structure reminiscent of the great hall of Todai-ji in Nara; the silhouettes of the gigantic megastructures attached to the vertebrae-like transportation elements recalled traditional Japanese roofs. Yet what the metabolists, in their effort to construct a modern and the same time a national identity, saw as the most characteristic regionalist element of his work, and by extension of theirs, was 'movement' and 'process', which they claimed to be deeply rooted in the Japanese identity. And for this reason, of all non-Japanese architects, the one they admired most at that time (apart from Team X, who also idolized him) was Louis Kahn. In this case, it was his theories related to movement and flow exemplified in his 1959 talk in Otterloo that the Japanese, in their own way, identified with.

Chapter 12

Regionalism Now

The 1959 Otterlo meeting invited Louis Kahn to give a keynote address. Kahn presented his Richard's Laboratories in the University of Pennsylvania, Philadelphia. His long and poetic talk touched on many topics but focused on 'movement' and built form, a theme that fitted very well with the preoccupation of Team X members, who looked at movement as one of dimensions through which to tackle the problem of the 'greater number' and regionalism. The International Style was still the enemy. When Wendell H. Lovett presented a well-designed but vacuous mainstream 'International Style' project, he received a hostile reaction from a frustrated audience of the 'generation of 1956'.

But there was also another, small but important, movement in American architecture that searched for answers to almost the same questions as those that preoccupied the Otterlo audience. Paul Rudolph, who could have been the leader of this movement, was by then absorbed in his own professional career. Edward Larrabee Barnes, after the war an assistant to Henry Dreyfuss, designing mass-housing prototypes, continued to keep a distance from the neo-monumentalist trend of the 1950s in the United States, turning to vernacular New England precedents.[1] In a talk at Yale in March 1964, Barnes argued for 'architecture in harmony with its environment', involving 'color, scale, and mood', whereby each building 'is part of a process, not a world in itself.' As an example, he presented his Haystack Mountain School of Arts and Crafts on Deer Isle, Maine (1959–1961), a complex of small buildings, a kind of 'Maine fishing village' of shingled cottages linked by a grid of wooden decks leading to a spectacular ocean view. Its plain Yankee farmhouse-like volumes with inclined roofs, recalling the rigorist ideals of the highly influential nineteenth-century American sculptor and essayist Horatio Greenough, fitted into the environment but also made the viewer reflect on the value of a symbiosis with nature in the Mumfordian but also in the Henry Thoreau sense.

More than an educational facility, the Haystack School was a community in the tradition of progressive artists' schools, whose purpose, in the words of Percival and Paul Goodman, was to 'irradiate society with people who have been profoundly touched with the excitement of community life'.

Like Barnes's project, the Sea Ranch by Moore, Lyndon, Turnbull, Whitaker (MLTW) and Lawrence Halprin (1963–1965) was conceived in this critical regionalist framework. In the words of Halprin, the Sea Ranch aspired

Figure 12.01 Edward
Larrabee Barnes,
Haystack Mountain
School of Arts and Crafts,
Deer Island, Maine
(1959–1961).

to become an 'organic community' in harmonious relation with the natural lie of the land. Every level of the original design bore the mark of the 'native character' of the site, the houses, linked by fences, rising gently from the meadow to meet with hedgerows serving as windbreaks, a common practice in the vernacular of barns and sheep sheds in the region. As Halprin wrote, the intention was to preserve the coastline and the beaches, 'the Sea Ranch ... becom[ing] a place where wild nature and human habitation could interact in a kind of intense symbiosis'.

As the construction of the Sea Ranch was coming to a close, in 1964, an exhibition was held in MoMA, New York, entitled 'Architecture without Architects'. It was organized by Bernard Rudofsky, an architect writer and traveler educated in Vienna who had finally settled in New York and celebrated the richness of vernacular architecture around the world.

Rudofsky's show did not mark a new beginning for MoMA or for the regionalist movement. Soon afterwards, the May Revolution in France and equivalent uprisings in most parts of the world, including the United States, absorbed the interest of young architects, who looked at regionalism sympathetically but not as a priority. As for the 1970s, they were dominated by postmodernism, a trend equally indifferent to regionalism.

But the vacuity of postmodernism demonstrated in numerous projects carried out during the 1970s and the growing wave of globalization led a younger generation of architects to renew the issue of regionalism around the beginning of the 1980s. This coincided with a massive 'rediscovery' of Spanish architecture, which had been relatively unknown internationally up to that moment, owing to Franco's isolationist fascist regime.

As we have already seen, regionalism has deep roots in Spain, revitalizing, as with the *Renaixença* modernism in Catalonia, or regressive, as with Franco's program for *regiones devastadas*. Franco imposed nationalist regionalist architecture in Spain, coinciding with the imposition of *Heimat* and 'Vichy' regionalism in Germany and France at the end of the 1930s. Inside the highly confined ideological framework, there were quality products such as the Vegaviana Village (1954–1958) by José Luis Fernández del Amo.

Figure 12.02 Charles Moore, Donlyn Lyndon, William Turnbull Jr, Richard Whitaker, and Lawrence Halprin, Sea Ranch, Big Sur, California (1963–1965).

Figure 12.03 Antoni Gaudí, roof of the 'Small Schools', next to the Sagrada Família, Barcelona (1936).

Figure 12.04 Lluís Domènech i Montaner, Palau de la Musica Catalana, 1908.

The situation changed radically around the mid-1970s:[2] for example, the exiled architect Josep Lluís Sert returned officially in 1975, and the Basque Country and Catalonia were recognized as autonomous regions in 1980. But architectural developments were not so abrupt. Before the unprecedented urbanization and building boom of the 1980s, Spanish architecture was free to develop in parallel with that of the rest of the Western nations. As early as 1958, the Spanish pavilion at the Brussels Expo by José Antonio Corrales and Ramón Vásquez Molezún surprised everybody by its newness and by the absence of any Franco-inspired references to the rural-feudal past or monumentalist 'Escorialismo'. The same year, Coderch and Valls presented a tourist project in Torre Valentina on the Costa Brava. The work fitted into the landscape following Le Corbusier's regionalist precedents but, back home, numerous projects tried to develop a more original approach to Mediterranean regionalism, drawing from the local vernacular.

The generation of the last years of the regime succeeded in surviving the intellectual sclerosis of the Franco era but also, in its effort to join the outside, free world, avoided becoming a thoughtless, passive importer of fashionable icons, including the trendy postmodern ones. Its members

Figure 12.05 José Luis Fernández del Amo (I.N.C.) Houses in Vegaviana, Cáceres, Spain (c.1956).

developed an original 'critical regionalist' approach that rethought moderniza-tion, combining it with Spanish precedents and adapting it intelligently to the particular constraints of specific situations. Such is the case of Alejandro de la Sota's Gimnasio del Colegio Maravillas in Madrid (1961), Antonio Fernández Alba's Convento del Rollo in Salamanca (1962), and Francisco Javier Sáenz de Oiza's Banco de Bilbao in Madrid (1971–1978).

A unique regionalist project combining public space and mytho-poeic Basque waterfront landscape with sculpture, El Peine del Viento ('Comb of the Wind', 1975–1977), was designed during the period of transition to democracy, the result of a collaboration between the artist Eduardo Chillida and the architect Luis Peña Ganchegui, both Basques, on the western tip of the horseshoe bay of San Sebastian, overlooking the Atlantic Ocean. Equally unique was the urban furniture for the poor fishing village of Combarro (1971–1974) in Galicia[3] by Pascuala Campos. The project, reminiscent of Gian-carlo de Carlo's buildings in Matera, intended to recognize the identity and

Figure 12.06 José Antonio Coderch, photomontage.

Figure 12.07 Juan Antonio Fernandez-Alba, Convento del Rollo, Salamanca (1962).

value of the community, inviting them not to emigrate but to stay in the region and struggle to change its economic and social conditions. More recently, the renovation of the Santa Catarina Market in Barcelona by Enric Miralles and Benedetta Tagliabue (1997–2005), photographed on the cover of the present book, serves as a means of celebrating and preserving the quality of traditional markets and traditional agricultural produce – the colors on the roof refer to the colors of the fruits and vegetables sold there – in an urban world encroached on by a socially and nutritionally challenged globalized food culture.

In Madrid, Antonio Vélez Catrain's (1979–1983) cubic block of Yeserias fused modern functional apartment services with the regional element of the patio, as it is known, a microclimatic control device as well as a medium for face-to-face social interaction. A similar fusion of regional and modern elements is demonstrated in a residential complex, the Arturo Soria Apartment, designed by Bayón, Aroca, and Bisquert & Martín (1976–1978), situated in the lush green park-like environment of the Ciudad Lineal, and in the Social Housing Block by Antonio Cruz Villalón and Antonio Ortiz García on Dona Maria Coronell Street (1974–1976) in the heart of historic Seville.

By the beginning of the 1990s, as global organizations and institutions were unleashed around the world, determining through universal design models and routines the shape of buildings, cities, and landscapes and depleting natural and cultural resources, 'flattening' by brute force singular peaks and unique valleys of biological diversity and ways of life, regionalism – critical and not regressive – became the focus of numerous architects around the world.

An example is Renzo Piano's Jean-Marie Tjibaou Cultural Centre in Noumea, New Caledonia (1993–1998). At the request of New Caledonia, the French government agreed to finance the construction in Noumea of a center devoted to the memory of the political leader Jean-Marie Tjibaou, a student of ethnology in the Sorbonne and a supporter of activities promoting Kanak identity who had been assassinated in 1989. Piano tried to pay homage to New Caledonia's culture, traditions, and history, while putting European technology and expertise at the service of this goal, a synthesis between local and global. He used the shape of traditional Caledonian huts, regional materials and building methods, and local beliefs about wind, light, and vegetation. The center is composed of ten 'houses' or huts serving different functions and evoking different themes: exhibitions, an auditorium, an amphitheater, research areas, a conference room, a library, and a group of huts for traditional music, dance, painting, and sculpture.

In a similar way, Jacques Ferrier and Jean-François Irissou employed high-technology construction and function devices to house the Siège social de Total Énergie à La Tour-de-Salvagny, a high-tech company on the outskirts of Lyon. Ferrier inventively employed cutting-edge fabric and function while recruiting the configuration of agricultural buildings, 'functional structures in the rural French landscape shaped ... in the course of time'.

Eastgate, a mixed office and shopping center in Harare designed by Mick Pearce, was a unique project ventilated, cooled, and heated entirely through natural means.[4] No pristine glass of global architecture here. Eastgate was modeled on the termite mounds that dot the Zimbabwean savanna,

Figure 12.08 Renzo Piano, Jean-Marie Tjibaou Cultural Centre, Noumea, New Caledonia (1993–1998).

emulating a structure that has a constant temperature of exactly 30–31°C. As temperatures in their environment fluctuate from 1.7°C at night to 40°C during the day, the termites dig a kind of breeze-catcher at the base of their mound which cools the air by means of chambers carved out of the wet mud below, and sends hot air out through a flue at the top.

Similarly, Ken Yeang, an architect, researcher, and writer, has been struggling with innovative high-rise projects defined as bioclimatic skyscrapers: passive-mode, low-energy buildings with zero dependency on non-renewable sources of energy.[5]

By contrast, the Bedok Court (1985) in Singapore by Theng Jian Fenn and Design Link Associates uses, like the 1973 Woh Hup, the most 'natural means' of environmental control. In contrast to its predecessor, this is a strictly residential complex concerned with social quality. The scheme draws from the regional Malay kampong (village) low-rise tropical dwelling precedents, such as veranda and front entrance porch and gardens in semi-detached and single houses, reused within a new high-rise framework that achieves high environmental as well as social quality. Each apartment has a sheltered and ventilated forecourt where everyday activities occur, accessible visually from adjacent circulation corridors and other forecourts. As Philip Bay,[6] who carried out a post-occupancy study of the project, observed, familiarity and social contacts are enhanced, contributing to a strong sense of community and security.

Site and region constraints were even stronger when building just outside the walls of the Old City of Jerusalem in Israel. Moshe Safdie designed the Hebrew Union College campus (1976–1988)[7] using the local stone, stone arcades, sunscreens, courtyards, and smaller gardens to provide outdoor 'rooms' well suited for study and teaching in this climate. The scheme is a microcosmic version of the real city, interweaving its own small

Figure 12.09 Ken Yeang, Guthrie Pavilion, Shah-Alam, Malaysia (2000).

Figure 12.10 Theng Jian Fenn and Design Link Associates, Bedok Court, Singapore, 1973.

community with the larger urban one. Likewise, in a different setting, Christopher Benninger in his Mahindra United World College, in Pune, India (1997–2000), one of the ten United World College public schools, a 'global village', used local stone materials, gently sloping masonry surfaces and Mangalore tile roofs to provide a village-like spatial organization permitting, between the buildings, views of the mountains surrounding the campus.

One of the characteristic of these end-of-the-century regionalist projects is the degree of involvement with the landscape. The craft of making a structure less intrusive while advancing its functionality has been greatly advanced, an excellent example being La Granja Escalator, Toledo, Spain (1997–2000) by José Antonio Martínez Lapeña and Elías Torres Tur, which minimizes the disruption of a historical setting, leaving the medieval walls of the city intact.

Figure 12.11 Moshe Safdie, Hebrew Union College, Jerusalem, Israel (1976–1988).

A new development enriching the critical regionalist approach goes beyond the objective of just minimizing the disruption of the landscape or hiding or blending the new structure, methods known since the picturesque, but engaging the new structure in a critical 'dialogue' with the site, fore-grounding its particularity. The means of engagement are either through the design of a 'path' – 'land art', following the example of Benton MacKaye and Pikionis – or through abstract means.

Navarra Office Walk Architecture took an approach to design simi-lar in spirit to the footpaths of Dimitris Pikionis. The Strip Park between Calta-girone and Piazza Armerina, Catania, Italy (2001) consisted of a bicycle, skating, and jogging track, or trekking trail, part of a program to put to new use the 35 kilometers of a former railway track that had passed through agri-cultural land and natural landscape between Caltagirone and Piazza Armerina, in central Sicily. The path encountered on its way spectacular viaducts, tunnels, and bridges from the 1920s and 1930s, and rugged landscape along-side traditional rural buildings. As the architect said, the railway line 'cut into the landscape like a wound, imposing its own laws in accordance with the needs of the machine age'.

German del Sol's Hot Springs Landscape, Hotel and Horse Stables, San Petro de Atacama, Chile (1998–2000) also deals with the relation between landscape and path. The project is located a short distance from where the Loa River flows through a valley with a semi-desert climate halfway between Antofagasta and Valparaíso, an area known for its river, its natural hot springs, and wells. The tourist activities form a complex linked through a zigzagging path that follows the winding river bed, congruent with the land formation. Raised boardwalks treat the grass gently and provide a rare viewpoint for gazing at the long, winding river, paying homage to the beauty of the land and making sustainable use of the pools.

Kengo Kuma's relation to the environment involves more senses, Kuma 'listening' as carefully as possible to the site before proceeding with the design. Only then does he place the building upon it, relating the struc-ture to the scale of the surroundings in a manner that seems like a natural tribute to the centuries-old tradition of Japanese wood architecture. In the case of his museum in the Batoh, Tochigi Prefecture, in Japan (1998–2000), dedicated to the artist Ando Hiroshige (1797–1858), Kuma composed a series of grid wooden structures for roof and walls. The character of the grid changes as the light pouring into the space changes: sometimes the grid pat-terns are transformed into a solid translucent pane and at other times they become transparent, changing the feeling and color of material from day to day. 'By creating the architecture entirely from a grid system,' the architect writes, 'we have aimed at a building that is a "sensor" of light', a bridge linking the work of the painter to that of the architect. 'The work of Hiroshige is characterized by ... changes in nature,' Kuma states. 'The character and essence of natural elements such as light, wind, rain and fog are continu-ously changing.'

Even more abstract and demanding is the experience offered by the Live Oak Friends Meeting house in Houston, Texas (1995–2001), the result of a collaboration between local architect Leslie Elkins and the light and space artist James Turrell. The project consists of a modest, traditional, vernacular gray wooden house, a traditional housing type in Houston, nestled among typical trees of that city, namely oaks, and crowned by a low-pitched roof also typical of Houston. Turrell installed a 'Skyspace', a skylight in the center of the ceiling. This serves the purpose of the building as a Friends Meeting Hall, to reinforce the community ties between Quakers. At the same time, the opening frames the view of the ever-changing sky and brings the onlooker to meditate on humankind's particular place in the changing environment, earthly and heavenly.

In addition to their environmental and cultural identity with their region, all the projects we have discussed so far in this chapter are constructed within an imaginary preconstructed landscape of memory, a most significant factor, as Ruskin stressed in the middle of the nineteenth century. As we have seen, reconstructed memory played an extremely important role in the construction of the new German state and continued to play one in most cases of nation and state construction in the nineteenth and twentieth centuries, creating new communities but also destroying old ones after centuries of harmonious coexistence.

The architects of the post-apartheid South Africa faced an enormous task in constructing housing and civic facilities for a new society, but they also needed to generate public spaces that creatively and critically addressed aspects of memory and identity intimately linked with repairing the wrong of the apartheid era.

Regionalist architecture had a long history in the area. Colonizers built 'Cape Dutch' houses intruding into South Africa as early as the seventeenth century. A different regionalism emerged in the pages of the *South African Architectural Record*, starting with the publications of Betty Spence in the 1940s and 1950s. Spence inquired into features of the culture and lifestyle of the non-Western local South African population, aiming at advancing the efficiency of construction and comfort in housing.

Figure 12.12 Leslie Elkins and James Turrell, facade and interior space with view of the sky of the Live Oaks Friends Meeting Hall, Houston, Texas (1995–2001).

The buildings designed by a group of architects – Rex Martienssen, Gordon McIntosh, Norman Hanson or Norman Eaton – had a common focus on developing a modern architecture fit for the South African region and considering functional organization of space within a comfortable microenvironmental environment. Their approach was inspired by Le Corbusier's regionalist experiments as well as a celebrated exhibition at MoMA in New York in 1943, 'Brazil Builds', resulting in what Nikolaus Pevsner called, in *Architectural Review* in 1953, 'a little Brazil within the Commonwealth'. In considering the region, social and cultural aspects were not central to their investigations, with the exception of the 1952 Meat Board building by Stauch & Partners, who tried to incorporate in their scheme, together with the facade of the building as an environmental control mechanism, a public passage linking entrance hall and stairs, paved using vernacular techniques and patterns.

Yet by the second half of the 1950s, the rise of the National Party and the pastoralist, farmer-populist Afrikaner Voortrekker ideology, in some ways very close to Nazism, which created super-ideological architecture such as Gerard Moerdijk's Voortrekker Monument, the pass laws, and the planning policies of 'separate development' and 'homelands' in South Africa, made clear to the younger generation of architects that the politics- and culture-blind regionalist approach had no future for them. Many of them – Julian Beinart, Issy Benjamin, Rusty Bernstein, Arthur Goldreich, Ike Horvitch, Ted Levy, and Alan Lipman – left the country.

The Constitution Hill project was the most ambitious architectural work of the new South Africa. The complex, physically and conceptually, is an epic that spans over a century of dramatic history, embodying components of an original fort that served as a prison for political prisoners and the new structure that serves as the home of South Africa's highest court. Restoration and constitution were most successfully transformed into a new unitary place with a dual function: sustaining memory without monumentality and upholding justice. The success was the result of the creative work of the OMM Design Workshop in partnership with Urban Solutions, but also of the committee that conceived the program and organized the international competition in 1997. Among its members were Charles Correa and Justice Albie Sachs. The work was partly preservation, partly reconstruction, and partly new structure. The scheme never became a coherent composition. It unfolds and shifts in response to the uniqueness of the specific events of the site, which are not accidental but history-specific.

A similar approach was followed in preservation, reuse, and innovation projects such as the Walter Sisulu Square of Dedication, designed by studioMAS Architects and Urban Designers and located in the heart of Kliptown, the oldest settlement in Soweto, and the Nelson Mandela Centre by Peter Rich, located in Alexandra. The scheme, next to a room-shed where Nelson Mandela slept and studied in the early 1940s, is a self-effacing long orthogonal concrete path with an entrance ramp picking visitors up from the pavement and taking them onto a bridge across the road. Inside the center there are historical exhibits about Mandela and the people of Alexandra.

'We may live without architecture,' Ruskin wrote, 'but we cannot remember without her.' He was referring, as we saw, to the problem of fake restoration of Gothic architecture in his time. South Africa decided that one

cannot construct a good society without knowing about the historical foundations it is built on. The role of memory here is not the same as in the nationalist movements, where, as we saw, a newly constructed memory helps the
construction of a new identity reusing fragments of the past. Memory is part
of the 'region' within which future buildings and cities are to be born or
present structures are reused. It has to be taken into account, just as the soil,
the microclimate, and the configuration of the site are taken into account.

For the fast-growing cities of East Asia, a precondition of their
growth is 'creative destruction'. Hong Kong faced it in the extreme.

Gary Chang, one of the most creative Hong Kong architects, published a book about his apartment in Hong Kong, a 32-square-meter one-room
space,[8] in which he tried to preserve its memory. The book gives the history
of the transformations of the apartment in 1976, 1988, 1998, and 2007, dates
that correspond to critical phases in the life of the author: birth, childhood,
exploration and dreaming, years of struggle, experimentation, and recognition.
But they also correspond to important periods in the evolution of Hong Kong:
from the years of austerity, overcrowding, and overworking to the years of
consumer spectacles and panegyric emporia, and from the period of tensions
and uncertainties to the establishment of Hong Kong as a Special Administrative Region of China.

Throughout those years, Chang redesigned the apartment, redefining its space and contents, adapting them to the changing users and changing
uses, as his grandparents died, and his sisters and parents left, leaving him as
the sole occupant of the apartment. However, throughout this remodeling
Chang kept the apartment's regional identity, an inward-looking niche within
which a collection of utensils and gadgets are compacted, as if stuffed in a
suitcase; in this manner, he produced a collective representation of the Hong
Kong people, to a great extent 'people of the suitcase' in their history, a history of coming and going.

Yet like a suitcase, the apartment has an infinite capacity for
unpacking, reaching out thousands of kilometers through the projectors and
screens that constitute the basic furniture of the windowless one-room apartment, devices that enable one to enjoy any media-borne distant views of the
world. It is a tradition of the Hong Kong home: just two years after the founding of the first wireless and television broadcasting, in 1969, it was reported
that nine out of ten of the densely packed Hong Kong homes were reached
by broadcasting services. Gary Chang has once more redone his apartment,
which he has now left, as a historical palimpsest to save, as in the book, its
historical transformations.

The most significant construction during the twenty-first century
has taken place in mainland China, enabled by the government but driven by
developers. Rarely were considerations concerning the ecology and the
culture of the region taken into consideration. One of the rare exceptions was
a $24-million project, 'Commune by the Great Wall of China' (2000), developed
by Zhang Xin and Pan Shiyi, who commissioned Asian architects. In most
cases, the characteristic of these unprecedented projects is technical proficiency, speed, and gigantic scale. They are designed by a huge number of
firms from all over the world, dispensing with questions of urban and regional
continuity and history.

Figure 12.13 A McDonald's advertisement in front of the historic gate of Beijing.

Unsurprisingly, this has led to heated discussions about growth and the 'creative destruction' that is turning China into an ecological and cultural flatland, and about regionalism. One of the key figures in this historical event has been Wu Liangyong.[9] Born in Nanjing in 1922, he witnessed the destruction of the city and its population by the Japanese. After studying architecture at National Central University, Chongqing, he graduated in 1944. In 1946, he started working with Professor Liang Sicheng in Beijing in founding the Department of Architecture of Tsinghua University. Liang Sicheng, a University of Pennsylvania graduate, is considered the 'father of Chinese architectural history' and is the author, with his wife, Lin Huiyin, of the first comprehensive history of Chinese architecture. Wu interrupted his work there to travel to the United States and study at the Cranbrook Academy of Art, Bloomfield Hills, Michigan, under Eliel Saarinen, obtaining a second degree in 1949, the year the civil war in China ended. After working with Eero Saarinen, assisting in the design of the General Motors Technical and Research Center in Detroit (1950), he returned to Tsinhua, resuming his research and teaching with Liang Sicheng in 1951.

Both Liang Sicheng's and Eliel Saarinen's commitment to regionalism influenced the direction of Wu's lifelong engagement with the problem of regionalism in the context of the new China. The question of what kind of architecture should be built in contemporary China arose with the abdication of the Qing emperor in 1911 and the proclamation of the Chinese Republic led by Sun Yatsen and, in 1919, the May 4 Movement, which called for a new popular approach to culture. The May 4 Movement, however, was driven by the goal of modernization while tormented by doubt as to whether Western civilization was superior to that of China and whether the ties with Chinese tradition ought to be severed.[10]

Among the architects who posed this question was an American, Henry Murphy (1877–1954).[11] A graduate of Yale College, Murphy arrived in China in 1914 at the age of thirty-seven to help design a Yale-in-China, known in Chinese as 'Yali' campus, at Changsha in Hunan Province. Murphy stayed in China for thirty years, up to the Japanese invasion in 1937. Interestingly, following his stay in China he designed one last series of buildings in the United States in Chinese style at Coral Gables, Florida, in 1926.[12]

As Jeffrey Cody points out, Murphy was captivated by the architecture of Beijing's Forbidden City. He argued that just as classical and Gothic architecture were adapted to meet the needs of modern scientific planning and construction, so 'it was not logical to deny to Chinese architecture a similar adaptability'. Murphy, who had practiced 'adapting' classical colonial and revival styles in the United States prior to his arrival in China, undertook to do the same in China.

Many of the Chinese architects who worked at Murphy's office had studied in the United States, mostly receiving Paul Cret's École des Beaux-Arts classicist education at the University of Pennsylvania. Typical of the naïveté of the situation, not very different from that in the United States at this time, Lu Yanzhi, who graduated from Cornell in 1918, won the design competition for the mausoleum of Sun Yatsen at the foot of the Purple Mountain near Nanjing by proposing a plan whose outline pictured a bell, a known symbol of Sun Yatsen, calling the Chinese people to a new epoch (1926–1929).[13] Murphy's buildings for Changsha University and Peking University, both constructed in the mid-1920s, although they did not solve the problem of creating a regionalist or a national architecture, were serious buildings, some decently representing the Western tradition.

By the 1930s, patience was running out with the Chinese/Renaissance style of Murphy and his followers, and his overall approach to architecture, which produced many low-quality cultural products such as the 'Yale-in-China' building, which used an incongruous regional idiom[14] associated with the fallen Qing Dynasty. Another irritant was the imitation in concrete of traditional wooden construction details, the *dougong*, as Murphy did in the fake pagoda water tower at Peking University. A similar imitation of regional wooden details caused comparable irritation in France at about that time.[15]

Tong Jun, an American-educated architect, returned to China and wrote in 1937 about the need to transcend decoration and concentrate on structure. He called for a new Chinese architecture that would contribute to twentieth-century world architecture. In his essay 'Architecture Chronicle', he denounced the false debates about 'a Chinese or modern exterior', saying that the 'plan can only be one thing: a logical and scientific arrangement.... Any attempt to give the [facade] local "colour" will require study, research, and originality'.[16]

This was the task undertaken by Liang Sicheng from the end of the 1920s onwards, interrupted by World War II. In 1946 in Tsinghua, he wrote: 'Chinese architecture' between tradition and modernity 'faces a grave situation'. 'Something new must come out of it, or Chinese architecture will become extinct.'[17]

Very little time for thinking about architecture was available during the period of wars and conflicts that led to the establishment of the People's Republic of China in 1949. Because of ideological and political affinities and of the vacuum left by the war devastation, China relied on Soviet and East German assistance in building, both technological and theoretical. The rhetoric might have been different but Soviet 'classicism' was not very distant from Murphy's Beaux-Arts theory of 'adaptability'. The East German legacy left behind some structures of technical rigor such as the 1952 'Project 157' military factory in Beijing, now '798 Art Zone', but not much food for thought.

It was for Chinese architects to carry out the task of identifying a direction for the architecture of the country. Wu Liangyong continued his research, teaching, and designing, being based at Tsinghua University with an interruption during the Cultural Revolution. As China's economy and cities began to grow at an unprecedented scale following 1978, a new problem emerged that brought back the regionalist question to the heart of Beijing. The problem involved the fate of the *hutongs*, traditional small blocks of high-density courtyard housing, developed between a multitude of narrow lanes within the main streets that divide the city into a rigid grid pattern. Seventy years of wars had had a severe impact on the *hutongs*, an impact only exacerbated by the recent phenomenal economic growth.

In the framework of his study on the planning of Beijing, Wu recommended preservation of the original community structure, building in continuity with the traditional courtyard system, and 'organic replacement' rather than conservation of the old urban tissue, developing a new prototype for housing, the 'basic courtyard'. He implemented it in his project for the rehabilitation of the historical Ju'er Hutong (Chrysanthemum Path Hutong, 1987–1993) in the heart of Beijing, pioneering a new approach to urban renewal in China that avoided the need for wholesale demolition of historic

Figure 12.14 Liangyong Wu, interior courts of his Rehabilitation of the Juer'Er Hutong (Chrysanthemum Path Hutong), Beijing (1987–1993).

but dilapidated inner-city housing. To increase the density of the neighborhood and to provide modern standards of privacy while maintaining community, Wu used two- and three-story walk-up apartments forming a courtyard and recruited the fishbone circulation pattern from southern China.

The scheme tried to satisfy modern requirements of privacy while retaining traditional patterns of community. A collaborative dialogue established between residents, architect-planners and local government was part of the design process. Wu succeeded in modernizing the urban tissue while sustaining cultural diversity and local identity.

Regionalist concerns, whether environmental or cultural, continue to be rare in fast-growing urban China, where globalization has taken over. However, important examples can be found outside cities, examples designed by a new generation of practitioners starting about the beginning of the new millennium.

Tiantai Museum, Tiantai (1999–2000) by Wang Lu is located about 200 kilometres from Shanghai on the coast of the East China Sea, a most important site in Chinese history containing the sixth-century Sui Dynasty Temple of Guoqing at the foot of the Tiantai Mountain, the cradle of the Tiantai sect of Buddhism, and a number of other significant buildings. Many famous Chinese calligraphers and poets have left inscriptions on the mountain. The museum houses a collection of scrolls and other cultural treasures. Wang Lu avoided the pursuit of a historicist/regionalist 'Chinese national style'. He chose instead to understand what problems are presented when a new structure is inserted into a region with a rich but fragile natural and cultural environment. The building was 'embedded' in the landscape 'through discovering, adjusting and restoring' the 'relationship and texture' of 'the past and the future'. The scheme reused the low-profile *hutong* courtyard type,

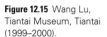

Figure 12.15 Wang Lu, Tiantai Museum, Tiantai (1999–2000).

which is certainly most felicitous for any museum. The surface of the building was also carefully designed, rough-hewn stones of local granite being chosen and given a deliberately a rough, natural feel.

The Zhuantang Campus of the China Academy of Art, Hangzhou, China (2002–2004) by Wang Shu – whose firm is called 'Amateur Architects' in the belief that 'spontaneously, illegally and temporarily constructed architecture by an amateur architect is equal to professional architecture' – was conceived as a town nestled in a landscape. Each of the buildings is a variation on the template of the regional courtyard house. The scheme is in 'continuity' with its environment, to quote the Ernesto Rogers expression, in space, each building being positioned at the foot of the Xiangshan (Elephant) Mountain in such a way that it enters into a different dialogue with the mountain.

In the project, the materials and techniques were chosen in order to minimize 'long-term adverse effects on the natural environment'. This is an additional reason why, instead of employing new materials, Wang Shu preserved and reused 2 million old tiles and bricks from all over Shejiang Province in dialogue with the memory of the old, now demolished structures that once stood in the region. He reported that after the buildings had gone up, the environment recovered.

> The streams, earth dams and fish ponds originally on the hillside were restored. Soil from desilting was used for land covering around buildings. Reeds were replanted on the sides of streams and ponds. The new campus turns Zhuantang from an edge condition to a newly central place with a sense of belonging and carries on the local construction tradition. In a sense it is the rebirth of Xiangshan Hill.

Figure 12.16 Wang Shu, one building of the China Academy of Art campus in Hangzhou (2000–2004).

Similar ideas lay behind the design process and form of his museum in Ningbo. Once more

> I collected and recycled building materials from the area in the eastern part of this province, near the sea, people suffer from typhoons, which cause many houses to collapse. They don't have a lot of time to rebuild them, so they put the bricks back together randomly. I find the resulting architecture very beautiful.[18]

As in his previous educational project, the Yuhu Primary School in Lijang in southwest China, and in the 'Bridge School' in Xiashi, Li Xiaodong created an original and seminal project in a peripheral country community. The project bridges the two parts of the small village. Each part is a *toulou* – a large, circular traditional residential building – sitting on one side of a small stream that divides the village. Its structure consists of two steel trusses that span the stream, with the space between containing the compact multipurpose educational facility. The structure reconnected the village, generating on each side an interstitial social place in front of each *toulou*, which historically have been inward-looking fortresses. The resulting in-between public places can be used informally on an everyday basis or on special days as areas for festivities, one side of the school opening up to offer a stage for performances. While the construction scheme and the details are cutting-edge contemporary, the irregular geometry of the circulation paths across the water draws from traditional Chinese precedents, the discipline, grace, and freedom of Zhang Chih's Grass Style calligraphy.

Figure 12.17 Li Xiaodong, Bridge School, Xiashi, Fujian Province (2010).

Most importantly, the project, as a articulated volume but also as an urban intervention, not only is congruent with the physical environment and the way of living of the village but also acts as a vital force for regenerating its cultural, social, and economic life. As one can see already happening, the new building has engendered a feeling of community and hope for the future among the inhabitants of this small rural community.

Like the Bridge School, a project in Daze Village, Linchi, Tibet (2009), designed by 'Standardarchitecture', a Chinese firm founded by Zhang Ke in 2001,[19] focuses on problems where contextual, regional constraints – environmental and cultural – invite highly innovative inventions.

The small tourist facility, designed by Zhang Ke, the principal of the firm, and Zhao Yang, the designer in charge of it, serves as a welcoming place for visitors intending to explore the Brahmaptra Canyon, the unique terrain and landscape of the Niyang River. In contrast to the Bridge School, the construction technology is based on local materials and regional Tibetan techniques of making a timber roof resting on stone load-bearing wall.

Rather than conforming to the contours of the surrounding landscape, as in a 'picturesque' design, this Tibetan building by Zhang Ke and Zhao Yang 'echoes' the environment through its irregularly shaped configuration and engages in a 'dialogue' with the region. One might compare this approach with that of Le Corbusier in designing the chopped and 'carved' space of Ronchamp Chapel. The designer of the center considered color to be an important aspect of Tibetan visual culture. He decided to paint the stone surfaces of the interior public space of the building using local mineral pigments. In addition, the color interacts with the sunlight penetrating the building, and the sun's changing positions mark with their hue the hours of the day. The designer insisted that there was no symbolism in the choice and combination of the colors, which enhance sensual appreciation not only of the building but also, through the building, of the surrounding landscape.

In contrast to the significant but rather small-scale projects located in remote rural areas we have discussed so far in this chapter, the projects designed by Yu Kongjian, a landscape architect but also designer of buildings, are large-scale developments, very often next to dense urban areas.[20] He has called his approach to design the radical 'Big Foot' (as opposed to the 'Small Foot' which women with bound feet once had). His reaction to tradition was the result not of a simple-minded desire for modernization, which is often

Figure 12.18 Zhang Ke and Standardarchitecture in cooperation with Zhaoyang Studio, Niyang River Visitor Center, Daze Village, Linchi, Tibet (2009).

encountered in the construction of the cities of new China, but of a deep worry about the future of the ecological environment of the country and the world. Responding to this problem, Yu offered one of the most up-to-date redefinitions of regionalism.

Yu returned to fundamental questions about the impact of 'the big number' put forth by the generation of 1956 immediately after World War II. While at that time the focus was to provide shelter, Yu turned to the total environment. As he pointed out, 65 percent of China's 1.3 billion people will live in cities within twenty years. Two-thirds of the 662 Chinese cities lack sufficient water, and all urban and suburban rivers are polluted. Each year, 3,500 square kilometers of land is lost to the desert and 5 billion tonnes of soil erodes into the ocean. In fifty years, 50 percent of China's wetlands will have disappeared and 40 percent of the surviving wetlands will be polluted. Taking into consideration these figures is not merely an option but is the heart of the identity of contemporary design, the framework redefining the idea of region and regionalism.

Not surprisingly, Yu Kongjian is vehemently opposed to projects such as Rem Koolhaas's China Central Television Headquarters, projects that have mushroomed in the Chinese cities with no consideration of cost and, more importantly, of their impact on the environment, ecological and cultural, built as if without context in a desert and turning one of the most important human centers into a desert. Characteristically, another European architect, also building mega-projects in Beijing, called sustainability a 'boring issue'.

Born a peasant's son, Yu Kongjian grew up working in agricultural fields. Land was both part of the daily life and the source of livelihood. His hometown is situated in the heart of Zhejiang Province, a region famous for its scenic mountain-water and its richness in vernacular architecture. Educated in China and at Harvard as a designer and as a scholar (receiving his Doctor of Design in 1995), he begun practicing in China in 1997, researching and teaching as a professor at Beijing University. In his investigations, he has tried to synthesize knowledge drawn from modern as well as traditional design methodology; his first book, *Tracing the Origin of Ideal Landscapes: The Cultural Meanings of Feng-shui and Ideal Landscape* (1998), deals with traditional landscape theory in China.

A typical problem that Yu faced was the recuperation of a site as Red Ribbon on a Garbage Dump, Qinghuangdao, Hebei Province (2008), a deserted garbage dump and slum area along the banks of the Tanghe River, on the eastern urban fringe of Qinhuangdao. The solution called for a minimal intervention achieving a dramatic improvement: a multifunctional 'red ribbon', made out of fiber steel, lit from the inside, spanning half a kilometer for lighting and seating, and the same time acting as a piece of environmental art. Four pavilions in the shape of clouds were distributed across the ribbon; 'various plant specimens are grown in strategically placed holes', and along it four perennial flower gardens of white, yellow, purple and blue act as a patchwork on what were formerly open fields, and turn the deserted garbage dumps and slum sites into attractions.

The Red Ribbon was a relatively small-scale project of relatively low complexity, demonstrating the direction of a therapeutic regionalist work. Most of Yu's design projects are on a larger scale but the tasks remains the

Figure 12.19 Yu Kongjian, Red Ribbon on a Garbage Dump, Qinghuangdao, Hebei Province (2008).

same. The Shanghai Houtan Park is also therapeutic but at the same time it advanced development. It involved recovering and reinvigorating the degraded waterfront of a former industrial site, constructing the wetland, controlling the ecological flood, a 'living machine' to treat contaminated water from the Huangpu River, and bringing in urban agriculture. At the same time, the project was a reflective, critical exercise. It was intended to demonstrate to the 2010 Expo visitors what 'green technologies' can do for the world we live in – in the words of the designer, how 'ecological infrastructure can provide multiple services for society and nature', and how productive landscape can evoke memories of the past and thinking about the future of ecological civilization.

Coda

Our historical overview has shown that from the Roman Empire to our contemporary era of globalization, there are two constants of regionalism. One is the opposition to global systems, such as classical architecture and, more recently, the International Style; and the other is an adherence to the individual identity of regions. The overview has also established that regionalism has a variable. This variable is a function of the succession of dissimilar political and cultural movements that have recruited it as their own.

During the past two centuries, for instance, regionalism became deeply involved with nationalist movements, to the degree that it became synonymous with them, providing settings for the construction of make-believe national identities and real national state-building. But through its ability to fabricate imagined worlds, it has also been employed to advance commerce, building 'as if' sceneries in emporia, fairs, for-profit residences, and sham tourist paradises. In both senses it has been used to 'retribalize' people, fenced them into 'ghost communities', or trapped them in phantom worlds of consumerism.

But during the same period, regionalism has also been involved in developing an environmental and ecological view of the world and has helped identify the long-range and long-term impact of globalization in architecture, threatening cultural and ecological diversity.

Our final chapter showed how *critical regionalism* emerged after World War II as a reaction to a new wave of globalization related to the brute force of vast programs of reconstruction and urban renewal of the time. In an effort to create intelligent structures better adapted to the region, to environmental resources, and to cultural constraints, it reused and reinterpreted the precedents of local architecture, and forestalled the nationalist and commercial trappings of past uses of regionalism.

To this end, critical regionalism tried to develop an architecture that raised an awareness of reality instead of hypnotic illusions. It proceeded by making traditional regional elements appear strange rather than nostalgic and familiar.

On the other hand, as new nations have emerged out of disintegrating post-Cold War states, the idea of a 'national style' to express identity is still being discussed. We believe that these discussions are of diminishing significance.[1] The priority of these new states is to resolve problems that threaten their survival, political conflicts caused by their suppressed, unrecognized minorities, and economic crises caused by their inability to match their legal autarky with economic independence.

Finally, the major question confronting these states – indeed, all states around the world – this century is, next to the unprecedented world ecological and economic crises, the flattening of the world's natural and cultural diversity. This loss of diversity cannot be resolved by taking for granted boundaries between regions defined according to the old 'Westphalia' criteria of sovereignty. Within this perspective, regions must be redefined in terms of their unique resources and particular constraints. Rather than being subordinated and flattened by globalization, regions should be embedded in a world system of complex interdependencies that are physical, social, cultural, and, above all today, ecological.

Notes

Preface: The Never-Ending Challenge of Regionalism

1   A. Tzonis, L. Lefaivre, and A. Alofsin, 'Die Frage des Regionalismus', in M. Andritzky, L. Burckhardt, and O. Hoffmann (eds) *Für eine andere Architektur*, vol. 1, Frankfurt am Main, 1981.
2   Eric Hobsbawm, *Nations and Nationalism since 1780: Programme, Myth, Reality*, Cambridge, 1990.

Introduction: The End of Geography?

1   Thomas Friedman, *The World Is Flat: A Brief History of the Twenty-First Century*, New York, 2005.
2   Walter Christaller, *Die zentralen Orte in Süddeutschland*, Jena, 1933.
3   Lösch's 'law of minimum effort' (1954) and Zipf's 'principle of least effort': George Kingsley Zipf, *Human Behavior and the Principle of Least Effort*, Boston, 1949.
4   Among the seminal studies taking into account modern types of transportation were C. Hammer and F. C. Iklé, 'Intercity Telephone and Airborn Traffic Related to Distance and the "Propensity to Interact"', *Sociometry*, vol. 20, no. 4, 1957, pp. 306–316; and Wesley H. Long, 'City Characteristics and the Demand for Interurban Air Travel', *Land Economics*, vol. 44, no. 2, 1968, pp. 197–204; and, on how cities interact in space, John Q. Stewart and William Warntz, 'Physics of Population Distribution' *Journal of Regional Sciences*, vol. 1, 1958, pp. 99–121.
5   Immanuel Wallerstein, *The Modern World-System*, New York, 1974.

1 The Regional and the Classical Imperial

1   Plutarch, *De Malignate Herodoti*, 12.1.
2   Alexander Tzonis and Phoebe Giannisi, *Classical Greek Architecture: The Construction of the Modern*, Paris, 2004.
3   T. Hamlin, *Architecture through the Ages*, New York, 1940.
4   M. Heidegger, *Aufenthalte*, Frankfurt am Main, 1989.
5   Jean-Pierre Vernant, *Mythe et pensée chez les Grecs: études de psychologie historique*, Paris, 1965.
6   Peregrine Horden and Nicholas Purcell, *The Corrupting Sea*, Oxford, 2000, p. 275.
7   A. M. Snodgrass, *Archaeology and the Rise of the Greek State*, New York, 1977.
8   C. M. Antonaccio, 'Placing the Past: The Bronze Age in the Cultic Topography of Early Greece', in S. E. Alcock and R. Osborne (eds) *Placing the Gods: Sanctuaries and Sacred Space in Ancient Greece*, Oxford, 1994.
9   F. de Polignac, *La Naissance de la cité grecque*, 1995.
10 C. Morgan, 'The Archaeology of Sanctuaries', in L. G. Mitchell and P. J. Rhodes (eds) *The Development of the Polis in Archaic Greece*, London, 1997.
11 J. Strauss Clay, *The Politics of Olympus: Form and Meaning in the Major Homeric Hymns*, London, 1989.
12 Alexander Tzonis and Liane Lefaivre, *Classical Architecture*, Cambridge, MA, 1986; Alexander Tzonis and Phoebe Giannisi, *Classical Greek Architecture: The Construction of the Modern*, Paris, 2004.
13 John E. Ziolkowski, 'National and Other Contrasts in the Athenian Funeral Orations', in H. A. Khan (ed). *The Birth of the European Identity: The Europe–Asia Contrast in Greek Thought, 490–322 B.C.*, Nottingham, 1994.

Notes

2 The First Regionalist Building-Manifesto

1   W. S. Heckscher, 'Relics of Pagan Antiquity in Mediæval Settings', *Journal of the Warburg Institute*, vol. 1, pp. 204–220, 1937–1938. The Casa dei Crescenzi is also discussed in R. Weiss, *The Renaissance Discovery of Classical Antiquity*, Oxford, 1973, p. 10. See also Richard Krautheimer, *Rome, Profile of a City, 312–1308*, Princeton, NJ, 1980.
2   Krautheimer, *Rome, Profile of a City*, pp. 120–121.
3   L. Heydenreich, 'Der Palazzo baronale der Colonna in Palestrina', in G. Kauffmann and W. Sauerlände (eds) *Walter Friedländer zum 90. Geburtstag*, Berlin, 1965, p. 87. See also the excellent M. Calvesi, *Il sogno di Polifilo prenestino*, Rome, 1983, especially pp. 34–65.
4   Krautheimer, *Rome, Profile of a City*, p. 198.
5   Rosalind B. Brooke, *The Coming of the Friars*, London, 1975.

3 A Flat Archipelago of Garden-Villas

1   David R. Coffin, *Gardens and Gardening in Papal Rome*, Princeton, NJ, 1991, p. 7.
2   Ibid., p. 61.
3   Alexander Tzonis and Liane Lefaivre, *Classical Architecture*, Cambridge, MA, 1984.
4   Coffin, *Gardens and Gardening*, p. 165.
5   Ibid., p. 71.
6   Anthony Blunt, *Philibert de l'Orme*, London, 1958.
7   Liane Lefaivre and Alexander Tzonis, *The Emergence of Modern Architecture: A Documentary History, from 1000 to 1800*, London, 2004.
8   Philibert de l'Orme, *The First Volume of Architecture*, 1567–1648.
9   Boris Porchnev, *Les Soulèvements populaires en France au XVIIe siècle*, Paris, 1972.
10 Roland Mousnier, *Fureurs paysannes: les paysans dans les révoltes du XVIIe siècle (France, Russie, Chine)*, Paris, 1968.
11 Erik Orsenna, *Le Portrait d'un homme heureux: Le Nôtre*, Paris, 2000.
12 Lefaivre and Tzonis, *The Emergence of Modern Architecture*.

4 'Consult the Genius of the Place in All'

1   Joseph Addison, *Spectator*, no. 69, May 19, 1711.
2   Liane Lefaivre and Alexander Tzonis, *The Emergence of Modern Architecture: A Documentary History, from 1000 to 1800*, London, 2004.
3   William Temple, *Spectator*, no. 414, June 25, 1712, Lefaivre and Tzonis, *The Emergence of Modern Architecture*, p. 273.
4   Lawrence Stone, *The Crisis of Aristocracy, 1588–1641*, Oxford, 1965, p. 15.
5   Pevsner was in of the first art historians to stress the political significance of the Picturesque: N. Pevsner, 'The Genesis of the Picturesque', *Architectural Review*, vol. 96, 1944, pp. 139–146.
6   William Mason, *The English Garden in Four Books*, 1772–1781, corrected edition 1783.

5 From the Decorated Farm to the Rise of Nationalist Regionalism

1   Fiske Kimball, *The Creation of the Rococo*, Philadelphia, 1943.
2   See Charles Nicolas Cochin, quoted in Liane Lefaivre and Alexander Tzonis, *The Emergence of Modern Architecture: A Documentary History, from 1000 to 1800*, London, 2004, p. 341.
3   See the J.-F. Blondel quotation in Lefaivre and Tzonis, *The Emergence of Modern Architecture*, p. 327.
4   Kimball, *The Creation of the Rococo*.
5   Jean Bodin, *Les Six Livres de la république*, 1576.
6   Lefaivre and Tzonis, *The Emergence of Modern Architecture*.
7   Johann Jacob Volkmann, *Neueste Reisen durch England*, 1782.
8   Alexander Pope, *Moral Essays: Epistle to Lord Burlington*, 1731; Lefaivre and Tzonis, *The Emergence of Modern Architecture*, p. 300.
9   W. D. Robson-Scott, *The Literary Background of the Gothic Revival in Germany*, Oxford, 1965.
10 Horace Walpole, *The History of the Modern Taste in Gardening*, 1771–1780.
11 Volkmann, *Neueste Reisen durch England*; John Alexander Kelly, *England and the Englishman in German Literature of the Eighteenth Century*, New York, 1921.

12 Justus Möser, *Patriotische Phantasien*, 1774–1778, Jerry Z. Muller, *The Mind and the Market: Capitalism in Modern European Thought*, New York, 2002; Jonathan B. Knudsen, *Justus Möser and the German Enlightenment*, Cambridge, 1986.

13 Lefaivre and Tzonis, *The Emergence of Modern Architecture*.

14 Robson-Scott, *The Literary Background of the Gothic Revival*, p. 80.

6 From Regions to Nation

1   Johann Gottfried von Herder, *Materials for the Philosophy of the History of Mankind*, 1784; Herder, *Ideen zur Philosophie*, 1784–1791; Herder, *Outlines of a Philosophy of the History of Man*, transl. T. O. Churchill, London, 1800, abridged as *Reflections on the Philosophy of the History of Mankind*, ed. Frank E. Manuel, Chicago, 1968.

2   Ibid.

3   Ibid.

4   Ibid.

5   Ibid.

6   Ibid.

7   Ibid.

8   Lionel Gossman, *Medievalism and the Ideologies of the Enlightenment: The World and Work of La Curne de Sainte-Palaye*, Baltimore, 1968.

9   J. Godechot, *La Grande Nation 1789–1799: l'expansion de la France dans le monde de 1789 à 1799*, Paris, 1981, vol. 1, p. 254.

10 Alexis de Tocqueville, *L' Ancien Régime et la révolution*, 1856.

11 Jacques Godechot, *The Counter-revolution: Doctrine and Action 1789–1804*, Princeton, NJ, 1981; Florence Gauthier, *La Voie paysanne dans la Révolution française: l'exemple de la Picardie*, Paris, 1977.

12 Karl Deutsch, *Nationalism and Its Alternatives*, New York, 1969.

13 *Views of the Lower Rhine, from Brabant, Flanders, Holland, England, and France in April, May and June*, three volumes, 1790.

14 In the entries 'Baukunst', 1792, and later in 'Kirche', 1796, in *Enzyklopädie*, 1792–1798; W. D. Robson-Scott, *The Literary Background of the Gothic Revival in Germany*, Oxford, 1965.

15 Robson-Scott, *The Literary Background of the Gothic* Revival, p. 245.

16 Ibid., p. 306.

7 Gothic Communalism and Nationalist Regionalism

1   Augustus Welby Northmore Pugin, *The True Principles of Pointed or Christian Architecture*, 1814, p. 61.

2   John Ruskin, 'The Lamp of Memory', in *Seven Lamps of Architecture*, London, 1849.

3   Nikolaus Pevsner, in the 1969 Walter Neurath Memorial Lecture, 'Ruskin and Viollet-Le-Duc'.

4   Liane Lefaivre and Alexander Tzonis, *The Emergence of Modern Architecture: A Documentary History, from 1000 to 1800*, London, 2004, pp. 411, 442, 444, 456.

5   Dora Wiebenson and J. Sisa, *The Architecture of Historic Hungary*, Cambridge, MA, 1998.

6   Ibid.

7   François Loyer and Bernard Toulier (eds) *Le Régionalisme: architecture et identité*, Paris, 2001.

8   J. Wright, *The Regionalist Movement in France, 1890–1914: Jean Charles-Brun and French Political Thought*, Oxford, 2003.

9   Frédéric Mistral, *Mes origines: mémoires et récits de Frédéric Mistral*, 1915–1925.

10 Maurice Barrès, *La Terre et les morts: sur quelles réalités fonder la conscience française*, troisième conférence, 1899.

11 Wright, *The Regionalist Movement in France*.

8 Homelands, World Fairs, Living-Spaces, and the Regional Cottage

1   Celia Applegate, *A Nation of Provincials: The German Idea of Heimat*, Berkeley, CA, 1990.

2   *Bund Heimatschutz Zweck im Schutz der deutsche[n] Heimat in ihrer natürlichen und geschichtlich gewordenen Eigenart*, 1904; Christian Otto, 'Modern Environment and Historical Continuity: Heimatschutz Discourse in Germany', *Art Journal*, vol. 43, no. 2, 1983, pp. 148–157; Winfried Nerdinger (ed.) *Architektur, Macht, Erinnerung.*, Munich, 2011.

Notes

3 Eric Storm, 'Region-Building in Stone: Nationalism, Regionalism and Architecture in Germany, France and Spain (1900–1920), Working Paper, Leiden, 2007; Eric Storm, 'Regionalism in History, 1890–1945: The Cultural Approach', *European History Quarterly*, vol. 33, no. 2, 2003, pp. 251–265.

4 Ernst Haeckel, *Generelle Morphologie der Organismen* (General morphology of organisms), 1866; Jost Hermand, 'Rousseau, Goethe, Humboldt', in Joachim Wolschke-Bulman (ed.) *Nature and Ideology: Natural Garden Design in the Twentieth Century*, Washington, DC, 1977; J. Hermand, *Old Dreams of a New Reich: Volkish Utopias and National Socialism*, Bloomingtom, IN, 1992.

5 P. Vidal de la Blache, *Tableau de la géographie de la France*, Paris, 1903; P. Vidal de la Blache, 'Pays de France', *Réforme Sociale*, vol. 48, no. 8, 1904, pp. 333–344; P. Vidal de la Blache, 'Les Régions françaises', *Revue de Paris*, December 15, 1910; P. Claval, *Introduction à la géographie régionale*, Paris, 1992; P. Claval, *Histoire de la géographie française de 1870 à nos jours*, Paris, 1998; P. Claval, *La Géographie du XXIe siècle*, Paris, 2003.

6 Mark Crinson, *Empire Building, Orientalism and Victorian Architecture*, London, 1996.

7 Gwendolyn Wright, *The Politics of Design in French Colonial Urbanism*, Chicago, 1991.

8 Paul Rabinow, *French Modern: Norms and Forms of the Social Environment*, Chicago, 1989.

9 Samuel Phillips, *Guide to the Crystal Palace and Park*, 1854: Paul Greenhalgh, *Ephemeral Vistas: The Expositions Universelles, Great Expositions and World's Fairs, 1851–1939*, Manchester, 1988.

10 Alfred Normand, *L'Architecture des nations étrangères: étude sur les principales constructions du parc à l'Exposition universelle de Paris*, 1867.

11 Ibid.

12 Alberto Villar Movelan, *Arquitectura del regionalismo en Sevilla (1900–1935)*, Seville, 2010; M. Trillo de Leyva, *La Exposición Iberoamericana: la transformación urbana de Sevilla*, Seville, 1980.

13 Philip Whalen, 'Burgundian Regionalism and French Republican Commercial Culture at the 1937 Paris Exposition', *Cultural Analysis*, vol. 6, 2007, pp. 31–62; Shanny L. Peer, *French Uses of Folklore: The Reinvention of Folklore in the 1937 International Exposition*, Bloomington, IN, 1989; Shanny L. Peer, *France on Display: Peasants, Provincials, and Folklore in the 1937 Paris World's Fair*, Albany, NY, 1998; Peter Feldman, 'Unity in Identity, Disunity in Execution: Expressions of French National Identity at the 1937 Paris World's Fair', *Penn History Review*, vol. 15, no. 1, 2007.

14 Jean-Paul Vigato, *L'Architecture régionaliste en France, 1890–1950*, Paris, 1994, p. 323.

15 Margaret Richardson, *Architects of the Arts and Crafts Movement*, London, 1983.

16 *Fortnightly Review*, March 1903.

17 Celia Applegate, 'A Europe of Regions: Reflections on the Historiography of Sub-national Places in Modern Times', *American Historical Review*, vol. 104, no. 4, 1999, pp. 1157–1182; Anthony D. Smith, *Nationalism and Modernism: A Critical Survey of Recent Theories of Nations and Nationalism*, London, 1998; Heinz-Gerhard Haupt, Michael G. Muller, and Stuart Woolf (eds) *Regional and National Identities in Europe in the XIXth and XXth Centuries*, Alphen aan den Rijn, the Netherlands, 1998.

9 International Style versus Regionalism

1 Lewis Mumford, *Sticks and Stones: American Architecture and Civilization*, New York, 1924.

2 Franz Schulze, *Philip Johnson, Life and Work*, New York, 1994, pp. 102–160. He in turn refers to Michael Sorkin's article 'Where Was Philip?', *Spy*, October 1988, pp. 138–1940, reprinted in his *Exquisite Corpse*, as the original source for this information.

3 See Elizabeth Mock, *Built in USA*, New York, 1947. This is the source for the chronology of all the exhiitions mentioned in the next few paragraphs (pp. 124–128).

4 Liane Lefaivre and Alexander Tzonis, 'Lewis Mumford's Regionalism', *Design Book Review*, vol. 19, Winter 1991, pp. 20–25; Liane Lefaivre and Alexander Tzonis, 'Tropical Lewis Mumford: The First Critical Regionalist Urban Planner', in Doug Kelbaugh and Kit Krankel McCullough (eds) *Writing Urbanism*, London, 2008; Lewis Mumford, 'The Regionalism of Richardson', in *The South in Architecture*, New York, 1941, reproduced in Mumford's *Roots of Contemporary American Architecture*, New York, 1952.

5   Lewis Mumford, 'Report on Honolulu', in *City Development*, New York, 1945.

6   Lewis Mumford, *City Development*, 1945, p. 77.

7   Ibid., p. 95.

8   Ibid., pp. 89–90.

9   The first studies of the introduction of regionalism to the Museum of Modern Art are in Liane Lefaivre and Alexander Tzonis, 'The Suppression and Rethinking of Regionalism and Tropicalism after 1945', in Alexander Tzonis, Liane Lefaivre, and Bruno Stagno (eds), *Tropical Architecture: Critical Regionalism in the Age of Globalization*, Chichester, UK, 2001, and in Liane Lefaivre, 'The Post War Suppression of Regionalism', in Liane Lefaivre and Alexander Tzonis, *Critical Regionalism Architecture and Identity in a Globalized World*, Munich, 2003. See also Keith Eggener's subsequent 'John McAndrew, the Museum of Modern Art, and the "Naturalization" of Modern Architecture in America, ca. 1940', in Peter Herrle and Erik Wegerhoff (eds), *Architecture and Identity*, Berlin, 2008.

10 John McAndrews, *Guide to Modern Architecture: North East States*, New York, 1940.

11 Elizabeth Mock mentions the street protests in her introduction to *Built in the USA since 1932*. See the next note.

12 There seems to be some discrepancy here. The MoMA Staff List, under Kassler, Elizabeth Bauer (Elizabeth Bauer Mock) mentions that her tenure was between 1942 and 1946. *Made in USA since 1932*, however, lists her as curator from 1943 on (see p. 128).

13 Catherine Bauer mentions that Elizabeth Mock is her sister in 'Bauer Speaks Her Mind', *Forum*, March 1946, p. 116.

14 In *The South in Architecture*, New York, 1941.

15 All the data concerning the exhibitions mentioned in the previous section are in *Built in USA since 1932*, edited by Elizabeth Mock, foreword by Philip L. Goodwin, New York, 1945, pp. 124–126.

16 Elizabeth Mock, *Built in USA since 1932*, New York, 1945. Translated into German as *In USA Erbaut 1932–44*, Wiesbaden, 1948.

17 See MoMA archive, Box 34 (1).

18 Concerning purely technical matters, more specifically, Mock chided Johnson and Hitchcock for not following a European model such as Richard Neutra's example in *Wie baut America* (How America Builds) of 1927, which had lauded the development of light steel and wood construction in the United States, and she praised Buckminster Fuller's Dymaxion house for its light construction.

19 Philip Goodwin, *Brazil Builds*, New York, 1943.

20 Bernard Rudofsky, *Architecture without Architects*, New York, 1964.

21 The first treatment of this subject is Zilah Quezado Deckker, *Brazil Built: The Architecture of the Modern Movement in Brazil*, London, 2001. Quezado, however, sees the exhibition as a continuation of the exhibition policies of Johnson and Hitchcock.

22 About the Good Neighbor policy, see Thomas Skidmore, *Politics in Brazil, 1930–1964*, Oxford, 2007 (first published 1967), pp. 44–46.

23 The quotes are from Goodwin, *Brazil Builds*, p. 98.

24 Jerzy Soltan, 'A Letter to Eduard F. Sekler: Reminiscences of Post-war Modernism at CIAM and the GSD', in Alexander von Hoffman (ed.), *Form, Modernism and History: Essays in Honor of Eduard Sekler*, Cambridge, MA, 1996. On p. 95, Soltan writes: 'Corbu himself being not available … guess who was at the top of the list? It was Brazilian architect Oscar Niemeyer. Again an unattainable aim! O. Niemeyer, considered a "registered" member of the Brazilian communist party, was off limits, not politically correct for the U.S., particularly in the fifities!'. The second on the list was Ernesto Rogers, who was 'not available'.

25 According to the architectural historian Franz Schulze, 'Whether she liked it or not, Mock was about to be gentled into the departmental shade. Philip recalled a luncheon he had had with her and Barr at which, by his own admission, he so pointedly ignored her that she was almost reduced to tears. She evidently never had a chance.' In his *Philip Johnson, Life and Work*, New York, 1994, p. 34.

26 Lewis Mumford, 'Sky Line', *New Yorker*, October 1947. We first mentioned this article in relation to critical regionalism in Alexander Tzonis and Liane Lefaivre, 'Die Frage des Regionalismus', in M. Andritsky, L. Burckhardt, and O. Hoffman (eds), *Für eine andere Architektur*, vol. 1, Frankfurt, 1981.

27 Lewis Mumford, *New Yorker*, October 11, 1947.

28 Paul Schultze-Naumburg *Uhu*, no. 7 (April 1926), pp. 30–40.

29 All quotations from pp. 12–18.

30 See Edgar Kaufmann Jr, 'What Is Happening to Modern Architecture?', *Arts and Architecture*, vol. 66, no. 9, September 1949, pp. 26–29.

31 Quoted in Stanford Anderson, 'The "New Empiricism–Bay Region Axis": Kay Fisker and Postwar Debates on Functionalism, Regionalism, and Monumentality', *Journal of Architectural Education*, vol. 50, no. 3, 1997, pp. 197–207 at p. 204.

32 Sigfried Giedion, 'A Decade of New Architecture', in *A Decade of New Architecture*, 1951, pp. 1–3.

33 pp. 16–17.

34 p. 17.

35 pp. 13–14.

36 p. 13.

37 In particular, the article of 1938 in which Mumford criticized monumentality.

38 See George Dudley, *A Workshop for Peace: Designing the United Nations Headquarters*, Cambridge, MA, 1994.

39 Henry-Russell Hitchcock, 'The International Style, Twenty Years Later', *Architectural Record*, August 1951, pp. 89–97.

40 p. 92.

41 *Built in the U.S.A: Post-war Architecture*, edited by Henry-Russell Hitchcock and Arthur Drexler, New York, 1952, p. 8.

42 p. 9.

43 Mumford, *Sticks and Stones*. In criticizing the 1893 World's Columbian Exposition in Chicago, he accused it of projecting an 'imperial façade' which was the 'very cloak and costume' of 'an imperialist approach to the environment' (p. 29).

44 Frances Stonor Saunders, *The Cultural Cold War: The CIA and the World of Arts and Letters*, London, 1999; New York, 2000, p. 258.

45 About this concept, see Peter van Ham, 'The Rise of the Brand State: The Postmodern Politics of Image and Reputation', *Foreign Affairs*, vol. 80, no. 5, 2001, pp. 2–6.

46 For more details on the role of MoMA in American expansionist projects during the 1950s, see Saunders, *The Cultural Cold War*.

47 See *Guide to the Records of the Department of Circulating Exhibitions*, Museum of Modern Art Archives, Box 34.

48 An interesting, although isolated, documented case of the impact of this program in India is reported to me by Rahul Merohtra, who, growing up in Bombay in the 1950s, recalls himself, as well as his immediate family entourage, made up of architects, being positively impressed by the catalogue.

49 Anonymous, 'Architecture for the State Department', *Arts and Architecture*, vol. 70, pp. 16–18, 1953. Quoted in Jane Loeffler, *The Architecture of Diplomacy: Building America's Embassies*, New York, 1998, pp. 7 and 206.

50 p. 11.

51 Steffen de Rudder, 'Modernistic US Consulates in Germany: Instruments of Self-Expression', in R. Quek and D. Deane (eds) *Architecture, Design and Nation*, Proceedings of the First Theoretical Currents Conference, Nottingham Trent University, September 14–15, 2010, Nottingham.

52 Jane Loeffler, *The Architecture of Diplomacy*, Princeton, NJ, 1998, p. 88.

53 See René Spitz, *HFG Ulm: The View behind the Foreground. The Political History of the Ulm School of Design 1953–1968*, Stuttgart, 2002.

54 Henry-Russell Hitchcock, *Latin American Architecture since 1945*, New York, 1955. See John Loomis, *Revolution of Forms: Cuba's Forgotten Art Schools*, New York, 1999, pp. 9–10, for a similar view of Hitchcock's book.

55 Hitchcock, *Latin American Architecture*, pp. 13 and 9 respectively.

56 Ibid., p. 111.

57 Ibid., p. 61.

58 Ibid., p. 61.

59 Philip Johnson, *Mies van der Rohe*, New York, 1953.

10 Regionalism Rising

1 Lewis Mumford, 'Sky Line', *New Yorker*, September 22, 1951; Lewis Mumford, 'The UN Assembly: How Do Architects Like It?', *Architectural Forum*, vol. 97, December 1952, pp. 114–115.

2 Jane Loeffler, *The Architecture of Diplomacy: Building America's Embassies*, New York, 1998, p. 108.

3 Paul Rudolph, 'UN General Assembly', *Architectural Forum*, vol. 97, October 1952, pp. 144–145.

4 See Nicolas Quintana, quoted in 'IX Annual Conference of the Cuban Cultural Center of New York', in *Miamiartzine.com*, May 22, 2010 by Irne Sperber.

5 Roberto Segre, 'La Habana di Sert: CIAM, Ron y Cha Cha Cha', unpublished typescript quoted in Josep Rovira, *Josep Lluís Sert*, London, p. 186.

6 See Styliane Philippou, 'Vanity Modern in Pre-revolutionary Havana: Cuban Nation and Architecture Imagined in the USA', in R. Quek and D. Deane (eds), *Architecture, Design and the Nation*, Proceedings of the First Theoretical Currents Conference, Nottingham Trent University, September 14–15, 2010, Nottingham. See also J. L. Scarpacci, R. Segre, and M. Coyula, *Havana: Two Faces of the Antillean Metropolis*, Chapel Hill, NC, 1997.

7 Quoted in Rovira, *Josep Lluís Sert*, p. 182.

8 Meredith Clausen, *The Pan Am Building*, Cambridge, MA, 1996.

9 Susan L. Klaus, *Modern Arcadia: Frederick Law Olmsted Jr. and the Plan for Forest Hills*, Boston, 2004.

10 Donald Miller, *Lewis Mumford: A Life*, New York, 1989, p. 345.

11 Ludwig Hilberseimer, *The New Regional Pattern: Industries and Gardens, Workshops and Farms*, Chicago, 1949.

12 Roger Clark, *School of Design: The Kamphoefer Years 1948–1973*, Raleigh, NC, 2007.

13 See Miller, *Lewis Mumford*, p. 444.

14 See Norma Evenson, *Chandigarh*, Berkeley, CA, 1966.

15 Roger Clark, *School of Design*.

16 Ibid.

17 Ibid.

18 Mary Mix went on to write a classic regionalist typology of American domestic architecture, introduced by James Marston Fitch at Columbia, called *The American House*, New York, 1980.

19 Mary Mix, *Americanische Architektur seit 1947*, St. Gallen, Switzerland, 1951, cited in Frank Hartmuth, 'The Late Victory of Neues Bauen: German Architecture after World War II', *Rassegna*, vol. 15, no. 54/2, June 1993, pp. 58–67. In relation to Raymond's building in Pondicheri, see Pankaj vir Gupta, Christine Mueller, and Cyrus Samii, *Golconde: The Introduction of Modernism in India*, Laurel, MD, 2010.

20 For a full overview of Rudolph's regionalist practice at this time, see Christopher Domin and Joseph King, *Paul Rudolph: The Florida Houses*, Princeton, NJ, 2002.

21 Rudolph, quoted in Domin and King, p. 140. The article appeared in *Architecture d'Aujourd'hui*, March 1949.

22 See 'Rudolph and the Roof: How to Make a Revolution on a Small Budget', *House and Home*, June 1953, pp. 140–141, and Guy Rothenstein, 'Sprayed on Vinyl Plastic Sheeting', *Progressive Architecture*, July 1953, pp. 98–99. See also Christopher Domin and Joseph King, *Paul Rudolph: The Florida Houses*, New York, 2002.

23   Paul Rudolph, *Perspecta* 4, Yale University, 1957.

24   Paul Rudolph, 'Focus on Regionalism at the Gulf States Conference', *Architectural Record*, vol. 114, no. 5, 1953. Quoted in Domin and King, *Paul Rudolph*.

25   Harwell Hamilton Harris, 'Regionalism and Nationalism', *Student Publication of the School of Design as North Carolina State College*, vol. 14, no. 5, 1964–1965, p. 27. Quoted in Domin and King, *Paul Rudolph*, p. 139.

26   Lucy Lippard, *The Lure of the Local: Senses of Place in a Multicultural Society*, New York, 1997.

27   Gilles A. Tiberghien, *Land Art*, New York, 1995.

28   J. B. Jackson (writing under the pseudonym H. G. West), *Landscape*, vol. 1, 1951, pp. 29–30. The authorship is confirmed in Helen Lefkowitz Horowitz, 'J. B. Jackson and the Discovery of the American Landscape', in Helen Lefkowitz Horowitz, *Landscape in Sight: Looking at America*, New Haven, CT, 1997.

29   Peter van Ham, 'The Rise of the Brand State: The Postmodern Politics of Image and Reputation', *Foreign Affairs*, vol. 80, no. 5, 2001, pp. 2–6.

30   Sigfried Giedion, 'The New Regional Approach', *Architectural Record*, January 1954, reprinted in his *Architecture, You and Me*, Cambridge, MA, 1958.

31   Ibid.

32   Henrique Mindlin, *Modern Architecture in Brazil*, New York, 1956. Here Giedion writes an introduction that praises Brazilian architecture for its ability to deal with regionalist matters, such as the tropical climate and the interracial issues (pp. 17–18).

33   Pietro Belluschi, 'The Meaning of Regionalism in Architecture', *Architectural Record*, December 1955, p. 132.

34   Ibid.

35   Jane Loeffler, *The Architecture of Diplomacy*, Princeton, NJ, 1998, p. 9.

36   Sert Archive. Quoted in Rovina, *Josep Lluís Sert*, p. 325.

37   Loeffler, *The Architecture of Diplomacy*, p. 152.

38   'US Architecture Abroad', *Architectural Forum*, vol. 3, 1953, pp. 101–115.

39   Loeffler, *The Architecture of Diplomacy*, p. 179.

40   Ron Robin, *Enclaves of America: The Rhetoric of American Political Architecture Abroad, 1900–1965*, Princeton, NJ, 1992.

41   Samuel Isenstadt, 'Faith in a Better Future: Jose Lluís Sert's Baghdad Embassy', *Journal of Architectural Education*, vol. 50, February 1997, pp. 172–178.

42   Belluschi, 'The Meaning of Regionalism in Architecture', pp. 132–139.

43   Jane Loeffler, *Designing Diplomacy*, Princeton, NJ, 1998, p. 81.

44   *The Mies van der Rohe Archive*, vol. 17, general editor Alexander Tzonis, consulting editor Franz Schultz, New York, 1992.

45   For a description of the incident, see Thomas Hines, *Richard Neutra and the Search for Modern Architecture*, Oxford, 1982, p. 244.

46   See Martin Schwartz, *Architectureandthelight ofday.Blogspot.com*.

47   Alessandra Latour (ed.) *Louis I. Kahn: Writings, Lectures, Interviews*, New York, 1991, pp. 122–123.

48   Ibid.

49   Ibid.

50   Ibid., p. 125.

51   Annabel Jane Wharton, *Building the Cold War: Hilton International Hotels and Modern Architecture*, Chicago, 2001, p. 37.

52   Conrad Hilton, *Be My Guest*, Englewood Cliffs, NJ, 1957. Quoted in Wharton, *Building the Cold War*, p. 8.

53   Hilton, *Be My Guest*, quoted in Wharton, *Building the Cold War*, p. 9.

54   Zeynep Çelik, *Displaying the Orient: Architecture of Islam at Nineteenth-Century World's Fairs*, Berkeley, California, 1992.

55   See Nathaniel Owings, *The Spaces in Between: An Architect's Journey*, Boston, 1973, p. 104. Quoted in Wharton, *Building the Cold War*, p. 21.

56 Wharton, *Building the Cold War*, p. 26.

57 Quoted in Vincent Scully, 'The Athens Hilton: A Study in Vandalism', *Architectural Forum*, vol. 119, 1963, pp. 101–102.

58 Scully, 'The Athens Hilton'.

59 Lefteris Theodosis, ' "Containing" Baghdad: Constantinos Doxiadis's Program for a Developing Nation', in Pedro Azara (ed.) *Ciudad del Espejismo: Bagdad, de Wright a Venturi*, Barcelona, 2008, pp. 167–172.

60 Constantinos Doxiadis, 'The Rising Tide and the Planner', *Ekistics*, vol. 7, no. 39, January 1959, pp. 4–10 at p. 6. Quoted in Panayiota I. Pyla, 'Baghdad's Urban Restructuring, 1958', in Sandy Isenstadt and Kishwar Rizvi, *Modernism and the Middle East: Architecture and Politics in the Twentieth Century*, Seattle, 2008, pp. 97–115 at p. 99.

61 Panayota I. Pyla, 'Baghdad's Urban Restructuring, 1958: Aesthetics and Politics of Nation Building', in Isenstadt and Rzvi, *Modernism and the Middle East*, p. 107.

62 Doxiadis, 'The Rising Tide and the Planner', p. 6. Quoted in Pyla, 'Baghdad's Urban Restructuring, 1958', p. 99.

63 See John C. Harkness, *The Walter Gropius Archive*, vol 4, general editor Alexander Tzonis, New York, 1991, pp. 189–192; see also Mira Marefat, 'The Unversal University: How Bauhaus Came to Baghdad', in Azara (ed.) *Ciudad del Espejismo*, pp. 157–166. See also Gwendolyn Wright, 'Global Ambition and Local Knowledge', in Isenstadt and Rizi, *Modernism and the Middle East*, pp. 221–254, and especially Magus T. Bernhardsson, 'Visions of Iraq: Modernizing the Past in 1950s Baghdad', in Isenstadt and Rizvi, *Modernism and the Middle East*, pp. 82–96.

64 Ernesto Rogers, 'Architecture of the Middle East', *Casabella*, vol. 242, August 1960, p. vii. Quoted in Marefat, 'The Universal University'. Marefat argues that Gropius was applying 'Bauhaus principles' and no regionalism in his design, although all the evidence is to the contrary, in particular this statement by Rogers which she quotes.

65 Walter Gropius, 'Planning a University', *Christian Science Monitor*, April 2, 1958, p. 9. Quoted in Marefat, 'The Universal University', p. 164.

66 The Frank Lloyd Wright quotation is in Bernhardsson, 'Visions of Iraq', p. 88. The episode as it is presented here is borrowed from Bernhardsson's account. See also Mina Marefat, 'Wright's Baghdad', in Anthony Alofsin (ed.) *Frank Lloyd Wright: Europe and Beyond*, Berkeley, CA, 1999.

11 Regionalism Redefined

1 Immanuel Kant, *Critique of Pure Reason*, trans. N. Kemp Smith, New York, 1965; *Critique of Practical Reason*, trans. L. White Beck, Indianapolis and New York, 1956; *Critique of Judgement*, trans. J. H. Bernard, New York, 1974. 'Defamiliarization' was a term introduced by Victor Shklovsky, member of the Russian Formalist group in Russia and influential in the emergence of avant-garde literary experiments in the 1910s and 1920s. See his 'Art as Technique' (1917) in L. T. Lemon and M. Reis (trans.) *Russian Formalist Criticism: Four Essays*, Lincoln, NE, 1965. For the definition of the concepts 'critical' and 'defamiliarization', see also Alexander Tzonis and Liane Lefaivre, *Classical Architecture*, Cambridge, 1986; Alexander Tzonis and Liane Lefaivre, 'Critical Regionalism', in S. Amourgis (ed.) *Critical Regionalism*, Pomona, CA.

2 See also Theodor Adorno, *Kant's Critique of Pure Reason*, ed. R. Tiedermann, transl. R. Livingstone, Stanford, CA, 2000.

3 The best history of the movement is the exhibition catalogue *Brasil 1920–1950: De la antropofagia*, Instituto Valenciano de Arte Moderno, Centro Julio González, 26 October 2000 – 14 January 2001. For the connection between Niemeyer and the Anthropofagist movement, see Styliane Philippou, *Oscar Niemeyer: Curves of Irreverence*, London, 2008.

4 David Underwood, *Oscar Niemeyer and Free-Form Modernism*, New York, Braziller, 1994, p. 48.

5 Lina Bo Bardi, *Lina Bo Bardi*, Milan, 1994.

6 James Stirling, 'Regionalism and Modern Architecture', *Architect's Yearbook*, 1950.

7 Ibid., p. 27.

8 Jerzy Soltan in conversation with Alexander Tzonis over the course of many years.

9   Minnette de Silva, *Minnette de Silva: The Life and Work of an Asian Woman Architect*, vol. 1, Kandy, 1998. All quotations and illustrations here are taken from that book. See also Bo Bardi, *Lina Bo Bardi*.

10 See Ijlal Muzaffar, 'The Periphery Within: Modern Architecture and the Making of the Third World', PhD dissertation, MIT, 2008.

11 See Pankaj vir Gupta, Christine Mueller and Cyrus Samii, *Golconde: The Introduction of Modernism in India*, Laurel, MD, 2010.

12 Jane Drew and Maxwell Fry, *Tropical Architecture in the Humid Zone*, London, 1956.

13 This is confirmed by one of the former owners of one of the original houses. See Manthia Diawara, *Maison Tropicale* (a film), Maumaus, Lisbon, 2009.

14 de Silva, *Minnette de Silva*, p. 126.

15 Ibid., p. 94.

16 Ibid., p. 190.

17 Gautam Bhatia, *Laurie Baker: Life, Work, Writings*, Harmonsdworth, UK, 1991. See also Laurie Baker's homepage.

18 Hassan-Udin Kahn, *Charles Correa*, London, 1987.

19 John Loomis, *Revolution of Forms: Cuba's Forgotten Art Schools*, Princeton, NJ, 1999.

20 Alexander Tzonis, Liane Lefaivre and Bruno Stagno (eds), *Tropical Architecture: Critical Regionalism in an Age of Globalization*, Chichester, UK, 2001.

21 See Chapter 9 for more on Lyautey and Prost.

22 Noriaki Kurokawa, 'Architecture of the Road', *Kenshiku Bunka*, January 1963.

23 See Udo Kultermann, *New Directions in African Architecture*, London, 1969, and Nnamdi Elleh, 'Architecture and Nationalism in Africa, 1945–1994', in Okwui Enwezor (ed.) *The Short Century: Independence and Liberation Movements in Africa, 1945–1994*, Munich, 2001.

24 See Philip Bay, 'Three Tropical Design Paradigms', in Tzonis *et al.* (eds), *Tropical Architecture*. The article quotes Lee Kuan Yu on p. 231.

25 Lewis Mumford, *The Brown Decades: A Study of the Arts of America, 1865–1895*, New York, 1931.

26 See Rem Koolhaas's 'Singapore Songlines' in Rem Koolhaas and Bruce Mau, *S,M,L,XL*, New York, 1995, pp. 1011–1087. He does not deal with them as tropicalist buildings, however.

27 See our 'Beyond Monuments, beyond Zip-a-tone, into Space/Time: Contextualizing Shadrach Woods's Berlin Free University, a Humanist Architecture', in *Free University, Berlin: Candilis, Josic, Woods, Schiedhelm*, London, 1999.

28 Tay Kheng Soon, 'Environment and Nation Building', in *65–67 SPUR*, Singapore, 1967, pp. 43–48 at p. 46.

29 Ibid., p. 44.

30 Ibid., p. 43.

31 Kisho Kurakawa, *Kenchiku Bunka*, January 1963, pp. 37–42 at p. 37.

32 Jean-Jacques Rousseau, *Les Rêveries du promeneur solitaire*, Geneva, 1782.

33 Alexander Tzonis and Liane Lefaivre, 'Dimitris Pikionis. Régionaliste des années 50', *Le Moniteur Architecture AMC*, no. 99, June–July 1999, pp. 60–69; Alexander Tzonis and Liane Lefaivre, 'Pikionis and Transvisibility', *Thresholds*, vol. 19, 1999, pp. 15–21.

34 Artur Glikson, unpublished letter to Lewis Mumford, February 19, 1952. With the permission of Sophia Mumford and Andrew Glikson.

35 Andrew Glikson, unpublished tribute to his father, Artur Glikson, in *'Dialogues': A Photographic Album Presented as a Gift to Lewis Mumford (1895–1990) by Artur Glikson (1911–1966)*. With the permission of Andrew Glikson, 1990.

36 Lewis Mumford, *The City in History*, Harmondsworth, UK, 1961. Graphic section 1, plates 10–12.

37 Izumi Kuroishi, 'Kon Wajiro: A Quest for the Architecture as a Container of Everyday Life', dissertation, January 1, 1998.

38 Arata Isozaki, *Japan-ness in Architecture*, Cambridge, MA, 2006, p. 11.

39 David B. Stewart, *The Making of a Modern Japanese Architecture*, Tokyo, 1987, pp. 1–129.

40 Isozaki, *Japan-ness in Architecture*.
41 Ibid., p. 17.

12 Regionalism Now

1 Alexander Tzonis, Liane Lefaivre and Richard Diamond, *Architecture in North America since 1960*, London, 1995.
2 '1975–1981: Years of Conflict', in Luis Fernández Galiano (ed.), *Spain Builds: Arquitectura en España 1975–2005*, Madrid, pp. 52–63.
3 Alexander Tzonis and Liane Lefaivre, 'El regionalismo crítico y la arquitectura española actual', *Arquitectura y Vivienda*, vol. 3, 1985, pp. 4–19.
4 Liane Lefaivre and Alexander Tzonis, 'Mick Pearce: Redefining Tropicalism as an Architecture of Diversity', *Prince Claus Fund Journal*, December 2003.
5 Ken Yeang, *The Green Skyscraper: The Basis for Designing Ecological Sustainable Buildings*, I999.
6 Philip Bay, *Towards a More Robust and Holistic Precedent Knowledge for Tropical Design: Semi-open Spaces in High-Rise Residential Development*, Singapore, National University of Singapore, 2004.
7 *Le Carré Bleu*, no. 3/4, 1999, *Architecture in Israel 1948–1998*, ed. Anna Orgel and Alexander Tzonis, pp. 5–9.
8 Alexander Tzonis, Introduction to Gary Chang, *My 32m² Apartment: A 30-Year Transformation*, Hong Kong, 2008.
9 Alexander Tzonis, 'An Architecture of Realism', *UIA Beijing Charter, The Future of Architecture*, July 2002, pp. 11–14.
10 Eduard Koegler, 'Using the Past to Serve the Future', in Peter Herrle and Erik Wegerhoff, *Architecture and Identity*, Berlin, 2008.
11 Jeffrey W. Cody, *Building in China: Henry K. Murphy's Adaptive Architecture, 1914–1935*, Hong Kong, 2001.
12 'Chinese Homes Proposed for Coral Gables', *Miami Daily News and Metropolis*, 5, January 1926, p. 28.
13 Eduard Koegler, 'Using the Past to Serve the Future: The Quest for an Architectural Chinese Renaissance Style Representing Republican China in the 1920s–1930s', in Herrle and Wegerhoff (eds), *Architecture and Identity*. See also Tan Zhengzhe, 'Liang Sicheng and Tong Jun', thesis, National University of Singapore, 2005.
14 Cody, *Building in China*, p. 44.
15 An impressive number of Shanghai magazines of architecture debated the question of Chinese identity in buildings among them, *The China Architects and Builders Compendium* (1924–1935), *The China Builder* (1930–1931), *The Chinese Architect* (1932–1937) and *The Builder* (1932–1937). Zhao Ling, personal communication.
16 Tong Chuin (Jr), 'Architecture Chronicle', *T'ien Hsia Monthly*, vol. 5, no. 3, October 1937, pp. 308–312.
17 Liang Sicheng, *A Pictorial History of Chinese Architecture: A Study of the Development of Its Structural System and the Evolution of Its Types*, ed. Wilma Fairbanks, Cambridge, MA, 1984.
18 Interview with Wangshu, *Frame* 19, Nils Groot, April 2009, pp. 54–63.
19 The offices of four principals, Zhang Ke, Zhang Hong, Hou Zhenghua, and Claudia Taborda.
20 Kongjian Yu and Mary Padua, *The Art of Survival: Recovering Landscape Architecture*, Beijing, 2006.

Coda

1 Jürgen Osterhammel and Niels P. Petersson, *Globalization: A Short History*, Princeton, NJ, 2005. Eruptions such as Masahiko Fujivara's *The Dignity of a Nation*, reviewed by David Pilling in the *Financial Times* of April 14, 2010, suggest that nationalism is not likely to vanish very soon, but as an architectural issue it appears to be taking a secondary place.

Index

Page numbers in **bold** denote figures.

Index

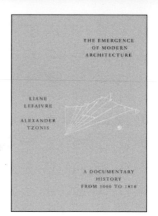

The Emergence of Modern Architecture:

A Documentary History, from 1000 to 1800

Edited by **Liane Lefaivre** & **Alexander Tzonis**

A cognitive history of the emergence of modern architecture. Cutting across disciplinarian and institutional divisions as we know them today, this book reconstructs developments within the framework of a cognitive history of the past. Modern is here taken to mean the radical re-thinking of architecture from the end of the tenth century in Europe to the end of the eighteenth century. Among the key debates that mark the period and explored in the book are those that oppose tradition to innovation, canon to discovery, geometrical formality to natural picturesqueness and the functional to the hedonistic.

March 2004: 552pp

Hb: 978-0-415-26024-4: **£95.00**   Pb: 978-0-415-26025-1: **£40.00**

To Order: Tel: +44 (0) 1235 400524 **Fax:** +44 (0) 1235 400525 **Email:** book.orders@tandf.co.uk

or Post: Taylor and Francis Customer Services, Bookpoint Ltd, Unit T1,

200 Milton Park, Abingdon, Oxon, OX14 4TA, UK

For a complete listing of all our titles visit:

www.tandf.co.uk

Taylor & Francis
Taylor & Francis Group